*Do-It-Yourself
Marketing
Research*

Do-It-Yourself Marketing Research

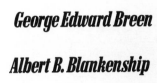

George Edward Breen

Albert B. Blankenship

Illustrated by Howard Munce

Third Edition

McGraw-Hill Publishing Company

New York St. Louis San Francisco Auckland
Bogotá Hamburg London Madrid Mexico
Milan Montreal New Delhi Panama
Paris São Paulo Singapore
Sydney Tokyo Toronto

Library of Congress Cataloging-in-Publication Data

Breen, George Edward, date.
  Do-it-yourself marketing research / George Edward Breen/Albert B.
Blankenship ; illustrated by Howard Munce.—3rd ed.

    p. cm.
    Includes index.
    ISBN 0-07-007450-X :
    1. Marketing research. I. Blankenship, Albert Breneman, date.
    II. Title.
  HF5415.2.B67 1989
  658.8'34–dc19   88-29223
                                           CIP

1234567890 KPKP 8954321098

ISBN 0-07-007450-X

*The editors for this book were William A. Sabin, James Bessent, and Virginia
Blair, the designer was Naomi Auerbach, and the production supervisor was
Dianne L. Walber. It was set in ITC Garamond Light by TCS.*

Printed and bound by The Kingsport Press.

*For more information about other McGraw-Hill materials,
call 1-800-2-MCGRAW in the United States. In other
countries, call your nearest McGraw-Hill office.*

Contents

Preface

The thesis of this book is simple. In many decisions that have to be made by small businesses (and larger ones, too), more marketing research *can* and *should* be done.

Since the second edition of this book, several major changes in marketing research are evident:

- New consumer products are coming to the market more rapidly, often without the extensive marketing research and test marketing once employed.

- There is often no marketing research specialist at all, even in fairly large firms. Many middle-management, white-collar departments (including marketing research specialists) in medium- and larger-sized firms have been drastically cut or eliminated to save costs. It seems likely that the trend will continue.

- There is a growing pervasiveness of computers throughout business and industry, definitely extending throughout marketing research.

These changes mean new emphases in this book.

New products are still failing in the marketplace. Failure can often be prevented by at least a minimum of good research. And good research does not necessarily require a professional to carry it out. Marketing research, as described in this book, consists of simple procedures for checking in advance the correctness of marketing, sales, and product decisions. If errors are made in such decisions, because of lack of judgment or lack of knowledge, resulting losses can sometimes be too great for a company of any size to bear comfortably.

This book, then, is a practical guide that shows the nonprofessional how to do *enough* marketing research—and how to do it in a semiprofessional and unbiased manner. It is not written for the professional researcher. It does not assume knowledge of statistics or anything except the ordinary mathematics common to all of us. In a sense, it is not meant to be "read" like an ordinary book, except for the first five chapters. It is to be kept handy for use when a problem arises that can be solved most readily and simply with techniques of marketing research.

Another purpose of the book is to warn the nonprofessional of possible pitfalls to avoid. Finally, the book gives enough background so that the reader can decide when professional help is really needed and how to go about finding it.

The book is divided into four major sections: *Section One* (Chapters 1 through 5) tells what marketing research is, how to evaluate your marketing problem which may benefit from research, how to plan your research study, and how to use the wealth of material provided by various government agencies, associations, and many other sources. The final chapter of this section describes how to plan and organize information that should continuously flow in from salespeople, suppliers, observations, daily press, magazines, and so on.

Section Two (Chapters 6 through 9) describes the kinds of research that may be found useful and profitable by manufacturers selling components and supplies to other business firms, research for manufacturers of consumer goods, simple research for major types of media, and research devices that will enable a retailer to determine more about his or her customers, future customers, and what can be done to increase sales and profits.

Section Three (Chapters 10 through 14) describes the various methods available for collecting pertinent and useful information. Four basic techniques are described in detail: the mail questionnaire, telephone interviewing, personal interviewing, and group interviewing. Chapter 12 is devoted to ways of ensuring an adequate sample for your purposes. Considerable attention is given to questionnaire design and testing and to data processing and analysis.

Section Four (Chapters 15 and 16) covers ways of writing or presenting a report that will get action. The final chapter tells how to recognize when outside professional help is needed for your study and how to find and use it.

Here is how the book can best be used. First, read the beginning five chapters. Then, as with any do-it-yourself manual, read those remaining chapters which will be useful to you. Select Chapters 6, 7, 8, or 9, depending on your own interest and need. Read *all* the techniques section (Chapters 10 through 14), which provides you with basic methods and procedures. For help in writing a good report or making a winning presentation to a group, see Chapter 15. And if a particular problem appears too big for you to handle yourself, read Chapter 16 on how to choose and work with an outside firm.

We repeat, for lesser marketing problems that beset businesspeople, this book shows that much marketing research can be done simply and inexpensively. Performed correctly, a little research is better than none. Often, a little marketing research is entirely sufficient—for example, when unexpected insurmountable problems suddenly show up in early research. Under these circumstances, a new product idea often can be killed early in the game, before substantial amounts of money have been spent.

None of the activities described in this book requires large sums of money. For the kind of questions addressed here, market studies can frequently be completed for a few hundred dollars. For many small or medium-sized businesses, research is less a matter of spending money than of using available information in an organized fashion or spending a little personal time. Certainly this is reasonable enough if it means stopping an action that would bring financially troublesome results.

Looking at the matter in a more positive way, a little marketing research is good when it can keep a potentially profitable idea alive, even though many people are lukewarm about it or actively negative.

Acknowledgments

The authors gratefully acknowledge key assistance from two people in the preparation of Chapter 4. Dr. John G. Keane, Director, Bureau of the Census, was kind enough to provide both overall and specific material about and from the census applicable to this chapter. Dr. Al Pozefsky, Director, UCF-STAC (University of Central Florida-State Technology Applications Center), carefully guided the authors through the maze of information available in data banks and how to tap the data banks for specific needs.

We would also like to express particular appreciation to Mr. Kirk M. W. Tyson for many of the ideas expressed in Chapter 5. Mr. Tyson, founder and President of The Competitor Intelligence Group (Oak Brook, Ill.), has authored *Business Intelligence* (Leading Edge Publications, 1986), a comprehensive text on the subject.

The authors are indebted to Ms. Peggy Kelcher, McKerracher Data Processing Services, Toronto, Ontario, for her helpful reading of and suggestions about Chapter 14.

In closing, we'd like to note that anyone who writes a book like this must acknowledge the hundreds of people who have taught him many things over many years. We wish we could thank every one of them. They have given us whatever wisdom we may have obtained. To each, let us now say thanks so much.

George Edward Breen

Albert B. Blankenship

Section One

Marketing

one

What Is Do-It-Yourself Marketing Research?

You can use simple research techniques to help solve your marketing problems. With a do-it-yourself approach, even people with no knowledge of modern marketing research methods can find better solutions to these problems and make fewer mistakes in judgment.

When you think of it, almost every business is constantly doing "market research." Most of the time, they are faced with a constant flow of relatively small questions which must be answered in one way or another. The merchant wonders whether a new line of goods should be stocked. A grocery, successful in one spot, contemplates a similar store on the other side of town. A lawyer believes that the office is not convenient for the types of desired clients. Where should the new office be located? A small manufacturer must decide whether to stick with selling agents or begin to field a sales force. These people wonder, ask friends and coworkers—and spouses. But this is not true research, and it could well lead to future trouble.

Wondering about the solutions to problems such as these is not good enough, especially if significant amounts of money and time are involved. You and all these other businesspeople can use simple but scientific research techniques to help solve your marketing problems. With a do-it-yourself approach, even people with no knowledge of modern marketing research methods can find better solutions to their problems and make fewer mistakes in judgment.

The purpose of this book, then, is to help people in small businesses make better decisions *based on facts.* This is true whether the person is in a small manufacturing business, at some point in the distribution channel, or in retailing. It is true for persons in service businesses. Many, many questions can be answered more wisely and correctly if a little do-it-yourself market research is used.

Large companies may have had extensive experience in market research, studying whether to put a new product on the market or deciding where to put a new branch store or factory, but even here, as the reader well knows, there have been some extremely expensive mistakes made in recent years. All business, whether large or small, needs the best possible analysis of present factors and probable future trends.

Let us give some examples. Does the package of a new product reach out and "grab" the browsing customer? It has become better known recently that most customers in stores, especially supermarkets, department stores, and discount chains, are likely to buy more than they came in for. The product that "reaches out" with its packaging is likely to attract attention and subsequent purchase.

Do the instructions which seem so simple to the product designers and engineers come across to the final buyer? A friend once said in desperation that "writers of instruction manuals must be born sadists; they *hate* people."

Is the store or office site really right for the kinds of customers or clients you want and the price levels and margins you wish to maintain? None of these questions should be answered by guesswork. All can be researched.

Lack of adequate research is suggested by observation of store turnover in a

With a do-it-yourself approach, even people with no knowledge of modern marketing research methods can find better solutions to these problems and make fewer mistakes in judgment.

shopping mall in a Midwestern city. Within 2 years of the mall opening, two large, independent supermarkets—one replacing the other—failed. One large discount chain, two dress shops, and a shoe store closed and were succeeded by similar stores. A men's clothing store and a waterbed store closed without replacement.

This is ridiculous. How much thought was given to these businesses? How much research, if any? Was the mall itself in a good location?

Nearby, an extremely large, but home-owned, supermarket was built and went out of business within a year. Across town, a franchised fast-food outlet stayed in business for about a year; two other types of restaurants have rented the same space since that time. One is still open, but with few customers.

All cities, large or small, have similar stories. Grand plans are made, money is spent, and failure results because the needed thorough research and planning were not done.

One or two errors in judgment will not put a large company out of business. Procter & Gamble had trouble with the original Pringles potato chips and is trying to bring them back. It also had trouble with its chocolate cookies. Its marketing people can pinpoint what went wrong, and the necessary changes in product and marketing can be carried out. But store shelves with products of less prosperous companies are all too familiar—products that come and go. Products aimed at the wrong market or packaged poorly. When even the large companies can make errors in judgment, smaller companies, with so much more at stake, should do research which might prevent unhappy, even disastrous, results.

A Little Introduction to the "Science" of Marketing Research

Marketing research is any planned and organized effort to gather new facts and new knowledge to help make better marketing decisions. Gathering of business knowledge can be done in a systematic and organized fashion. Facts, opinions, and attitudes can be sought from a sufficient number of sources so that the true answer to your problem appears to have been found and can be acted upon. The task of deciding on the size and nature of this "sample" is discussed in Chapter 12. It need not concern us here, for the moment.

Planning and organizing the search for knowledge, setting up clear and definite objectives, giving consideration to how the facts can be gathered as completely as possible (with due regard for the budget), and making sure that the results are as unbiased as possible make at least a semiscience of an activity that has been too often haphazard.

Over the years, a number of formal techniques have been developed for gathering market knowledge. These are nothing more than "tools" to help business people to do a better job. Some of the highly technical (and expensive) tools are outside the capability of the typical person with a small business. Nevertheless, the major part of the marketing research tool inventory is within grasp.

These techniques are the subject matter of this book. They are not exotic or

"Writers of instruction manuals must be born sadists; they hate people."

esoteric. With a little effort, in most situations, any businessperson can use them. There are a number of rules of the game to be covered when we get down to the "how" of marketing research. Even the word "rules" is too strong, since fresh approaches to a problem often yield surprising results. Still, many people have had a great amount of experience in marketing over the past century. You can benefit from their successes and failures, from the knowledge they have gained painfully and expensively.

As we said, few businesses today can afford to do without proper marketing research. For most smaller companies, and for most problems, this means a do-it-yourself approach. Even for large companies which have trimmed their middle-management staff so drastically, remaining product or marketing managers perhaps will have to assume the burden of proving that their decisions are indeed correct. No one else will be available to do the job.

When even large companies can make errors in judgment, smaller companies, with so much more at stake, should do research which might prevent unhappy, even disastrous, results.

Why Marketing Research Is So Often Neglected

If marketing research is so necessary, why has it not been used more for the everyday kinds of questions that businesses face? It is good to consider some prevalent attitudes among management people, people with small businesses, and even many marketing people themselves. Recognizing these, you may take steps to avoid them:

▪ Just because they are small entrepreneurs and independent by nature, people with small businesses may yield to the easy conclusion that they already know everything that is important to know. It seems to go with the territory: men and women who are willing to risk their savings, their families' future, and their business reputations are the ones most likely to feel self-confident about the extent of their knowledge and marketing ability.

▪ Statistics on business failures do not phase them; they and their businesses will be different. A real no-no in retailing is to start a new business in a location where a similar business has just failed. In the shopping mall mentioned earlier, however, this rule was largely ignored. We do not want to denigrate this great self-confidence and entrepreneurship, but we do suggest that even the most able small business operators do not know all they need to know and are quite able, even likely, to make expensive mistakes in judgment.

You must plan and organize the search for knowledge, set up clear and definite objectives, and give consideration to how the facts can be gathered as completely as possible.

▪ There is often a fear of a "science" that appears mathematical, involved, and mysterious. Most aspects, as we show, are simple, often just common sense. Reading professional journals in marketing research is enough to frighten anyone. This book will help allay that fear. Large studies conducted by professionals may be mathematical and involved, but the average study need not be so. The trouble is that as specialists have introduced new uses of computers and new mathematics, many simplicities of former years have been forgotten. Because of this fear of specialists, many smaller problems which *could* and *should* be researched have not been.

Even the most able small business operators do not know all they need to know and are quite able, even likely, to make expensive mistakes in judgment.

- There is often a real fear of seeming to waste time on research. Anxious to hit the market before a competitor does, sometimes even the smallest amount of market research has been sacrificed even by large companies who want national "rollout at the earliest possible date." Fear of market research is not irrational if others who are involved either directly or merely financially do not clearly understand the marketing questions that may be involved. Such people may show real impatience over further delay when a course of action appears so obviously "right." Perhaps they think that a market must be hit right now, while it is hot. But competitors already taking action may be making mistakes that could be avoided. Large companies make mistakes, but it is the small company that often feels the need for speed at any price.

- Often, as we have said, there is a failure to understand market research in its role of insurance. Even though a proposed course of action may be correct, it will be reassuring if a little market research shows that management was right all along. For a manufacturer, market research will also often point to things that were not known. Small and beneficial changes may result from marketing research: in product design, color scheme, or advertising themes. For the retailer, research can tell what kinds of customers are now dealing with the store, where they are coming from, and what they think of the store as a primary supply source. It also can indicate where the store should advertise and what the ads should say. This very basic knowledge is worth the little effort to get it.

- Finally, almost everyone fails to understand that most marketing research studies can be done quite adequately in a "cheap and dirty" manner. By no means does every study have to involve months of time and thousands of dollars; long and costly studies *are* and *should be* the exception. To make market research look so complex that only specialists can perform it is a real disservice to business. There is a need for specialists and consultants, but they are not needed for the solution of every problem that comes along. You can do most of the investigating yourself.

What Kinds of Problems Can Be Handled by Do-It-Yourself Marketing Research?

In this book we address all businesses that must market their goods and services, preferably at a decent profit. We speak to small business, but the methods can be used by everyone. They may be used by product or marketing managers in large companies, who now find themselves without a marketing research department of their own.

It may seem unnecessary to define a problem, but perhaps a few examples will set you thinking about your own situation and what you can do about it.

1. You have a new product in the design stage. Its sales may be potentially attractive, but at the beginning not large enough to warrant large rollout

By no means does every study have to involve months of time and thousands of dollars.

expenditures. It will be profitable from the beginning, you believe, if costs are kept down. What combination of product features, colors, and design will appeal to the most customers at the lowest cost? As a marketing person, you feel more comfortable if you are a little more sure about the information given to you by the product designers and engineers. It is possible that they want to provide even more features and quality than the typical customer wants or needs. It is also possible that research will show that the product has much greater sales potential than you had thought. A great first "push" may be indicated.

2. You have to make a decision, but two strong "sides" have made their appearance among your associates. Confirmation is needed so that you will not be hearing "I told you so" if something goes wrong. It would be nice to say, "My research shows. . . ." Thus, even if things turn out badly, you can demonstrate that you tried. It is more likely that the research will point to the proper road to take. Do not make the mistake that you can "buy a little research" from some small, local consulting firm with whose work you are not familiar. You must take part in the planning and execution of research even if the actual work is done by some outside person.

3. You may own or manage a retail store in a deteriorating neighborhood. Relocation is desirable. But where? Much local information may already be available, as you will see in Chapter 4.

4. Whether you are a manufacturer or retailer, the return on advertising is often questioned (and questionable). This can be a difficult kind of research, but you can still do enough, particularly if you are in retailing or are a small manufacturer, to get some idea of what, if anything, advertising is bringing you.

What combination of product features, colors, and design will appeal to the most customers at the lowest cost?

5. You feel the need for more knowledge about your share of market. Maybe you are not doing as well as you think you are. A little more effort could bring extra and profitable business. Complacency about share of market can be deadly. While studying your market share, you can easily find all sorts of information. What do customers *really* think about your company? What do they think about your product, your service, your pricing? Is it possible, even probable, that you are continuing to do some of the very things that have hurt you in the past? Are you like the golfer who practices his swing without the help of a "pro"? Sometimes the practice merely hardens the things the golfer was doing wrong in the first place.

6. If you are in banking, with all the fast-changing economic pressures you have, you will want to know how to maintain or increase that "bottom line." What are the prospects for residential and nonresidential building for the next 12 months in the area? Relative to the present and probable future mortgage rates? What are the plans of local builders for constructing high-priced or low-priced houses? Is there some disgruntlement among your depositors about the interest rate you are paying? Is there anything you can do to allay this dissatisfaction? What do customers think about the automatic teller machines? Are they using them? Why, or why not?

What do customers really think of your company, your product, your service, your pricing?

7. Small media (suburban newspapers, local radio stations) may wish to have a much clearer idea about their effect on their communities. Are the stories and ads in local papers being read? With what effect? What kind of programs do local radio listeners really want? Does every station have to stick with country and western? There are ways to obtain such information that will fill gaps left by ordinary rating systems.

There's no space to list all the possible marketing questions of various types of firms. A retailer would like to know the geographic and economic areas from which customers are being drawn, so that the store can merchandise more carefully for this group. A wholesaler would like to know whether he or she is considered a prime or secondary source for many customers—and why. And what can be done about it. A manufacturer wonders whether an older product with decreasing sales is on the way out, or whether the sales force is merely tired of it and are spending too much time on newer and more stimulating products. This could result in some change of emphasis in sales directions or sales incentives. The manufacturer has to *know* first, however.

The problems most readily solved by the methods described in this book are relatively simple, straightforward matters, where easily obtained facts, opinions, and knowledge can be organized in such a way that proper actions become obvious. Most active marketing people, at any level of distribution, do not have time for studies that demand weeks or months of effort. Regular work must go forward. So we talk about part-time methods that you and your associates can easily justify.

Retailers like to know the geographic and economic areas from which customers are being drawn.

Marketing people, at any level of management or distribution, will be stronger in their jobs if they do some market research on their own. Decision makers should "get out in the market" frequently. For a retailer, this includes some time on the floor. Do-it-yourself marketing research can be a *planned* way of learning about the market and can be the most instructive way of all.

Begin Putting the Problem on Paper

At this point, begin listing questions and problems on which you would like more information and about which you feel instinctively that more knowledge would lead to wiser decisions. You are not yet ready to think about *how* you will do the job of getting the information. You are only going to list areas in which you might make a weak or doubtful decision for want of facts.

A quick inspection of your list will point to situations which clearly require the services of a consultant or professional. You do not have the time or money to do the job yourself.

Other areas will be removed from your list because, in your own good judgment, they cannot be researched at all. You would like some definite knowledge about your competitor's plans, for example, but short of illegal industrial espionage, you may not be able to find out.

After these eliminations, you will probably be left with a list of questions that can be answered through a little organized effort on your part.

Summary

We have tried to lead you to the belief that much market research can be done without employment of a professional. If you have followed this preliminary discussion, you probably realize that you, too, have some decisions to make—decisions that can be more soundly made with more facts.

Remember the three things that are much too easy for all of us:

1. It is too easy to say no to a new product or a new idea. An action that is never taken can never fail. It might have been profitable, but no one will ever know.

2. It is too easy to take the simple road in reaching a decision—to talk to a few customers, your spouse, or a few people at a cocktail party, and then make a decision. This is not market research; it is no more than a cop-out.

3. And finally, it is too easy to say that there is no time for good marketing research. This is one of the most frequent situations. Having ruminated on an idea for weeks and months, suddenly you and all your associates want action *now*. Rarely is this sudden burst of speed really necessary. Moving rapidly ahead, saying "damn the torpedoes," can sink the ship.

Chapter 2 begins to explain *how* a problem can be identified and *how* work can be started on getting the necessary facts to solve the problem.

You will need to begin putting the problem on paper.

two

Most of the time, the facts and knowledge that you need are more easily obtainable than you probably realize. This information will come from published (secondary) sources or through some form of communication with people who know the answers. Or from people whose opinions and attitudes will affect the success of the proposed action. In later chapters we will cover all the standard methods of gathering information, including mail questionnaires, telephone interviews, and group sessions. To borrow an old expression, many times, all that is necessary to get started is a little "gumption"—and a little time and money.

Before you get started, it is important that you formulate a very clear and accurate definition of the problem that needs studying. Even the smallest problem—if it warrants studying at all—should be defined carefully and agreed on by all those who are now or *will* be concerned with the findings.

At this point, eliminate everything that you do not need to know to answer the main question. The manufacturing company that studies whether to switch from agents to its own sales force might wonder what kind of cars it might have to furnish to the new sales force. This is a secondary problem, however, one that need not be solved before the major problem is addressed. Eliminate, simplify, shorten: these are the things that need to be done at this stage.

An important first step in any research, large or small, is to get full agreement of the team. Effective human and business relations are possible only when the crew understands where the ship is going and why. Only the very smallest, one-person shops may proceed without this preliminary "sell." In most cases, the entire team must work together willingly, so that everyone can understand the problem involved and the reason why more information is needed in order to make a wise decision.

Statement of Why a Particular Problem Is Worth Studying

As part of your selling job with your associates, and also as a means of getting the precise problem into writing, there are some important preliminary steps that should be taken. These steps require no more than a few hours or a day or two, depending on the circumstances, how many people should be consulted, and the probable amount of money that will be involved or is at stake.

First, ask yourself some preliminary questions (we will assume that you have chosen one problem by now that you would like to work on):

1. What are the probable alternative actions that can be taken depending on the findings of the research project? If there are no alternatives, as sometimes happens, perhaps a study is useless.

2. If there are alternative actions, is there already some disagreement about them? Who is on each side? How important would their opposition or support be? In general, how thorough must your study be to convince some of the people involved? (All researchers know that sometimes a study must

Most of the time, the facts and knowledge you need are more easily obtainable than you probably realize.

Many times, all that is necessary to get started is a little "gumption."

be enlarged a bit more than necessary in order to convince some stubborn doubters.)

3. In your own opinion, do the several alternative actions have equal merit? Or are you leaning in one direction yourself? You must know yourself very well to do unbiased research.

4. What can go *wrong* if a bad decision is made? It is time to begin getting a numerical handle on the importance of the problem. This will determine how much can be spent for research.

5. What can go *right*? This is the opposite of question 4, but it requires separate thought. What can you do for your company, your store, your small business by helping to make the right decision?

6. Is the decision one that can really be made more wisely through research? A question can be very important, but it may not lend itself to research at all. It would be almost impossible, for example, to prove through research that salespeople in a manufacturing or wholesaling operation would sell more if they drove comfortable, middle-sized cars instead of small ones. It can be presumed that comfortable salespeople will do a better job, but even comparing one year of small cars with another year of larger ones would introduce so many variables that the results would be without value. The same would be true with other methods of constructing such a research study.

7. At this point—even though there is no final "go or no-go" in the particular study you have selected—it should begin to be clear whether a do-it-yourself marketing research project will be feasible. You may have a feeling by now that too much time will be required in light of the money value of the problem. Do not back away too quickly. In the pressure of daily events, it may be easy to decide not to go ahead with a study, but such a decision may well be wrong. You may have taken a short-run view at a time when your company would benefit more by your stepping back and considering long-range benefits. It has been widely said in recent years that American business has been too involved with short-range product development and short-range sales and profit considerations instead of building for longer-term financial strength. Even your smaller problem may benefit by consideration of this matter.

All the preceding is preliminary. The matters discussed below are for your own consideration before any formal proposal is made to your associates. It would be good to get even these in writing—questions and answers both—even though no other person will see them in this form.

You must ask yourself what can go wrong if a bad decision is made.

Getting the Opinion of Others

It is good sense to get as much advice from others as possible. If you are going to propose some do-it-yourself research, it is doubly important to do so if the whole field is new to your company. Even though you, the reader, may be the owner and boss, you know from experience that if other people are to act on research findings, their prior agreement as to purpose, methods, and procedures is essential.

Let us take an illustration from manufacturing. The same human actions and reactions could be expected in any type of business. Product ideas do not originate from nowhere. Someone in the factory or in marketing, sales, or some sort of development group first gets the notion. Or there is pressure to go quickly into a product line that a competitor has just opened. Having had the idea in the first place, the person no longer can be completely unbiased. Unless the idea is a foolish one, a group of other people at various levels will begin to lend support.

Naturally, an opposition group (an important group) will appear. The idea is good, they will say, but it will not sell. It was tried once in the 1970s and flopped. The competitor seems to be having rough sailing getting the product onto the market.

It is healthy for the company that these pro and con groups exist. If everyone was "for" everything, the company would be bankrupt in short order. If every new idea is killed off for the sake of safety and conservatism, however, the sheriff also could be expected at the door.

Marketing research, even the smallest do-it-yourself kind, will give everyone a say. What should be studied? What geographical area should be covered? What research methods are most likely to uncover the truth? What particular topics absolutely *must* be included? Each contending group has its turn at bat. The research will be better for it, and the results will be much less likely to be questioned.

Depending on the study itself and the kind of business you are in, such groups as those listed below should be consulted. If you are only going to do a small study, the consultation will be once-over-lightly. Even with a small study, however, you may regret it if you miss seeing someone who can later "knife" your findings.

The following list is for a small manufacturer. Other types of businesses should develop contacts more suitable for their own situation. The important thing is to use knowledgeable people in the planning and evaluation stages.

- *Product design and product engineering.* These people are likely to be biased in favor of their own ideas.

- *Sales and marketing.* In smaller companies, even in middle-sized companies, these departments are likely to be comprised of the same people. At all levels of distribution, the sales department can quickly prove that a product will not sell—by not selling it. Usually this is not conscious sabotage, but it is just as effective.

- *Advertising and packaging.* These people can tell you in advance about matters they would like to know to help them do a better job later on. It is good to listen to these creative folks.

It has been widely said in recent years that American business has been too involved in short-range product development and short-range sales and profit considerations instead of building for longer-term financial strength.

It is good sense to get as much advice from others as possible.

It is healthy for a company that both pro and con groups exist.

- *Manufacturing.* Your research can help people in manufacturing do a better job. They want to know acceptable colors, materials, configurations, and so on. There are many opportunities for cost cutting here. Attention should be paid at this point to possible foreign markets if exporting is in the cards at some future date. It may be possible to have some market research done by a European firm, for example, to see what features, product names, and so on will be acceptable over there.

- *A few good customers.* Manufacturers and wholesalers usually have a few very good customers who can advise them on a proposed study. Use these customers unless there is need to keep the proposed action confidential at the moment.

- *Your banker.* Almost every firm—from small retailer to large manufacturer—has a solid banking connection that can provide some guidance and advice about most problems.

Chapter 4 covers source material in much more detail.

Financial Importance of the Problem

Early in the planning stage (to be covered in Chapter 3) it is necessary to decide on the amount of time and money that can be spent. You should already have given some thought to this matter.

It would be nice to study and study and study or to get greater and greater accuracy, but this is impossible, even for situations that involve great risk. There always has to be an end to study and the beginning of action.

Before starting specific plans, therefore, you must arrive at some maximum dollar figure that this particular research can support. Consider these two questions:

1. *What are the likely short- and long-term costs of a wrong decision?* A new product, at any level of distribution, may "lay an egg" in spite of our best efforts. However, if only a few thousand dollars can possibly be lost, a $1,000 study is clearly not called for.

2. *What are likely to be the short- and long-term profits from a correct decision?* Even from this viewpoint, there are real limitations on research costs. What percentage of the greatest possible future profit can be spent to make sure? Consider a retailer who would like to devote some selling area to recreational goods. National figures may be available for average sales per square foot for this type of merchandise in this type of store. The total size of this particular store allows only a few hundred square feet for these goods. With the greatest success, therefore, we can still predict that sales and profits will be modest. Other local competitive factors also need consideration. How much is research worth in a situation like this? Probably not a great deal.

A new product, at any level of distribution, may "lay an egg" in spite of the best efforts.

Summary up to Now

If you have followed these first two chapters, here is where we now stand:

- You are interested in the possibility and the advantages of doing some marketing research yourself.

- You have listed a few problems where you would like more knowledge and facts.

- You have talked over the problems and their possible solutions with a number of people who have direct or indirect interest in their solution.

- You have made a preliminary decision about the amount of money you believe should be spent on this particular study.

Still to be decided is *how* the research is to be done. The remainder of this book concerns methods of research and how to present and use the findings.

But first, a few words of caution and painfully learned *wisdom:* Marketing research is wholly useless unless something is *done* with the results. Not only should there be a clear purpose for the research, but there should be a clear understanding *in advance* about how the findings will be used. Knowledge for the sake of knowledge can be precious to a scientist, but it can be waste of time and money for a commercial, profit-making organization. Not one bit of information should be collected that cannot be used, either now or in the near future. This does not mean that there never are surprises. Research may reveal a completely different marketing world from the one you had pictured. But this is clearly a useful finding.

To make a point, let us be a little ridiculous. If we should find that our product or our store is used slightly more by blue-eyed people than by brown-eyed people, this would be interesting to a sociologist. If we are in manufacturing, it *might* indicate that we should change our finish a bit, but the likelihood is that nothing can or will be done. Advertising cannot be directed only to blue-eyed people or only to brown-eyed people. We would have a case of fascinating futility.

The next chapter shows you how to write a research proposal. A clear, well-thought-out proposal is just as important in many ways as the completed study. You cannot have one without the other.

The research proposal should be prepared in written form even if you, the reader, are owner and boss. It will clear your head, make you think more deeply about the situation. Then you can "accept" your own proposal or not. You will see that you have not skipped any good sources of information. You have not overlooked important market segments that could make or break your idea.

Knowledge for the sake of knowledge can be a waste of time and money for a commercial, profit-making organization.

three

How to Plan Your Study

If you are now convinced that there are marketing questions which you could answer better with do-it-yourself research (and there *must* be), then it is important to get the problem and the plan of attack into writing. A small study that requires only a small amount of time and money will require only a short write-up. Larger, more important studies should be done with greater care and detail.

Even if you are a product line manager, or its equivalent, for a large corporation (lacking your own company market research department), you will be wise to follow the procedures outlined in this chapter. Knowing your own products so well, you may be tempted to shortcut these preliminaries. But don't.

There is something about *writing* that forces precise thinking. Aspects of the question at hand are not overlooked. Portions of the study that are really not vital show themselves and can be discarded.

Moreover (a point that needs reemphasizing), a written plan is likely to send you to others for guidance and help. We really cannot overstate the need for getting the team lined up in advance. This does not mean that everyone thinks alike at the start—or that complete agreement will even be reached when the study is over. But it can mean that everyone important sees the need for research, approves the method by which it will be accomplished, and has at least implied that he or she will abide by the results when the facts and recommendations are presented. Getting this agreement is half the battle.

The psychological principle is sound. The more people who become involved in one way or another, the better the study will be and the more likely it will be acted on.

Statement of Why the Study Needs Doing

The first portion of your plan should clearly outline the specific reasons why time and money should be devoted to this study:

1. What is the specific nature of the step that we want to take? A new product, a new store location, or whatever? Precise and clear-headed thinking is vital here.

2. What specific information do we lack? What facts, knowledge, or opinions will enable us to make wiser decisions?

3. What are the alternate actions that can be taken, either with research or without it? Exactly *how* will the information that we propose to get help us choose among these alternatives?

For the most part, just from your preliminary work discussed in Chapter 2, you are ready to write this section of your plan.

It is important to get the problem and the plan of attack into writing.

Statement of Money That Can Be Spent

On the basis of your own preliminary thinking and your discussions with other people, you have a pretty good idea of what this marketing research is really worth. You know the costs involved in a wrong decision. You have a fair notion of the profits that will develop if a "go" signal is given by research.

What, then, is this marketing research worth? Perhaps this is a decision that can bring an extra $100,000 in profits during the first 3 years. Can you afford just 1 percent of this sum to be sure you are right? Or 2 percent? Perhaps less than 1 percent? It is impossible to be definite here, since company attitudes vary greatly. If your company has never attempted marketing research, spending as little as possible will be wise as long as good research is done.

It also will be wise, in some cases, to have alternative plans ready. For $500 you can do this. For $1,000 you can do this much more (and be more sure of the accuracy of your results). The lower-cost study will take so many weeks; the higher-cost study will take longer but produce less subsequent risk of error. Management (if you need permission of a supervisor) or you yourself can then decide how much is enough and what degree of risk can be accepted for the sake of saving money and time.

The better and more complete your plan, the better chance you will have of doing a thorough study. The plan is a selling instrument to management, if necessary, or even to yourself. You are selling what you know is a good product or a better product for more money. On paper, right in front of you on your desk, it may well become obvious that the longer, more expensive study is the wiser way to go.

Sources of Information for the Plan

You now have reached the most interesting part of planning. You have a question that needs answering, you have a decision to make, and you want more facts. Somewhere out there in the great big world are your sources of knowledge. There are people who know how to help you. There are printed sources, if you only know where they are.

If you had hundreds of thousands of dollars to spend, you could throw out a huge study, like a big net to catch a small fish. But you probably do not have anywhere near that amount of money. Nor do you have the time, even if you did have the money. The trick is to know how to go to the right printed secondary sources—and how to communicate directly with those in the field who have the knowledge that you want.

Broadly, your sources will be divided into two groups:

1. Secondary sources—materials already available from the government, from associations, and so on.

2. Primary sources—materials you will have to develop yourself through one or another marketing research technique.

You have a question that needs answering, you have a decision to make, and you want more facts.

For already available sources, you may refer to some that are described in Chapter 4, or you may know of sources in your own industry. More often than can be imagined, companies that have belonged to their own trade associations for years have failed to use the facts that almost every association collects. More on this later.

For the work you will do yourself, you must decide which of the information-gathering methods described in later chapters will be appropriate. There should first be a very specific description of those people whom it is necessary to contact, such as buyers and sales managers of wholesale houses, people who use heavy construction tools and the purchasing agents who supply them, or households that appear close enough to use your shopping center. You may wish to do a sales test of a new product in a few selected markets—such markets must be carefully selected. By listing these people or these markets, you will free yourself to eliminate respondents who have interesting viewpoints that are not vital to the problem at hand.

The way you approach these people must be your own decision, based on the amount of money you have to spend, the type of information you need, and the time that can be spared to do the work. However, usually the information needed and the primary sources from which the information is available will dictate the kind of research you will use. These research methods are described in detail later in the book. Usually the choice of methods is not at all difficult to make.

Not to be disregarded, however, are other concerns that might be making demands on your time. Before deciding how to approach the primary sources, you also must consider the time it will take to summarize the questionnaires, for example. You would be wise to consider using computers for this work. We do not want to frighten you; most of the work will not be overly time-consuming. For the most part, we are talking about hours, rather than days, whether you are analyzing mail questionnaires, a few group interviews, or the result of a telephone study.

Read Chapters 10 through 14 on how to do various kinds of research, and then be very realistic about what can be done in your particular circumstances. Your plan must list both materials already available (secondary sources) and primary sources, and it must show how, in general, you intend to use these sources. As soon as you have read this chapter, be sure to read Chapters 4 and 5, covering, respectively, marketing information available from outside, usually printed sources, and marketing intelligence gathered from a number of other sources.

Where the Information Is

You are now well on your way to a good plan for research. You have clearly stated your purpose. You have made an estimate of the cost. You have developed some idea of primary and secondary sources. You have decided which method or methods you feel are best to tap both primary and secondary sources.

Now you must make a judgment about where you are going to go. It would be good if you could complete a "national survey" by visiting a few people around the corner. Unfortunately, more is usually required. Whether your business is in a national market, a local market in a shopping center, or a regional concern of

Not to be disregarded, however, are other concerns that might be making demands on your time.

some kind, there must be a good reason not to take your sample of opinions and facts from every part of your territory and from every important segment of your market.

Time and money enter the picture, and a judgment must be made. Would an eastern manufacturer of can openers really have to sample West Coast opinions? Or vice versa? Are can openers used in different ways in several parts of the country?

The first guess would be no. Yet it would be wise to check a few sources. In a surprising number of ways, various sections of the country hold fast to different lifestyles. In the west, the outdoor life is well known to anyone who has lived or worked in that area, but other things are less obvious. Houses look different and are decorated differently. Even the tools used in construction sometimes differ slightly. Customs and taste, in such things as coffee strength, vary markedly from coast to coast. Regional preferences for soups and fast foods present a marketing problem.

Radio and television have fortunately not completely destroyed the individuality of north, south, east, and west. One walks across a bridge from Cincinnati into Kentucky and feels in a different world. To some real extent, all these differences affect the purchase and use of many products. Maybe even *your* product.

You must still use judgment. Most manufacturers cannot produce separate models for east, west, north, and south. Shopping centers cannot have completely different stock and fixtures for separate sections of their markets. But many studies can still be done fairly close at hand, with reasonable certainty that the results in other areas would not be materially different. This book cannot solve these problems for you; just be careful in choosing where research needs to be done.

How to Time Your Study for Best Results

There is nothing worse for anyone conducting marketing research than to discover that the final decision was made before the study had been completed. Silly as this may sound, it has nevertheless happened to a great many fact finders who were too slow about their work.

Do not take this point too lightly. If yours is a company large enough to have departments, there may be the following scenario:

A great many fact finders are too slow about their work.

- You see the need for studying a question before some marketing decision is made. You decide to have it done, perhaps with the actual work being done by one of your subordinates or even by you yourself.

- Other departments may be making their own plans. If you are a manufacturing firm, product engineering may figure that it should go ahead on preliminary design or redesign work. What they are doing "can always be stopped or changed in direction. Why waste this time just waiting for a study?"

- The sales department makes preliminary plans. The ad agency is brought in for early "thought" sessions. All sorts of people are busy before the study is completed.

- A great momentum has been built up before the study has been completed. Stopping such "planning" becomes more difficult daily. People get caught in the moving tide, and the individual doing marketing research (even though he or she may run the company) may come to feel like the little Dutch boy with his finger in the dike.

We have no way of alleviating this type of situation. Speed in completing a study can be a very important element. To increase the speed, if young people from several departments are actually used in part of the study itself, a very good psychological atmosphere is created. Any department will be more willing to listen to its own people—even if you *are* the president. A study produced in time to be useful is certainly far better than a professionally ideal study that *follows* a decision rather than *leading* it.

Outline of Final Report

Now it is possible and advisable to write an outline of the final report to show yourself and others what it will be like. The outline could follow this plan:

1. Purpose of study—a short statement of questions that need research and why

2. Possible actions as a result of findings

3. Secondary sources covered

4. Primary sources covered and how

5. Extent of coverage

6. Findings and recommendations—possible alternative findings

7. Actions that should be taken in the case of each of the possible sets of findings.

This effort is simply a short version of your plan, but it is written as an outline of the final report and will make the writing easier when the time comes. It gives a prospective user a last chance to find a weakness or an area that was missed. For more on writing and presenting the final report, see Chapter 15.

These first three chapters have shown the value of communication and cooperation. It is often good, if you are the head of a company, to let someone else have the "credit" for a good study and resulting action. Such generosity can help build teamwork. When the company has reached the point at which someone regularly says, "Let's do a little research and get the facts," then you have accomplished something very good for the organization.

The next two chapters focus on sources of knowledge and how to tap them.

Giving others credit for a good study and resulting action can help build teamwork.

four

How to Find Existing Marketing Information

You want to use the work previously done by other people, if available and relevant to your problem. Otherwise you will be wasting your time and money. An almost unlimited amount of material is available from hundreds of sources.

But you must start by understanding the difference between "data" and "information." Anyone can collect data. But the data significant to your particular problem (Chapter 2) is information. It is relevant. It can help you. It is data with a goal, a purpose.

Available information can help you in several ways. It can provide background information. This information may solve part—even all—of your particular problem. Even if it does not, it can steer you to the unanswered questions which may be provided by further research. It also may provide a statistical base from which you can interpret whatever new material your own study uncovers.

Readily available forms of marketing information may be either in printed or data-bank (computer) form. This chapter gives you the flavor of it all. We cannot give a total answer; there are entire books on the subject. But we provide a starting point.

How to Start Your Information Search

There are distinct steps in the process.

Determine the kinds of information you need. Keep your search within the limits of your specific problem; otherwise, your possibilities of information will be overwhelming. Start with a list. Do not leave your information needs "open." If you do, you will never complete your study.

Decide whether to stay with print sources or go with on-line information. This is a tough decision, especially since you are not likely a computer expert. But let's consider how you should make this decision.

To the computer novice it may seem easier to depend on print sources. You feel at home with them. Few of those readily available cost anything. But checking out all these printed sources takes a tremendous amount of time. Use of on-line sources will provide far more comprehensive information. But such use will cost you some money, and you will need some expert assistance.

Check the library reference specialist. If you are in a metropolitan area, start with your *public library*. Even in a small community it may be the right place to begin, since the computer provides such a communications link. Better still, though, if you are close to a college or university, go to the *academic library*. Then there is also the *state library,* a possibility if it is within commuting distance.

How to deal with the library specialist. Make your session with the library specialist effective. Start by defining your specific needs. Ask for advice on whether print data or data-bank material will come closer to meeting your

You must start by understanding the difference between "data" and "information."

requirements. You had better ask, too, the possible cost of whatever route seems most desirable.

Be sure to ask advice on where to seek further specialist guidance. These may be someone in a higher library system, a so-called information broker (defined later in this chapter), or the nearest member of the Special Library Association.

Check your ad agency, if you have one. The person in charge of marketing research at your advertising agency may have discovered sources of information that you do not know about. If your agency happens to have a marketing research department, chances are that its library will be a good source of information, and the agency research director will be enthusiastic about following through for you.

How to Continue Your Print Information Search

If you go to the print information route, here's how to proceed.

Start by consulting some of the more promising printed "guides." It is tough to be definitive about these, since there are so many *good* guides as starting points. The most promising general guides are the *Reader's Guide to Periodical Literature* and *The New York Times Index.*

Follow these with more specific business guides. The *Business Periodical Index* covers most business subjects.

Consult the Standard Industrial Classification (SIC) Manual. Published by the *U.S. Department of Commerce,* this manual assigns classification numbers to all types of businesses within the country. Armed with the knowledge of the SIC number or numbers relative to your situation, you can readily isolate specific statistics you need from other sources.

The system is simple. For example, 275 means "commercial printing establishments generally," while 2751 denotes "commercial printing, letterpress."

Know about the major no-charge federal information source. This is the *Department of Commerce,* and within it, the *Bureau of the Census.*

The *Census Bureau* provides statistical data of incredibly broad use for the small businessperson in marketing efforts. However, there are so many varieties that there just is not enough space to list them all. We will start by giving you some examples and show how they can help solve specific marketing needs and problems.

An elderly couple visited a regional office of the *Census Bureau* to find out about the population of seniors and its distribution. By using census data, they were able to identify metropolitan areas having sufficient senior population numbers to warrant their service: a trade show presenting new and unusual travel and vacation opportunities for seniors.

In another case, a retail store consulted census tract data (a *census tract* is a small area of about 4,000 to 5,000 within a city of 50,000 or more inhabitants) on income, housing values, and ethnicity for its trading area. Its delicatessen and certain specialty items were then expanded. By studying growth trends in detailed production data over several years, a furniture manufacturer decided to offer a line of metal office furniture.

Census data also may be of help in determining business location. An entrepreneur in Chicago evaluated marital status and age distribution in deciding to open a singles' bar in a particular neighborhood. A lawn-mower firm set up its sales territories on the basis of census data showing single, detached dwelling units. The same sort of data could be used to set up sales quotas for sales personnel.

These examples give only a cursory idea of the broad range of census material available and the ways in which the information can be used. It is even possible to get statistics by blocks and neighborhoods. Here is a summary of the sources and types of census information:

Census of Population. Conducted every 10 years, this provides thorough detail on the nature of the U.S. population. It covers demographics such as sex, age, ethnicity, family size, marital status, occupation, income, and amount of education.

The information is available for every city, town, and village. It is even possible to get—at cost—data for specific neighborhoods, often useful for a small firm. Information is also available by ZIP code. But the *Census Bureau* warns that to make the most of its material, you must be sure that your own measurement concepts are reasonably similar to its own.

Census of Housing. This census provides information on number of rooms, whether owned or rented, value of home or rent paid, plumbing, air-conditioning, and number of cars owned. This sort of information is particularly useful for the firm examining the market for household items such as furniture, rugs, and washing machines.

Economic censuses. This is a catchall term that covers the Census of Manufactures, the Census of Retail Sales, the Census of Wholesale Sales, and the Census of Service Industries. The Census of Manufactures shows shipments (in both units and dollars) of thousands of products manufactured in the United States. Shown by Standard Industrial Classification numbers (and descriptions), such data can tell you geographically exactly where the products you are interested in are produced.

In the three other censuses—retail, wholesale, and service—sales and number of establishments are given by product line, by states and counties, and by SMSAs (Standard Metropolitan Statistical Areas). The SMSA is an area made up of a dominant city of 50,000 or more population and a less densely populated area socially and economically integrated with that city.

There is so much census data that the detail is almost overwhelming. So how do you find out exactly what you can use and how to get it?

The best bet is to start with your local library. If your librarian does not have the material or the answers on where to get it, there may be a field office of the *Department of Commerce* near you (there are 43 of these throughout the country). A shortcut is to use the 800 telephone listing for the *Bureau of the*

The U.S. Census of Population provides thorough detail on the nature of the U.S. population.

Census. Tell them your needs—and ask for their advice—and they can give you the nearest library that contains the information you want.

County business patterns.   These are a series of separate reports for each state and a summary for the entire country. They provide information on employment and size of firm reporting, including payrolls. These reports can be particularly useful in analyzing market potential, establishing sales territories and quotas, and locating where your establishment(s) should be.

Learn about other major federal government sources.   One of these is the *Statistical Abstract of the United States.* Published annually by the *Department of Commerce,* it provides over 1,000 pages of tables and data, and it is a basic starting point for statistical data about the United States. It gives a broad overview of the kinds of data available, including census material. However, it is only a starting point, to give you further ideas.

The Survey of Current Business is another federal information source you should know. This monthly publication covers important information such as gross national product, national income, and international balance of payments. It provides information on personal income, employment, and prices, and it carries a special section on current business statistics.

The Federal Reserve System publishes relevant publications. The *Federal Reserve Bulletin* is a national monthly publication emphasizing financial information. It may be of assistance in directing areas for research.

Learn about your major state sources.   State governments have a hodgepodge of departments and bureaus of varying competency. We suggest that you write to the Department of Commerce, the Department of Development, the State Librarian, or the state Chamber of Commerce in the state of your interest. At least you will get some leads to follow. But in all these bodies, publication of statistics is secondary to the job of attracting new businesses to the state and maintaining the health of companies already in the state. We have small hope for much helpful information for your particular needs, but a letter or two to determine what is available is worth trying.

Check your local government (county or city).   Local governments are rarely any better than states in having useful statistical information for you. Their information varies in quality and quantity, to be sure, but you should check them out. Your local government may have an economic development commission, a redevelopment commission, or a downtown planning committee. They *may* be able to supply vital statistics for you.

Check business and professional associations.   Business or professional associations may be good sources of statistics which can help you. But the quality of their help varies. Some are purely public relations firms, aimed at influencing legislative bodies and/or the public. But some really do collect and disseminate sound data that might be of assistance to you. One problem: Even if the particular

Business and professional associations may be good sources of statistics for you.

group *does* have sound, useful data, you may have to pay membership fees to get it.

Every industry or professional group seems to have one or more associations. For some product lines there are associations that both compete and overlap. The best information source about appropriate associations for your particular firm is your own firm. If you need information about associations in other fields, the best source is *The Encyclopedia of Associations* (Gale Research Company, Detroit, Mich.). It should be in your local library.

Check directories.   We must first define "directories," since we will be talking about two distinct types. The most common use of the term refers to specific lists, such as lists of firms, people, products, and communities. The other meaning, which will be more applicable to data-bank sources, refers to broad sources of information covering many, many detailed topics. We shall start with some examples of the list type of directory. These are specific lists of whatever the classification is. Some of these are free, in the sense that they are available to you in libraries. Others are available only on payment of a fee. Let's examine the specific possibilities for you.

There is the state industrial directory. This typically includes listings for all (or most) industrial firms, classified by firm name; by cities, towns, and villages; and by products. They vary in size, quality, and cost. Your local library likely has this publication, but if not, get in touch with the State Industrial Directories Corporation (New York City), where these are available for a fee.

There are telephone directories (both alphabetical and Yellow Pages listings). Either or both may be of considerable assistance in plotting your market or in planning whom to question in your survey (see Chapter 12).

The Dun & Bradstreet Million Dollar Directory, likely available in your local library, is one of the first sources you will want to consult to find out about companies within an industry. The first volume covers firms with a net worth of $1 million and more. The second lists businesses with a value of $500,000 to $999,999. Each listing gives the firm's name, trade names, state where incorporated, parent company (if any), headquarters address, division names and functions, annual sales, SIC code, and names and titles of the executives.

Moody's *Manuals* are also important list directories. Industries, public utilities, and transportation are covered in these; information is updated biweekly. They are good for getting a "feel" of an industry you are studying, although they cover only the largest corporations. They are not a source about small, privately held companies. Published by Moody's Investors Services, these manuals are available in most banks and brokerage firms.

A most important directory is the *Thomas Register of American Manufacturers.* Available in your library, this is a 17-volume list of some 123,000 manufacturers classified by products and by state and city. Total assets are listed, as well as trademarks and subsidiaries. This is a great source to determine the nature of your competitors or market.

There are city directories. Typically, these concentrate on residential listings.

Directories may be of considerable assistance in plotting your market or in planning whom to question in your survey.

However, they go farther than the telephone book, for they usually include a crisscross listing, showing names and numbers by blocks.

There are also specialized directories published by media and associations. One is the annual issue of *Advertising Age* (Chicago, Ill.) which lists all ad agencies, their billings, major personnel, and clients. This same publication has another annual issue listing major advertisers, with their advertising personnel, and describing their spending and programs for major products. But let's mention at least one broader-scale directory, one that provides a bit more than merely a specific list. This is the *Directory of Industry Data Sources,* published by Ballinger (Cambridge, Mass.). This provides sources primarily by industry, from furniture to wood and wood products. It also has a section listing data publishers and producers by various industry topics. Each specific listing gives the name of the publisher, the specific title, a brief abstract of contents, and price.

Check other commercial printed sources. The *Sales Management Annual Survey of Buying Power* (New York, N.Y.) provides useful local information on population, individual income, certain types of retail sales, and an index of market potential. It is included with an annual subscription to *Sales Management* or is usually available in your local library.

The *Editor & Publisher Market Guide* (New York, N.Y.) provides information on household incomes, retail sales, and other market data relevant to over 1,500 newspapers.

Other commercial data are also available, most of which are in print (hard copy) form, but not in libraries. You have to buy them. Here are a few:

Census tract data by ZIP code from a firm such as Donnelley Marketing Information Services (Stamford, Conn.). They can provide you with current information, whether about consumers or businesses. CACI/Source Products (Arlington, Va.) offers an annual publication entitled *The Sourcebook of Demographics and Buying Power for Every ZIP Code in the U.S.* They also publish a similar county handbook.

Donnelley's *American Profile* provides an updated summary of demos (vehicle registrations, socioeconomic status indicators, mobility, and so on) by whatever your requirements are: ZIP codes, census tracts, counties, circles, bands, whatever—you name it.

MarketPac, offered by National Decision Systems (Encinatas, Calif.), provides business counts by SIC, demographic and socioeconomic categories, employment counts, and consumer spending. You can get these by states, SMSAs, ZIP codes, or ADIs (areas of dominant influence; see Chapter 8).

A few firms offer specific industry studies. FIND/SVP, Inc. (Bethesda, Md.), publishes a monthly directory of available reports. These include industry and market and company studies, and business and marketing reference sources. They will put you on their mailing list without charge. Business Trend Analysis (Commack, N.Y.) offers a similar service.

Local Chambers of Commerce can fill you in on their thinking about expansion, environmental control, and transportation facility plans.

Getting the "Feel" of a Local Community. Generally, the local Chamber of Commerce or local Industrial Board offers more enthusiasm than facts. But you *can* get their assistance in understanding the *psychology* of the community—what their thinking is about expansion, environmental control (and its likely cost to you), and transportation facility plans. But do not count on much hard data.

How to Continue Your On-Line Search

By "on-line," we mean a completely organized system of storing information in a computer memory that permits easy and almost instantaneous playback of the information. The "expert" may talk about a "data-base retrieval system." It is really only a systematic file of information that has been put into a computer memory.

Do you need your own computer to use such files? Not at all. You may be far better off if you do not attempt it, even if you have your own computer. The process requires considerable computer skill, and you do not want to take considerable time off from your major role in the business to learn the system. Even if you have your own computer expert within the firm, before assigning him or her this responsibility, make sure he or she has the time to handle it.

There *are* special options you might want to consider if you have your own computer. There are programs available for computer use which, if you have a continuing need for them, might make it worthwhile to purchase and use them. Such programs are available for sales analysis, sales forecasting, tracking of sales or advertising campaigns, and mapping of your marketing area. But all these have to do with entering your own data into the system and using the computer for analysis. This is different from on-line searching, where the information already exists and merely awaits your tying into it.

Learn enough about existing data banks. There are over 5,000 data banks covering topics as broad as aborigines to zoology; as narrow as economics, management, and marketing; as marketing-oriented as advertising, markets, and marketing research. There are many subbreaks. Unless you are an expert, it is a confusing world out there. The nature of information may be bibliographic, a list (directory or dictionary), news, or statistics. A particular data bank may cover items for a period of 10 years or only 6 months.

There *are* directories of on-line resources, and your local librarian should be able to help you spot these, so you can get acquainted. We will mention just two, to give you an idea. One is the *Directory of On-Line Information Resources,* published annually by CSG Press (Rockville, Md.). This provides, under each subject—the topics are broad but specific, such as "alcohol" and "newspaper"—a statement about the years of coverage and, for each sublisting, specific contents and the organization offering access to the data base. The *Database Catalog,* published by Dialog (Palo Alto, Calif.), an information retrieval service, lists data-base sources by topic (the marketing areas, found in their general listings under many different headings) from advertising to trade opportunities. In each case, the specific listing provides the organization source, dates of coverage, types of information available, and costs. The one specialized list for federal data bases is Information USA (Chevy Chase, Md.).

The information broker is a specialist in retrieving data-base material.

It may require drudgery to get the information you need to get your firm on the best possible marketing path.

Select the right specialist with whom to work. We have already discussed—in connection with your search for print sources—the various library facilities: local, academic, state. Many public libraries, particularly in larger communities, offer data-base searches. Some charge a fee.

If your local library does not handle such searches, ask for advice on where to seek such help. There may be a nearby academic library with such facilities. If not, the state library almost surely will have them. In each case, the head reference librarian is the right place to start.

In recent years, a specialist (the information broker) in retrieving data-base material has emerged. You will not yet find such a listing in the Yellow Pages, so you will have to ask the librarian where to find one. While the information broker deals primarily in retrieval of data-base material, some also work in locating printed information. The information broker may be an independent firm or even a specialist librarian.

Know how to deal with the computer search expert. In your first meeting with an information broker, be thoroughly prepared to define your problem—and therefore your information needs. Have at least a cursory knowledge of some of the data banks that might be relevant for you, so that you can suggest some possibilities.

Understand the difference between an *exploratory* request (looking only for leads) and a *definitive* request (where you seek specific information relevant to your problem).

Understand and use appropriate key words. The computer is a machine, lacking human intelligence. It blindly follows specific orders, searching for information listed under words it is given. If you do not have the right words, you will not get the right answers. If you miss some terms, you will miss some data. A *Thesaurus of Key Words* is available for each data bank. By examining this carefully for your particular needs, you can make sure that you do not ask for too much or too little.

Finally, do not forget to get some estimate of cost. While the expert probably will not charge you a fortune, some of the data banks are expensive to use, and you need to know this in advance of any possible use.

Summary

As we have said several times, it is impossible for any book to give all sources of information for every product line and every sales situation. You must do much searching for yourself.

What we have tried to do is to get you off to a good start. The business of finding good sources is an attitude of mind. After a bit of experience it is possible to figure out what is *probably* available and where to get it.

If you are like most of us, when you buy a put-it-together-yourself product, you are likely to read the directions, throw up your hands, and tackle it on your own. Do not do this with seeking marketing information. If we can persuade you to do one thing, it is to reread this chapter carefully. It may be one of the dullest in the book, but it is also one of the most important.

It will take courage and determination to follow through. Most of us do not find it intriguing to dig into source material this way, to accumulate facts gathered by others, even though such information may be crucial to survival and growth of the business. It may require drudgery to get the information you need to get your firm on the best possible marketing path.

five

Marketing Intelligence and How to Use It

On a pleasant June evening, many automobile company executives were at a large cocktail party in Detroit. A Chrysler executive overheard a comment that Ford's top advertising photographer was in Paris. That seemed curious, since June was the month when automobile company photographers were usually involved in helping to implement the fall ad campaign. The Chrysler representative in Paris was alerted and learned that new Fords were being photographed with the Eiffel Tower as background and that Hong Kong was the next stop.

Chrysler "scooped" the Ford campaign with an ad campaign that highlighted its cars at U.S. landmarks, figuring that the American public could identify more easily with these than with foreign landmarks.

What Is Competitive Marketing Intelligence?

Let's start by defining the broad term *competitive intelligence*. This is the collection, evaluation, synthesis, and interpretation of information about a specific competitor which is useful for your company planning and operation. Note the focus on an individual competitor. Generally, the information is not readily available. Unlike the search for existing information outlined in Chapter 4, competitive intelligence includes not only published material (usually of obscure nature), but also may include first-hand observation, as in the Chrysler example. Whatever the method of getting the information, all is legitimate. There is little of the cloak-and-dagger variety.

The term *competitive marketing intelligence* covers competitive intelligence of a marketing nature. This includes information that may help your firm in its marketing efforts against a competitor. It may provide an early warning of some specific competitive move.

Marketing intelligence is widely used. As a shopper, you may have noticed a person in a grocery store with a handheld computer walking down an aisle. Kirk Tyson, president of The Competitive Intelligence Group (Oak Brook, Ill.), estimates that as many as one-fourth of these are employees of competing retail stores. Others are employees of firms who sell information about brand share and movement to grocery producers and chains.

Your competitors are watching you, so you had better be watching them. The manufacturer of a shaving lather had its research lab working hard on a hot lather product. The company placed a limited number of samples of the first product— for trial—with consumers. Each sample was picked up following the trial, to prevent any possible pickup by competitive manufacturers. After four such tests, consumers gave such glowing reports that the manufacturer decided that since the product was ready for marketing, there was no longer a need to pick up the samples in what would be the fifth and final consumer test.

Within 24 hours, the company president had a telephone call from the president of his major competitor congratulating him on the fine product, a sample of which was on the competitor's desk.

Your competitors are watching you, so you had better be watching them.

Is your competitor really aggressively pushing the product or just allowing it to sit quietly in the marketplace?

The Key Information Areas of Marketing Intelligence

There are several key information areas about your competitor crucial in understanding the firm's role in the marketplace.

The Product Commitment. For each of its major products or services—since company philosophy may vary by product—you need to know how committed your competitor is to the product. Is the firm really aggressively pushing the product or just allowing it to sit quietly in the marketplace? However, it may be a growing product category where the firm takes an aggressive stance. It may be a product category that is slipping within the marketplace, with the firm's accepting sales and profits as they occur, without marketing push.

Product Quality. Your competitor may stress top quality in some or all products or may have a policy simply of acceptable quality. Where top quality is stressed, top price is likely to be stressed as well. Acceptable quality is more likely to mean a moderately-priced item. Whatever the attitude, you need to know it to evaluate your role vis-à-vis the competitor.

The Competitor's Attitude about New Products. Some firms are, by intent, followers, rarely spending the money to develop their own new products. They are content to follow the lead of others. But your particular competitor may spend considerable funds on product development and may like to be among the leaders in new product introduction. You have got to know which role your competitor plays if you are to compete successfully.

Attitude Toward the Bottom Line. Does your competitor show more interest in immediate profits, or does the firm take a long-range viewpoint? Only if you know this can you understand how to operate in the marketplace against this firm.

Specific Nature of the Competitor's Market. Whether you are in the consumer or the business market, you need to know the particular kinds of customers served by your competitor. If it is the consumer market, you will want to know the geography and demographics (sex, age, income, and the like). If it is the business market, in addition to geography, you will want to know how the market is split by types of business, size, and the like. In the case of the business market, you may even be able to get information on major accounts and key customers.

Market Share and Trend. What is the total market share of the competitor? Is the firm or brand dominant within the product category? Is the competitor's share rising or falling? If you are a medium- to large-sized firm, you can buy such reports. If you are a smaller firm, you may have to make your own observations.

Distribution Channels. Is your competitor using distribution channels virtually identical with your own so that you meet head-on at all levels of marketing? Or

Does your competitor show more interest in immediate profits, or does the firm take a long-range viewpoint?

does your competitor have such marked differences in channels that you really meet competitively only, perhaps, at one level, such as the retail store shelf? You need a full understanding to make your own competitive plans and moves.

Flexibility in Marketing Strategy. Is the competitor a wheeler-dealer, responding quickly, decisively, and aggressively to pressures of the marketplace? Is the firm likely to use such tactics as pricing and advertising to respond quickly? Does the firm have the funds to use such tools and to continue to use them as long as it thinks the end justifies the means? Your understanding of the firm's marketing flexibility and muscle will greatly affect your own strategy and tactics in the competitive arena.

The Two Basic Sources of Competitive Marketing Intelligence

One is the *already-available source.* This is the kind of information described in Chapter 4. In the case of competitive marketing intelligence, however, such sources are mainly "unobtrusive" sources, the sort that you do not easily come by in the usual search for market information. The other is *first-hand collection of information,* where the intelligence exists only when you collect your own original information.

The Already-Available Source. Sometimes termed "desk research" or "secondary information," this is published information. While Chapter 4 has discussed such sources, you do not easily come across relevant detailed information about a specific competitor. These sources are not widely recognized and sometimes are not easily available. You have to know what the source is and where to get it. Your trusty reference librarian may be able to help you.

There's rich government information available, but you have to know what it is and how to get to it.

Specialized published material. This material is available from data-base sources, described in Chapter 4. Trinet (Parsippany, N.J.), for instance, provides marketing, sales, and financial data on U.S. firms with 20 or more employees. Investext offers reports on specific firms published by financial analysts.

Federal government information. There's rich government information available, but you have to know what it is and how to get it.

There are frequent *congressional committee hearings* on various topics that may reveal competitive information. Telephone your congressional or senatorial office. The people in the offices are delighted to check out such sources for constituents. The *Environmental Protection Agency* makes studies of firms that might pollute. The *Consumer Product Safety Commission* may have competitive information from its investigations of products considered potentially hazardous. Studies by the *National Institute for Occupational Safety and Health* may reveal interesting intelligence about specific firms.

If your competitor is large enough to be publicly traded on a stock exchange, the *Securities and Exchange Commission* is a fertile source. The firm must reveal many of the facts it would prefer competitors not to have—not only specific financial information, but many operational details as well.

Determining the locations of owners of automobile license numbers can help you determine the geography of your competitor's customers.

If you need information about a small firm, you may be able to get it from the *Small Business Administration* (Washington, D.C.). Any small firm that moves through *Small Business Administration* (SBA) in seeking primary or subcontracting work from the federal government must reveal many details of its operation, such as its type of business, number of employees, products and services produced, when established, current year's sales, and type of ownership. All this is included in the SBA's Procurement Automated Source System (PASS). In addition, the *Department of Commerce* (Washington, D.C.) maintains files on some 27,000 minority businesses.

State government information. One possibility is *court records*. If your competitor has been involved in court cases, the firm is almost certain to have revealed information about itself that is available nowhere else. Telephone your attorney to determine where to learn whether the firm has been in court and how to obtain or review the transcripts.

A second possibility is *determining the locations of owners of automobile license numbers*. What are the geographic locations of your competitor's customers? If customers drive to the place of business, you can record license numbers and then check the location of registration. (If you lack other means of checking the geography of your own market, you can use this system to check your own customers.) While most states do not provide such information directly to you, you can buy it from R. L. Polk & Company (Detroit, Mich.).

Your competitor as a marketing intelligence source. If your competitor publishes an *annual company report,* this can be a useful intelligence source. This report sometimes provides information you otherwise would not get. Be careful, though. There are ways to present financial data in a misleading manner. Firms typically publish the positives, not the negatives, whether about financial or other operations. An annual report certainly is not going to tell you any secrets, but it might tell you news of which you are not yet aware.

Look for *press reports and articles.* For past news, consult your local library or newspaper. If you need and want ongoing items, either do it yourself or subscribe to a good press-clipping service. At a nominal charge (Tyson mentions $30 monthly plus $0.70 per clip), such a service will provide you with press clippings about your competitor.

Media reports. Studies covering your competitor may have been conducted by your local advertising medium (newspaper, television, or radio station). It may have been a marketing or consumer survey which shows where your competitor ranks in your particular market and perhaps the strengths and weaknesses of that competitor according to reactions within the marketplace. Or it may be a "desk" study examining the firms within the market and describing them and their operations based on available information.

Broker reports. Chances are you have a stockbroker. Your broker may be able to get you one of the Investext checks referred to earlier in this chapter, which will provide a detailed and insightful analysis of the broad operational aspects of selected firms, one of which might be your competitor.

Credit reports. Credit reports (from Dun & Bradstreet or a local credit bureau) may be an aid in competitive marketing intelligence. The main value of such

A running check on the nature and frequency of competitors' advertising can give you a focused idea on what they are trying to do in their marketing efforts.

reports is in providing credit history and creditworthiness. Occasionally, they provide information you would not pick up elsewhere.

Dun & Bradstreet sometimes provides—when updating a report—material from an interview with one or more company executives. The input is limited and biased to present the firm's best case, but occasionally, new plans are revealed.

Advertising by your competitor. Three types of advertising may provide you with key leads about your competitor's marketing-related plans. One is *general advertising.* By keeping a running check on the nature and frequency of competitors' advertising, you can get a focused idea on what they are trying to do in their marketing effort. A scrapbook will help you maintain such records.

Make it specific. Keep monthly records on a company's efforts, specifying media (newspaper, radio, television) by space or time and estimated monthly figures (your local media, if you are a customer, will be of help). Keep notes on the *nature* of the effort.

Check the *Yellow Pages.* Says Leonard Fuld, managing director of a firm specializing in seeking out competitive marketing intelligence, "If you don't know the trading area of a competitor, open up the Yellow Pages to get a better map. It's one of the best references available." Check the Yellow Pages of various communities to determine how extensively your competitor is advertising. That's your competitor's definition of the company's marketing area.

If your competitor markets so broadly that you cannot be sure what directories to check, there's another possibility: the *Electronic Yellow Pages,* a data-base source available through Dialog. Check your knowledgeable librarian.

Check *local want ads.* If you regularly watch such ads by your competitor, you can spot when the firm is adding employees and the kinds of employees being added. This may give vital clues on new marketing effort.

Collecting Your Own Information about Your Competitor's Marketing. Sometimes the available information does not tell you all you need to know about your competitor's marketing. You may have to collect your own information first hand.

Formal surveillance. This is a structured observation of what is going on at your competitor's premises. It is expensive and not often necessary, so it is used sparingly.

A Canadian gasoline company conducted a massive controlled observation study of four service stations–restaurants along a major Ontario highway over a 2-week period. Observations were made of each station–restaurant (during all hours of operation of the outlet, often around the clock) from a post across the highway. No attempt was made to get cooperation from the stations. One parent firm even sent out observers to observe the observers!

Specific information was obtained on each service station and its restaurant. Service station data covered vehicle counts (at islands, bays, parking lots), recording of license numbers, gallons of gasoline pumped, and gallons received. Restaurant information included vehicle counts in parking lots, numbers of people entering the restaurant, and dollar amounts of purchases (from cash register observation).

You can make less elaborate observations of your competitor's premises. You

Formal surveillance is a structured observation of what is going on at your competitor's premises.

can observe traffic flow. As discussed earlier, you can determine where the vehicles come from. If you need an estimate of the number of employees, check employee parking lots by shift and by number of people within each car. It is simple to arrive at a pretty good figure on total employees.

Leonard Fuld, managing director of Information Data Search (Cambridge, Mass.), has found that counting shipping boxes can tell you a lot about a firm. Says Fuld, "The [bottom of a] box has a seal and numbers, and the name of the manufacturer. So all you have to do is to call the supplier. Usually you'll be told how many boxes they produced for the company in a certain time period. Then you can generate pretty reliable estimates of production runs and unit shipment sales."

If your business is retailing or consumer service (restaurant, hotel, motel, and so on), you have additional options. You can do comparison shopping (visiting your competitors' premises to find out what is going on, to learn their offerings versus yours, their services, their pricing). You may even decide to make use of a professional service to handle this for you.

Informal observation. Most first-hand marketing intelligence is less structured than what we have been talking about. The term is broad: it means keeping all your antennae open for what is going on competitively. Information observation is largely "listening in," although some is slightly more structured.

The Chrysler story at the start of this chapter is an example. Bacardi, maker of the world's best-selling rum, has an organized approach. Representatives visit "trendy" bars and listen to customer orders to bartenders, waiters, and waitresses. The reports provide a guide to what is happening to drinking patterns among the trendsetters.

By "listening in," you may get wind of significant events or possibilities about your competitor. The waitress in a coffee shop mentions a layoff at the nearby plant and comments that it is too bad that there is no promise of when the "poor fellows" may be called back to work. A regular there says that the problem is poor sale of a new product. While such sources may be entirely wrong, they provide clues to be followed.

This sort of "listening in" can be well planned. Spot business places that cater to employees and families of your competitor. These are generally easy to spot, since they will be convenient to your competitor's location. Choose types of businesses where people linger and chat, mainly restaurants and bars. Check those crisscross telephone directories we talked about in Chapter 4 to put together your list of such possible places of business.

Informal observation means keeping your antennae open for what is going on competitively.

Imagination is your only limit in informal observation. One automobile dealership had its service personnel record the radio dial setting for each car brought in for servicing. The dealership placed its radio advertising accordingly.

Direct Questioning. When we mention "direct questioning" as a tool for gathering marketing intelligence, we are not talking about the survey approach discussed in Sections Two and Three, later in this book. The sort of questioning here is more informal and unstructured. There is no specific list of people ("population") you should be questioning. In short, it is much more up to you as to where to go and how to do it.

One form is *networking*. Tyson suggests that you start by building a "who knows who" list. Build a list of every person you know who might obtain nonpublished information from outsiders.

This list may include *your peers in other firms*. Such people, in addition to suggesting other sources, may be able to give you public information about what their firm is doing that you might not yet know. They also may be able to give you information on the immediate competitor of your inquiry.

If you build peer contacts in other geographic areas, your search may be even easier. Your peer in a removed geographic area may be able to obtain and provide information about your competitor that you cannot get locally. Naturally, you will be expected to reciprocate.

One researcher in a manufacturing firm developed such a responsive group of peers in other similar firms that he was able easily to determine market shares and to spot when a firm was developing a new or improved product. Again, you have to be willing and able to reciprocate when asked; otherwise, the contact will wither.

The *media sales representative* from your newspaper or radio or television station is another important source of direct questioning. The media rep can give you important information about your competitor, most obviously about advertising plans or results of a particular advertising effort. The astute media rep can go well beyond this, however.

The *real estate agent* often knows of a firm's expansion plans. The agent is often the first to know not only about the kind of real estate being sought (location and size), but also about the plans of the firm leading to such needs.

The *shopping mall manager* is another good source, assuming that your competitor is either a current or an incoming tenant. The manager may know general plans for the firm, but will definitely know square footage, cost per square foot, and lease arrangements.

Do not overlook *associations*. The association executive is likely to know about specific plans for your competitor and may be willing to discuss these, assuming he or she has not been told in confidence. Being an active member of your association—local, regional, or national—will mean that you hear many things about your competitor that you would not pick up for yourself. Sometimes, too, publications of the association reveal information about your competitor.

You can get marketing information about your competitor from *customers*. This might be either your own customers (who also use other sources, such as your competitor) or your competitor's customers (whether or not they happen to deal with you).

Do not use your own customers for a study of your competitor. They are your own loyal, continuing clientele. Whatever they tell you about your competitor is biased in your favor. (You *do* want the reactions of your customers to how well you serve them, but this is a separate discussion, considered in Chapter 9). If you really want first-hand customer reactions about your competitor's efforts, then go to *the competitor's customers*.

Here is the way to do it: Locate a local research firm (or maybe a member of the marketing faculty at your local college or university) who can recruit qualified

Real estate agents are often the first to know of a firm's expansion plans.

participants and set up a *focus group interview*. This tool is particularly useful if you are thinking about entering a new geographic market area and need a view of the competitive customer market. Properly designed and conducted, the focus group interview can quickly uncover customer perceptions about your major competition. But you will need to be mighty careful. You do not want to disclose who you are. There are many more procedures you will need to have followed. (See the discussions about focus group interviews in Chapter 11.)

Outside Assistance in Collecting Marketing Intelligence

In reading this chapter, you may have decided that you have neither the time nor the energy to collect competitive marketing intelligence. You have the option of using outside specialists.

The Specialist in Secondary (Existing) Information.   This is a specialist information broker (the dealer in information banks described in Chapter 4). Such firms do not stress marketing information, but you can use such a firm—if it has such resources—to get such intelligence. Such a firm—with your direction—will be delighted to get you marketing intelligence about your specific competitor.

While we cannot make specific recommendations, some of the more frequently named firms are the Competitor Intelligence Group (Chicago, Ill.), FIND/SVP (New York City), Predicasts (Cleveland, Ohio), and Washington Researchers (Washington, D.C.).

The Specialist in Primary Information.   There is only one firm we are aware of, and it has a good press. This firm is Information Data Search (Cambridge, Mass.). We have quoted Fuld, its managing director.

Make your own search.   Do make your own search. But it is not all that easy. Do not figure on picking up the Yellow Pages and locating a source. It is too soon for that.

If you deal with an *advertising agency, management consultant firm, or marketing research firm,* start there. If you do not have such contacts, go to the Yellow Pages. You will recognize names of the more prominent firms. They should be able to handle a search for you or to suggest possibilities.

Use *networking facilities.* One or more of your peers will have had valuable experience to guide you.

Do not be shy about approaching *knowledgeable people in major companies* for their ideas. Fortune 500 firms are the way to go. Start by getting the name of the marketing research director or director of corporate planning. Then telephone. Do not write, for response is indefinite. And do not be embarrassed about your direct approach. Generally, the person will be flattered to respond.

Do not be shy about approaching knowledgeable people in major companies for their ideas.

How Marketing Research Can Help Your Business

How Marketing Research Can Help Your Business Market to Business Firms

This chapter concerns market research for business firms dealing with other business firms. It deals with products that are used by other manufacturers, either for their own use or for inclusion in their own products. It also deals with the special problems of research with concerns that buy products for resale.

Not long ago we had lunch with the marketing department of a middle-sized manufacturing company. It says something about the company that the marketing department also was the sales department and the whole lot of us could fit around one of the smaller tables in a restaurant. Three men were responsible for "moving product" (their term). The reason for the meeting was that one of the products was not moving at all.

This happens sooner or later to almost every company in the manufacturing field. Even the largest company will sometimes labor and labor and produce a mouse. The largest companies can shrug it off (and shrug off some personnel along with it perhaps). The birth of a mouse for a small company can be an unhappy day—a birthday that will not be celebrated in years to come.

The marketing department had "hired some research" from a small local professional researcher and then had blindly followed the recommendations. Busy with other matters, the company felt that it could not take the time either to do any research itself or to know that the research was being done well and thoroughly (it was not). The sad ending of the story: $2 million unavailable for products in greater demand, use of valuable space in a warehouse. The company might have avoided this dreadful situation if it had either done its own research (after all, who knew the product better?) or at least worked with the researcher, who undoubtedly did his best with an unfamiliar problem.

It is possible that many companies that now have dispensed with their marketing research departments in the interest of cutting costs will be tempted to follow the lead of this manufacturer. Either they will do no marketing research at all or they will attempt to "buy some research" which may or may not be done well.

In all the situations to be described in this chapter, the owner, manager, product line manager, or someone else in the firm can perform do-it-yourself marketing research. Failing that, the company which chooses to "go outside," possibly to a local researcher describing himself or herself as a business consultant in the Yellow Pages, would be extremely well advised to know what is going on, supervise what is going on, and indeed take some part in the research itself, if possible. This approach gives the research a chance of being meaningful, useful, and not too dangerous in terms of reaching unwarranted assumptions and conclusions.

The scope of this chapter therefore becomes clear. The "situations" described cover relatively small manufacturing companies, but they also will be familiar to larger companies which no longer have a professional staff to do the job. In light of the fierce cost cutting of recent years, leading to the dismissal or early retirement of large numbers of middle managers, we must assume that no research at all will often be the case. Furthermore, there appears to be a

Even the largest company will sometimes labor and labor and produce a mouse.

competitive push to get product to market much faster than formerly was true for both consumer and industrial goods.

But market research is still worthwhile and can often save a product which might have been successful. Or produce findings that will make the product more profitable. Or stop a badly conceived product before great harm is done. Not one of these situations may exactly duplicate your own particular headache, but the chapter will have done its work if you, the reader, can be urged to make a transition from this book to *your* problem.

Our own fundamental outline of how to organize a study starts with some very simple questions. Almost all marketing research will begin this way:

1. What is it I need to know to make a correct decision?

2. Who knows the answers (including already-available secondary sources)?

3. What is the best, least expensive, and most thorough way of communicating with these sources?

4. How much is the answer worth, in light of the risks and probable profits involved?

Situation One

You are a manufacturer of construction tools with over a century of successful experience. Sales and profits have grown continuously except for a period during the Great Depression. Now you contemplate entering the market for other products which become a part of both residential and commercial buildings. A way of doing this is by the purchase of a small company with a good name, but not one of the sales leaders in its field. You believe that with your marketing experience and ability, you can lead this new company/division to greater success.

Admittedly, more than marketing problems are involved. But marketing research can add knowledge that will make the ultimate decision to purchase or not to purchase more sound. Secrecy may be necessary at that point. A dummy name may be useful for research purposes, as long as no fraud is involved.

These questions should arise:

1. What strengths and weaknesses does this small company have in its own market?

2. How does this new product go to market? Is there any way that our own market strength can help this new product?

3. What do distributors and installers think of this new company's product line? Specific weaknesses and strengths?

4. How do the ultimate consumers of this product feel about this product line? Is brand name important to them? Or is brand name most important to distributors and installers?

5. What pricing policies has this company followed, as compared with larger

Market research can often save a product which might have been successful or stop a badly conceived product before great harm is done.

competitors? Can a bad pricing policy in the past be overcome through our efforts?

6. What is the probable future of this industry in the near and longer term? To borrow terms from the Boston Consulting Group, will it become a "Cash Cow," a "Star," a "Question Mark," or a "Dog"?

Such questions as these can be answered more soundly with the help of some marketing research. Ways of conducting this research will be found in Chapter 10.

With top-drawer researchers now getting from $500 to $1,000 or more per day, plus expenses, this problem might better (in this particular case) be approached by members of the buying company marketing group. As a former advertising columnist might have said, the company should do "the old hat trick." Get out in the field. A first decision might be to limit the area to be researched. It will be possible, in many cases, to determine some area that has a larger than average number of potential customers. Will these be similar to customers in other areas? We do not know. And a matter of judgment enters in. However, it is fairly safe to assume that this cluster of business-type customers will be similar enough to allow some decision to be made. If there is sufficient disparity in the results, it may be necessary to widen the research until some form begins to appear in the responses.

It will be necessary here, as with other situations to be discussed, to determine who the real decision makers are among the potential customers. It would be incorrect, in many cases, to assume that the purchasing agent or one of his or her people is the right one. Your proposed product may be so relatively unimportant the purchasing agent may ask and follow the advice of those who use the product. They are the ones who should be contacted by one means or another.

Now is the time to make a choice of means for making contact: interview, mail questionnaire, or telephone. In this case, personal interviews may appear to be the best approach.

You cannot get away from some judgment at the start, however. There must be some idea of what profit or loss might come from a good or bad judgment. Research, as we said before, must find its place somewhere within these boundaries.

One thing to be careful of is the proper mix of respondents. Even a 75 percent response is of no value if the company that purchases over 50 percent of this particular product line chooses not to talk to you meaningfully or answer your questionnaire. A little detective work among that company's competitors may be in order. Call it research or just plain common sense. Here, see Chapter 5 of this book.

The company that you prepare to buy has its list of customers—but you will not limit your research to them. There are ways of getting names of people to receive questionnaires or to be interviewed. The *Thomas Register* is a source. Associations are a source. An association may not be willing to give you a membership list, but someone else may be willing to part with last year's list, which is good enough. We cannot go into all the methods of research here. Chapters 4, 5, and 10 will be useful.

A company often must do "the old hat trick" and get out in the field.

An open, honest approach is crucial—and, where possible, an approach that allows the respondents to see some future value for themselves. Some new information about the market may be passed on—without destroying confidentiality.

It has been our experience stretching over many, many years that the average businessperson really wants to help if he or she sees your need, knows that you are not going to hurt him or her in any way, and finds your approach friendly and disarming. This is not to say that you cannot use standard research techniques such as printing a questionnaire on different colors of paper for different kinds of customers or some other device to help you sort out the responses to a mail questionnaire. None of these techniques is dishonest or harmful to the person who answers such a questionnaire. What would be dishonest would be to promise confidentiality and then use the results only as a sales device. Sales actions that disguise themselves as market research are not used as much as formerly. They are dishonest, they annoy and may harm the respondent, and certainly they harm the companies which want to do a legitimate job of fact finding in a true and responsible marketing research project.

Acquisition fever comes and goes in cycles that correspond roughly to the business situation. Even the largest of companies have frequently had much bloodletting. The word "growth" often carries an emotional tone similar to "motherhood" and "American flag." To be against growth is to be un-American. But growth that means a poor new product or a bad acquisition is not good for the country, and definitely not good for you. Very large companies can give much top executive attention to an acquisition, with help from bankers, consultants, and other helpers. You—presumably a smaller company—may not have all this expertise at your beck and call. You must depend on marketing research, often done by yourself or some other member of your small staff.

The important thing is to *do* the research before you get carried away by growth, acquisition, motherhood, and the American flag. If a new product line, a new acquisition, is part of a well-thought-out long-range plan, marketing research may still be required. If there is no formal long-range plan and no marketing research, however, then may heaven help you. You may be lucky enough or smart enough to carry it off, but luck, plus the smarts, will be much better if pertinent facts are also available.

In the particular and true circumstances that served as the foundation for this case study, no research in the market was done at all. As with so many situations, there appeared to be the necessity for speed or some other company would make the buy. And, even more important, there was fear that any rumor of a buy-out would harm the market prospects of the company to be bought. Also important was the belief that news of an impending purchase would hurt the morale of the employees of the target firm.

In this particular case, also, the purchase was not a success. The buying company found that there was no synergy between the market strengths of either firm. Moreover, the older company was not aware of the tremendous marketing strength of a large competitor in this field—marketing strength among distributors and installers that could not be overcome. The new division continued to

The word "growth" often carries an emotional tone similar to "motherhood" and the "American flag."

lose money and subsequently was sold. Marketing research of only the simplest and most direct form could have prevented this disaster.

Situation Two

You can only guess at the true share of the market for one of your highest selling and most profitable products. There is no trade association reporting industry sales. And anyway, you would not trust such figures, having reason to believe that some competitors would fudge their figures.

Marketing research can help solve this problem with at least some degree of accuracy. Most businesspeople are likely to give as accurate answers as possible. A mail questionnaire among customers can reveal reasonably accurate figures for the percentage of purchases of your product versus the total of competitors' products. These questionnaires can be supplemented by some visits to customers. Some customers will not tell the truth or will refuse to answer, but you will be surprised at the accuracy about the entire market that can be obtained from interviews and questionnaires if the sample is carefully selected.

One company thought that its share of market for one of its most profitable products was more than 70 percent. Careful analysis in the market showed that the true share of the market was less than 50 percent. The 70 percent share led to a comfortable lack of aggressiveness. The 50 percent share led to a much greater sales push. Without market research, the company might well have continued in its slow pace, probably gradually losing its market to much more aggressive competitors aware of their situation.

Luck, plus the smarts, will be much better if pertinent facts are also available.

Situation Three

You would like to know just what the attitude of your distributors toward your company really is. Are you the favored, first-line supplier? Are they satisfied with your performance and unlikely to go elsewhere? What can you do to improve your performance with them?

Read Chapter 10 for specific ways to use marketing research. However, in a situation such as this, some selected field calls may be helpful in determining the true situation. Such calls should not, obviously, be made by the territorial salespeople. Better would be a top executive of the company. For many companies, however, particularly large corporations, such executive field work is unlikely. We have found that a marketing research director, if such a person exists, or one of the marketing people lower in corporate job level can more often than realized loosen the tongues of persons being interviewed and approach the "truth." A number of interviews tend to even out the responses. One or two respondents may have been too busy to do more than produce a few generalities. Another may be upset over some recent incident of bad delivery, and so on. Somewhere along the line, however, the same stories, the same gripes, the same praises will be heard. The findings become more organized, and what needs to be done becomes more clear.

A mail questionnaire among customers can reveal reasonably accurate figures for the percentage of purchases of your product versus the total of competitors' products.

People are often surprised at the small size of samples used by professional pollsters.

People are often surprised at the small size of samples used by professional pollsters. Sooner than seems possible, however, the final study results begin to be apparent. This is also true in business-to-business research.

It is vital to convince respondents that their most truthful answers are what is being sought. "Your delivery stinks." "Your local salespeople should know more about our requirements." And so on. Only by convincing the people being interviewed that this is what you want can you go home with a real feel for what is needed—and how your company stands as compared with your competitors.

Situation Four

You are not a brand new manufacturer, but you have a new product about which you have some doubts. You already have good distribution of your present line, which goes to the same channels. You do not feel that a broad consumer study is necessary, but you would like to know the probable acceptance in the distribution channel.

A big temptation here is to use your sales personnel as marketing researchers. We may say emphatically that, for most situations, the use of the sales force for marketing research is a bad mistake. Your salespeople are by nature and training optimistic folks who think positively. Their relations with buyers are entirely different from those of true fact finders. A researcher may deliberately seek negative aspects of the market for your new product. What can go wrong? What is wrong with this product as compared with others already on the market? Is the proposed price too high? Is the design poor—or could it be improved? Thinking of such things goes against the grain of a good sales representative.

Of course, we are speaking in general terms and not about all salespeople at all times. Some people can be good salespeople and good researchers at the same time, but they are the exception rather than the rule. This point must be given careful consideration in the choice of how to do your study.

Moreover, it is unfair to many salespeople to ask them to spend their time unproductively (in their opinion) doing a job which they were not hired for. If they have the choice of being in Detroit for a research interview or in Cincinnati for a sales windup, where do you think they will be? They will choose sales, and that is what the company wants them to do. Moreover, for many salespeople, an incentive is part of their total income. To ask them to give up selling time is to ask them to give up part of their income.

The one advantage an established manufacturer has is a knowledge of its customers, names of people, ways of trade, and so on. Whether the manufacturer chooses to go the route of a mail questionnaire, a telephone study, or a series of personal interviews, it already has one leg up on the problem.

One thing that must be watched for—particularly for the do-it-yourselfer to whom this book is addressed—is the tendency to ask Old Joe in Kansas City what he thinks and then take his answer as gospel truth. Joe, smart as he may be, can only answer for himself. He is one man, old, in one part of the country. There is a strong temptation, however, which must be resisted with all willpower, to call Old Joe for the answer. "Joe," you would say, "would our product XXX, which you know, be better if we redesigned it and added a transducer?" "A what?" asks Old Joe, who may still be using his Atwater Kent radio. Well, we need to carry this no further; Old Joe, as good a customer as he has been, as fine a fellow as he is, can give you no help on this particular project. The trouble is that being a friendly fellow, he will *try*. You, being a busy person, also will try to pretend to yourself that you have had a productive interview. We had a word for such research in the Navy, but we won't use it in print.

A mail questionnaire can be useful for this problem—if done correctly. So is a telephone study—if your relations with the customers are close and good. See Figures 6.1 and 6.2 for examples of the use of a telephone in marketing research.

Not everyone can do a telephone study properly, and some people will never learn how. A telephone call can be a nuisance to a busy executive. A conversation with a busy executive's busy secretary can cause both of you to tear your hair out. It happens frequently that a would-be researcher tells a secretary that he or she is doing some marketing research, would like some information that would help both sides, and so on. The secretary usually gets on the intercom and tells the boss that someone from the XX Company is on the phone. That is all; you have wasted your words on an unwilling ear. Now you have to start all over again—and you had better be good or you will get nothing.

The important thing with either a mail questionnaire or a telephone study is to be *prepared*. Be prepared for any eventuality—a grumpy secretary, a grumpy boss, a busy boss with no time for you, a suspicious person who does not really believe you are honest, and so on.

Perhaps you have a new product about which you have some doubts, and you want to know the probable acceptance in an already established distribution channel.

Probably the best research in this case is, if possible, to take a model of the new product out into the field. This makes a much more interesting interview for both sides and is much more likely to achieve worthwhile results.

Situation Five

You are successful in a small part of the total market for electrical goods used in homes and offices. You would like to enlarge your field, perhaps running the risk of meeting serious competition from the very large companies. What can you do?

Methods of searching for answers will be similar to the preceding situation. This is not simply a problem for the sales and marketing departments. A significant move into new product lines will require the thought and action of financial people, top management, and perhaps even the board of directors.

The possibility that a new product line will cut into the sales of a presently profitable product must be studied. It may still be a wise decision to go ahead to prevent ultimate disaster as the present line begins to become "old hat" with customers, salespeople, and even management.

One thing that you must determine early on is whether the proposed new product line is bought by the same buyer as your present line. This might involve doubling the time used by your salespeople in one customer's office. Or it might even mean the need for a separate sales force for the new product line. This might not kill the new product idea, but you would then have to see possible sales and profits that would warrant separate salespeople.

In telephone research, you sometimes waste your words on an unwilling ear.

WOODWORKING MACHINERY/TOOLING
FUTURES STUDY

DATE _____ Personal _____ Telephone _____ PHONE # (___) _____

NAME _____ TITLE _____ DIST. _____

COMPANY _____

ADDRESS _____

My name is _____ with Construction Resources Inc.,
a market research firm in Birmingham, Mich. I would like your help. We are working on an
assignment for a major U.S. manufacturer of tools and machines for the woodworking industry to
identify the needs of the marketplace over the next 5 to 10 years.

Your inputs will help them to better plan engineering and R&D to meet your and the woodworking industry's future needs.

(PHONE) Do you have a few minutes or could I call you at a more convenient time?

A. Have there been any recent changes in your molding and shaping processes within the last
    2 or 3 years? Yes _____ No _____ What? Why? Replaced what?
    1. Tooling (Steel vs. carbide vs. diamonds vs. hot isostatic pressing, etc.)

    _____

    _____

        * Tried diamonds? Results? _____

    2. Machinery (i.e., Weinig, etc.) _____

    _____

    3. Raw materials (i.e., p'board, mdf, etc.) _____

    _____

    4. Other (i.e., computers, lasers, etc.) _____

    _____

FUTURE CHANGE

B. What new technologies might change your molding and shaping operations in the next 5 to
    10 years?

    1. Your changes in raw materials (such as particleboard or medium density fiber board, etc.)

    _____
                                                    CONSTRUCTION
    _____   RESOURCES INC.

FIGURE 6.1. *Example of a well-designed questionnaire to be used in either
telephone or personal interviewing. (Courtesy of Construction Resources, Inc.,
Birmingham, Mich.)*

B. 2. Your changes in tooling materials (i.e., Hot isostatic pressing, ceramics, GE "Compax," diamond, lasers, etc.)

_____

_____

3. Changes in machine technology (i.e., Weinig and Leiser techniques of using standard tools, or complete systems, etc.)

_____

_____

4. Changes in tool holders/tool changes (i.e., hydraulic holders, etc.)

_____

5. Changes in materials handling? _____

_____

6. Changes in controls/systems/CAD-CAM/etc.

_____

COMPANY BACKGROUND

C. 1. Product Produced:

HH furniture	_____	Moldings	_____
Office furniture	_____	Cabinets	_____
Wood windows	_____	Flooring	_____
Wood doors	_____	Misc. (Specify_____)	_____

2. Number of Employees _____

3. Type(s) of machinery using cutter knives or shapers? Which are most important tool users?

Molder _____

Shaper _____

Double end tenoner _____

Finger jointer _____

Planer _____

4. What types of tooling is used on what equipment?

	Knife Inserts/heads		Shapers		Other (Explain)	
	Steel	Carbide	Steel	Carbide		
Molder	_____	_____	_____	_____	_____	_____
Shaper	_____	_____	_____	_____	_____	_____
D.E. Tenoner	_____	_____	_____	_____	_____	_____
F. Jointer	_____	_____	_____	_____	_____	_____
Planer	_____	_____	_____	_____	_____	_____

C. 5. Approximately how many cutter or shaper tool sets are owned _____

EXPLORE WHY _____

_____

6. How many equipment changeovers per day? Trends?

	No. of Changes	Discussion
Molder	_____	_____
Shaper	_____	_____
D.E. Tenoner	_____	_____
F. Jointer	_____	_____
Planer	_____	_____

7. Approximately what volume do you turn out in a typical hour, day, year? _____
   lin. ft. per _____

8. What type cutting edge do you use most?
   Tool steel _____ Carbide _____ Diamond _____

   Other (describe) _____

   Why? _____

9. Shape/mold tooling expenditures per year now? In 5 years? Why a change?

	Now $	1995 $	Why a possible change?
New tooling	_____	_____	_____
Resharpening	_____	_____	_____
Total	_____	_____	_____

10. What is the primary type of wood used in your process?

Dimension	_____	Med. density fiberboard	_____
(Species _____)		Waferboard	_____
Particleboard	_____	Other (Plastic/plas. lami./etc.)	_____
Hardboard	_____	(Specify _____)	_____

BUYING PRACTICES

D. 1. Concerning your molding and shaping tools, do you typically specify:

		WHY?
Custom design	_____	_____
Standard design	_____	_____
A complete system	_____	_____

a. Is there a trend in any direction? WHY? _____

_____

2. Where do you buy your molding and shaping tools?

What manufacturer(s) _____

a. Direct _____ b. Mfgr. rep. _____ c. Dealer _____

3. What services are performed by your source of supply, the manufacturer?

_____

a. Are you happy with your present system for tool buying? Why? Why not? Changes?

_____

_____

OTHER

E. 1. What firms/individuals should be contacted that are on the leading edge of wood machining change?

_____

_____

2. Are there any further emerging technologies, comments, suggestions you'd like to pass along to the engineering and R&D people?

_____

_____

Thanks for your help.

For situations such as this, mail questionnaires have been successfully used. Possibly a combination of personal interviews and mail questionnaires would do the trick. It would be advisable, in this case, to do some personal interviews first to get material to use in the questionnaire. Careful attention must be given to the preparation of the mail questionnaire, as described in Chapter 10.

Not a matter for the market researcher, but one that would be important in this case, is the problem of financing a new line, providing manufacturing and warehousing facilities, and so on. However, marketing research should definitely provide answers to the person or persons making the final decision.

Situation Six

An older product's sales are slipping. Why? Sales boredom? Market change?

This is always a ticklish and iffy sort of problem. Salespeople do get tired of the same old thing. Something new is exciting. An old product may still have a natural market, but it may need more push rather than less. With more push, the potential profit is large, since early costs have all been written off.

Should you drop the line or change your sales tactics? This is not a question

An old product may still have a natural market, but it may need more push rather than less.

PMG PROJECT NO. 84-7001

LARGE OUTBOARD MOTORS

DEALERSHIP _____ DATE _____

LOCATION _____ RESPONDENT _____

PHONE _____ TITLE _____

Hello, I'm _____ from Price Marketing Group, a market research firm. We're doing a study on large outboard motors (those of more than 100 HP). We're trying to understand how important various kinds of boats are to the sale of these larger outboards.

May I speak with the sales manager (OR general manager OR owner)?

I'd like to talk about this for 10 to 15 minutes. Is this a convenient time? If not, when...

Date	Time	Person	Title	Action*
_____	_____	_____	_____	_____
_____	_____	_____	_____	_____
_____	_____	_____	_____	_____

*Call back, interview, etc.

Interview No. _____ (1-3)

Section of U.S. _____(4)

FIGURE 6.2. *Another example of a well-designed questionnaire. (Courtesy of Price Marketing Group, Evanston, Ill.)*

1. What brands of outboard motors do you sell?
   If more than one brand, which is your primary brand for the larger motors?

Brand	(Col. 5) Primary Brand	(Col. 6) Secondary Brand
Johnson or Evinrude	1	1
Mercury or Mariner	2	2
Yamaha	3	3
Suzuki	4	4
Other brands	5	5

2. What size motors in the (primary brand) do you carry, that is, sizes larger than 100 HP?
   How about in the secondary brand?

Size (HP)	(Col. 7) Primary Brand	(Col. 8) Secondary Brand
100	1	1
115	2	2
140	3	3
150	4	4
175	5	5
185	6	6
200	7	7
220	8	8
235	9	9
300	0	0

3. Which of the following kinds of outboard-powered boats do you carry?

   (   ) bass boats _____   (   ) fiberglass
                                            (   ) aluminum
                                            (   ) both

   (   ) off-shore fishing boats
   (   ) off-shore/high performance runabouts
   (   ) family runabouts _____(   ) fiberglass
                                            (   ) aluminum
                                            (   ) both

4. For the current model year, how many outboards of all sizes (under and over 100 HP) do you expect to sell?

   _____
   (Col. 9-11)

		115HP	140/150HP	175/185/200 HP	220/225/235HP	300 HP

PRIMARY BRAND _____ _____ | CARD 2 DUP COL. 1-3
(Name)   (Code No.)

	115HP	140/150HP	175/185/200 HP	220/225/235HP	300 HP
5. No. motors sold in 1984	(12-14)	(33-35)	(54-56)	(75-76)	(18-19)
5-1. BASS BOATS					
5-1(a). Aluminum Hull	(15-16)	(36-37)	(57-58)	(77-78)	(20-21)
Fiberglass Hull	(17-18)	(38-39)	(59-60)	(79-80)	(22-23)
5-2. OFF-SHORE FISHING (Center-console and walk around cabin)					
5-2(a). Single-engine	(19-20)	(40-41)	(61-62)	(4-5)	(24-25)
Twin-engine	(21-22)	(42-43)	(63-64)	(6-7)	(26-27)
5-3. OFF-SHORE/HIGH PERFORMANCE OUT-BOARD RUNABOUTS					
5-3(a). Single -engine	(23-24)	(44-45)	(65-66)	(8-9)	(28-29)
Twin-engine	(25-26)	(46-47)	(67-68)	(10-11)	(30-31)
5-4. FAMILY RUNABOUTS/ SKI BOATS					
5-4(a). Aluminum Hull	(27-28)	(48-49)	(69-70)	(12-13)	(32-33)
Fiberglass Hull	(29-30)	(50-51)	(71-72)	(14-15)	(34-35)
5-5. ALL OTHER outboard powered boats	(31-32)	(52-53)	(73-74)	(16-17)	(36-37)

6. Now that I have a pretty good idea of the kinds of boats on which your 100+ HP outboards are used, I'd like to explore another topic with you; that is, the degree to which each of these types of boats are rigged with the largest allowable size offered by the brands you carry, given the maximum HP rating specified for that boat?

6-1. When you put a 115HP motor on a BASS BOAT, on what percent of those boats is that the largest motor you can install given the maximum HP specified for that boat?

Then go on for each of the other size motors installed on BASS BOATS.			
125/115HP	140/150HP	175/185HP	200HP

	125/115HP	140/150HP	175/185HP	200HP
Percent rigged maximum rating when rigged with that motor	(38-39)	(40-41)	(42-43)	(44-45)

6-2. Now, with regard to OFF-SHORE FISHING BOATS, when you rig a SINGLE-ENGINE 115HP, on what percent of these off-shore fishing boats is this 115HP motor the largest you can install given the maximum HP specified for the boat?

And so on for the other size motors.			
125/115HP	140/150HP	175/185HP	200HP

	125/115HP	140/150HP	175/185HP	200HP
Single-engine off-shore fishing	(46-47)	(48-49)	(50-51)	(52-53)
	220/225HP	235HP	300HP	
	(54-55)	(56-57)	(58-59)	

6-3. When you rig TWIN 140/150 MOTORS on an OFF-SHORE FISHING BOAT on what percent of these boats is the configuration the largest motor you can install given the max HP specified for the boat?

(AND SO ON FOR THE OTHER SIZES)

	Twin 140/ 150's	Twin 175/ 180's	Twin 200's	Twin 220/ 225's
Twin-engine off-shore fishing	(60-61)	(62-63)	(64-65)	(66-67)
	TWIN125's/ 115's	Twin 235's	Twin 300's	
	(goes on Cd4)	(68-69)	(70-71)	

6-4. When you rig a 115HP motor on a FAMILY RUNABOUT, on what percent of these boats is this 115HP motor the largest motor you can install given the max HP specified for the boat?

And so on for the other size motors.			
125/115HP	140/150HP	175/185HP	200HP

	125/115HP	140/150HP	175/185HP	200HP
Runabouts	(72-73)	(74-75)	(76-77)	(78-79)

that salespeople can answer, largely because they really do not know. Personal interviews by someone from the home office are almost a necessity. Are we losing our share of a somewhat stable market simply because everyone is tired of the product? This situation is similar to the need to determine share of market.

There are fads in products for business, as there are in consumer products. There are rushes to develop new departments, new methods, new training ways, new accounting techniques, and so on. There have been fads in such approaches as brainstorming sessions and operations research. Each fad, in turn, may call for equipment and supplies. Each may fade away, leaving a worthwhile residue. Manufacturing marketing research with business firms must take into account that not all change is necessarily a forward movement. Sometimes change occurs because everyone is a bit bored with the old. People may be eager to drop old ways and old product lines and leap toward the new.

Not the least bored may be your own salespeople. However, to drop a line entirely or to stop pushing it because everyone has jumped into something new may be the worst thing that can be done to retain good profit levels.

How to find out? As we said, some personal calls could be the best way of getting a feel for what is going on. Small manufacturers may very well make a nice profit by continuing to supply the smaller market that larger companies no longer find attractive. General Electric may not be able to manufacture and sell some item that you could make profitably in a back corner of your factory. Both companies would be happy, and a good product would still be available for a market big enough to keep you well in the black.

Situation Seven

Are we offering too many or too few price lines? Are our price lines at the proper level for best sales in today's market?

Carrying too many price lines can be the death of profits for a small or middle-sized manufacturer, and this situation is far too easy to fall into. Because of attempts to meet competition in the past, new variations of products or new price lines may have caused inventory growth beyond all reasonable limits. Too much inventory will be accompanied by too much wasted sales time, too much paperwork, and too many other things that could be easily dispensed with. Yet even the largest manufacturers are guilty of carrying too many price lines—each fearing that dropping certain lines will cause customer loss.

How to find out? You know your own sales figures by price line. You have a pretty good idea of competitors' sales by price line. Competitors, too, may have inventory and paper up to their ears.

A little personal interviewing may be all that is necessary. Could a significant number of customers be just as happy with a product nearly the same as the one they are using? Or do they care at all? Perhaps their purchases have been based merely on habit; another size or shape would do equally well. Switching these folks would be no problem. A few might care, but they would nevertheless be able to alter their own routine to fit your new, simplified product line (especially if it meant somewhat lower prices). A few might absolutely refuse to consider

Could a significant number of customers be just as happy with another size or shape of a product they are already using?

anything else. How important, how profitable are these stubborn ones for you? The loss of customer A, who buys 12 dozen of a certain product line (exactly so many inches long) and will take no other may be an easy sacrifice. If customer A buys a half million, then you have another problem—but at least you will have the facts to guide you.

The manufacturer of a product that included a hardwood handle had been using Brazilian rosewood, imported at some expense, in the belief that users would have nothing else. A quick questioning foray into the field found that users were not even aware of the kind of wood they were using and would be just as happy with plain old hardwood from this country. This was accomplished in short order, allowing the manufacturer to make a higher profit and to have the opportunity to meet competition with lower prices if it became necessary.

A manufacturer of electric motors with various horsepower ratings found by some intensive research questioning in the field that one complete line of motors could be eliminated. Only a few customers objected at first, and they were won over to the next horsepower size without too much trouble, especially since they found that the price would be lower and the new motors would be quite as satisfactory. Up to then, the equipment manufacturer had been convinced that this one motor was an essential offering.

Cases like this seem obvious, yet doing the "old hat trick," getting out into the field with a fresh, unbiased mind and with a willingness to seek the bad as well as the good, can often pay handsomely. And this is indeed market research.

Situation Eight

You are uncertain about the effectiveness of your promotion and advertising. Is it really increasing sales and profits? Is it improving your image among your customers? How could it be improved?

This problem is mentioned here only because it is a matter that worries both small and large companies. Measuring advertising will be the subject of Chapter 8. However, there are things you can do with *coded return coupons, special offers* in certain advertising pieces that require action by customers, and so on.

Especially worrisome, often enough, is the need to join in expensive trade shows. There are professional research firms that will offer to do this job for you, but no one has yet to work up a really objective and useful "handle" on this problem. Often you feel that you are "damned if you do, and damned if you don't." What will customers think if they do not see your booth at the show? However, do they buy more because you are there? Would they buy less if you were not there?

Interviews with people visiting your booth can be helpful. Follow-up records of such people to see their buying habits is possible. Perhaps all you can hope for is that the customers will think of you first when they get around to buying your type of product. We have no ready-made answer for most companies, but we do believe that the problem of trade shows deserves more research than it has often had.

A large firm with several different lines to sell may find itself being urged to

Is your promotion and advertising really increasing sales and profits?

enter several trade shows. Cost of space, building the booths, staffing the booths at all times, hospitality rooms, food and beverages, and paying unionized construction crews at the trade show buildings all can add up to enormous costs. As we said, these considerations deserve more serious thought than has been given in the past.

Summary

No single chapter such as this can cover all the situations faced by small manufacturers selling products to other manufacturers or to distributors. If this chapter has done its work, it will have pushed smaller firms (and larger ones, too) into using more marketing research to help reduce costs and increase profits.

We think the important things to remember from this chapter are

1. The major questions proposed earlier in the chapter: what are the facts we need to know to help us make a proper decision? Who out there knows these facts? What is the best way of communicating with these sources of knowledge? How much is the project worth in terms of marketing research cost?

2. The few basic ways for businesses to communicate with other businesses. These will be covered in detail in Chapters 9 through 12. They include personal interviewing, telephoning, mail questionnaires, and others. A great deal of juggling of sales statistics can now be done by computers, and almost every business can now afford a small personal computer. However, the problem of finding and learning how to use the proper software is somewhat daunting, and the standard methods of market research are still as important as ever.

Finally, we must point out once again that even in large companies, after the recent wholesale elimination of middle management, product line managers and market managers may have to solve some of these problems themselves, doing their own research as best they can and knowing when research is necessary, advisable, and possible within their situation.

seven

How Marketing Research Can Help the Manufacturer Market to the Public

The "public," as we use the term, means what professional marketers call the "consumer market." It is the segment or segments of the general public that may purchase the particular manufactured item. All purchasing is done for personal rather than business use. As opposed to the buyers described in Chapter 6, these people are not skilled in their buying. There are many more of them, too.

The public (we shall call them that instead of using the "consumer market") generally includes those buying fast-moving items, such as foods, drugs, and beverages. Also included are buyers of more durable goods, including appliances and automobiles. As you might expect, the survey methods are somewhat different.

There are three broad areas in which survey research can help provide answers about a manufacturer's marketing to the public: about your product, about the market, and about promotion of the product.

In this chapter we tell you how to handle manufacturer research about the public market in several respects: the development of new products, the testing of new or existing products, market definition, and product (or service) promotion.

Developing and Evaluating New Products

The public cannot invent new technical items. The public did not invent the airplane or the computer. What the public *can* do is to provide ideas for product improvements and even occasionally define a product that is needed. There are also sound procedures for measuring responses to ideas.

Getting Ideas for New Products. Consider bacon. Bacon, a popular choice for many years, lost favor as medical studies showed the risks of fat. Based on focus group interviews, a major meat packer decided to reduce the amount of fat in sliced bacon.

The focus group interview may be a productive way to develop consumer ideas for new or modified products (see the discussion about focus groups as a technique in Chapter 10). It takes a skilled approach to make the focus group work well for this purpose (or for any other). In this case, the moderator moved gradually into a discussion of bacon by first getting participants to talk about their breakfast habits and then going into the area of bacon preparation and serving. The moderator then probed—and continued to probe—into the problems of preparation and serving of the product.

Careful examination of what participants reported about the preparation, serving, and use showed that major objections included time and messiness of handling and preparation (spattering of grease, pouring off of grease, and so on) and greasiness of the end product. Cleanup time also was a big problem, as was the unhealthiness of a product of that amount of saturated fat.

When all these problems were summarized to the group, and participants were

The "public" means what professional marketers call the "consumer market."

A concept test may answer your research needs by letting you know which way the wind is blowing.

asked their suggestions, it was no surprise that a less fatty bacon was the unanimous idea.

Response to a New Product Idea. You may have an idea for a new product or service, but you hesitate to spend a lot of money on it unless it seems promising. A concept test may answer your research needs by letting you know which way the wind is blowing. The *concept test* presents the *idea* of a new product and asks for a reaction.

One form of the concept test is entirely *verbal.* It is descriptive entirely through words. There is a statement as to what the product is and what it does, virtually a definition. Another form is *visual,* with an illustration presented along with the description. This may take the form of a photograph or drawing, with the verbal description as an aside. Or it may take the form of a draft advertisement, which combines the description and an illustration, generally in the form of a print ad.

The third form uses a *mockup* of the product. This is something that passes for a prototype, but it is merely a dummy product (not in usable form) to help get across the idea of the product.

Eric Marder Associates, Inc. (New York City), offers a concept testing procedure using a mail survey in which questionnaires are sent to potential users of a new product. An enclosed booklet covers many products other than the one being examined. The obvious reason is to minimize the amount of attention paid to the new product idea.

Each page of the booklet shows a picture of the product, provides a brief description, and indicates its price. Consumers first describe their frequency of use of the product within the past month. For each alternative, the respondent is then asked whether the picture is interesting, whether the description impresses favorably, and whether the product is worth the price shown.

These questions are merely to "sensitize" consumers to the concept (price, picture, and theme). The key question follows, with the person telling how likely he or she is to buy each item.

Ten stickers—only 10—are enclosed with each booklet. The person has the choice of placing all 10 against a single product, placing a single sticker against each, or sorting them out otherwise. The booklet is set up mechanically so that only one sticker can be handled at a time. The consumer who wants to "bloc vote" has to work at it.

One sample of respondents is mailed booklet A. A matching sample receives booklet B. While 9 of the 10 pages are identical, the tenth page is different. The procedure means that you can be sure that basic comparisons between the samples assure you that the products and their characteristics are similar and that the differences in response to the concept are true differences.

If you can afford it, have your ad agency produce a mockup of an ad to use in the test. On a more modest basis, you can have a very rough visual draft. In either case you will have an oral statement provided by the interviewer or on the screen in the group interview facility. We admit some prejudice against this visual approach, since the results depend so much on the enthusiasm of the copywriters and illustrators.

Whatever you present to respondents, ask for their reactions and ask about their possible interest in purchase. Note that with the use of visuals you almost have to have a personal contact with the respondent, since you want to display the visual. This means in-mall or in-home interviewing.

There are risks involved in using the concept test. While the concept test can definitely kill bad ideas, it also may lead you down the garden path to follow what seems to be a good idea, only to have a poor reception once the product has been developed. In one concept test, the idea of a peanut butter pudding was tested. Mothers roundly rejected the idea. Generally, it was visualized as a product that would be sticky, gooey, and icky. The company decided—probably quite rightly—not to proceed with the product, believing it would never leave the store shelf. This decision was made despite the fact that actual taste trials of the developed product showed that both children and their mothers found the product both delicious and smooth.

Then there was the case of dry cereals containing freeze-dried fruits. Concept tests suggested that this was a most acceptable idea, and the cereals were introduced. They did not last long. They turned out to be a novelty item, and in the cereal business that's just what you do not need. You need repeat buying.

Testing of New or Existing Products (Consumer Product Testing)

As opposed to the concept test, you may need to know what your potential consumers think about your proposed new or existing product after trying it. This is getting down to earth—*consumer product testing*.

A general warning: This sort of test is not necessarily a sound prediction of success or failure in the marketplace. Your product may be excellently received in the test situation but fail because of other marketing problems. A poor or marginal product may make it in the marketplace because of massive marketing efforts, whereas a superior product may fail because of ineffective marketing. One major-selling beer brand consistently scores low in blind product tests (where people try samples without brand identification).

Consumer product testing takes many forms. For a food or beverage, the test may be as simple as a one-time taste test, perhaps conducted at a mall. For a laundry detergent, only a longer-term in-home test can get the right answer. You may place the product with people at a mall, have them try it at home over an extended time period, and perhaps even conduct the call-back interview—getting their reactions—by telephone.

Whatever form your consumer product testing takes, there are a few warnings on the procedure. One is to test the product only with people who use the particular product category. Since heavy users account for the bulk of sales, it is most desirable for you to make heavy usage—defined in some specific quantitative terms—a requirement. Results based on this sort of selective sampling will give far more significant results.

There is almost always a need for blind testing. Rarely should you reveal the brand name or proposed brand name, for this will mean that the person being

Whatever you present to respondents, ask for their reactions and ask about their possible interest in purchase.

tested will be reacting at least in part to that name and what it stands for. For most consumer product tests, therefore, you will need special packaging, generally showing only an identifying symbol, such as a letter or number. Even here there are problems. If you are testing only variants of your own product, that's no great problem. If you are testing against one or more competitors, however, you may have real problems. It is pretty difficult to repackage a soft drink in another container, yet your competitor's bottle may give away the game.

There are basically two different test designs for consumer product tests, each requiring a somewhat different questioning procedure. One is the monadic test, and the other is the paired comparison.

In the *monadic test,* the tester uses a single product. You simply ask about reactions to that product, and you may use scaling questions (described in Chapter 13) in which you get a numerical overall rating for the item, along with similar ratings for various qualities of the product. On the other hand, you may simply use a qualitative scale, where you ask about stated degrees of feelings rather than for a numerical response.

In the *paired-comparison test,* the tester tries two products (sometimes more, in which case the name is a misnomer), and while testers are asked to make overall choices between (among) the products, along the way they also may be asked to make numerical scale judgments for each one.

If you are testing your product or service against a competitive one, set up a procedure that says "try me first," "try me second," and so on and rotate products for equal average position. You need this control because the first product tried has an advantage.

Be careful about the product attributes you included in the questioning. There is no simple prescription. If you have the time and money, the real way to go is to use the focus group interview (see Chapter 11) as the first step, so that you can determine just what qualities people think are important before you construct your questionnaire. Short of this, if you are reasonably expert in your field—as you likely are—you may be able to build a pretty good list of qualities based on your own judgment.

Taste Testing. This common form of product testing is different enough to require special discussion. If all you need is a simple test to determine which of two (or more) flavors is preferred, then perhaps a central-location test, such as in a mall, may fill the bill. When you are in a location with a large volume of continuing traffic, all you need do is to intercept people, qualify them (make sure they are users, preferably heavy users), and get their reactions.

In this rather simple sort of study, you have two choices. As in the consumer product test, you can use either a monadic or paired-comparison test design.

Three successive questionnaires for a potato chip taste test are shown later in the chapter. While this is scarcely a guide to putting together a taste questionnaire, it is an example of how it might be done. This started as a mall-intercept study. There were three distinct phases to the study, the first two of which were handled within a shopping mall: (1) potential respondents were qualified; (2) those who qualified were given samples of each of two products to try, along with

In taste testing, all you need to do is intercept people, qualify them, and get their reactions.

a statement about how these were to be tried, and a questionnaire to be filled out immediately following trial; and (3) a follow-up telephone questionnaire was conducted with triers. However, this was more than a simple taste test.

The qualifying questionnaire (Figure 7.1) reflects the wishes of the sponsor. Those under the age of 18 were to be excluded (question A). Anyone who might spread the news about such a study also was to be excluded (questions B and C). Since the last phase of the study involved telephone calls, those living outside the local calling area were to be excluded, to save telephone costs (question D). Since the telephone call would be within the following week or so, families planning to be out of town then were excluded (question E).

Questions 1 and 2 set limits on selection based on frequency of use of the product class. Questions 3, 4, and 5 provide information that makes it possible to analyze preferences by present brand used, frequency of use with dips, and social versus home use of chips and dips.

At this point, the second page of materials was handed the respondent (Figure 7.2). It starts by setting an agreed-upon time for the follow-up telephone call and brief instructions about order of trial of the two products. From that point on, the remainder of the form is aimed at having the person record responses close to the time of trial, while impressions are still fresh in the mind.

The third form (Figure 7.3), is the follow-up telephone questionnaire. It is pretty clear and self-explanatory.

Testing a Manufacturer's Servicing.   Figure 7.4 shows the questionnaire used in a telephone survey by Mercedes-Benz to evaluate customer satisfaction. Owners of cars 1 to 2 years old were covered.

The questionnaire includes identifying items about the dealer, car, and the owner. There are queries about the purchasing situation, delivery, servicing and repairs, parts, and warranty. All in all, says Robert S. Baxter, manager of marketing research for Mercedes-Benz of North America, the results "are used as benchmark measures for individual dealer evaluations. . . . Dealerships selling 250–400 cars [are] compared with those of comparable retail unit volumes. Areas of strength and deficiency are pointed out and corrective measures . . . recommended."

Market Definition

Market definition measures the characteristics of your actual or potential buyers. You need to know the size and nature of your clientele so that you can build a marketing program aimed right at them, planning all your marketing efforts to reach and satisfy them. Your promotional efforts (advertising and other steps), your merchandise, your service—these and all the other aspects of your marketing program must be geared to your actual or potential market. There are three basic measurement areas.

1. *How many buyers (and potential buyers) do you have?* To plan and have an effective marketing program, you should know the number of buyers and the

Market definition *measures the characteristics of your actual or potential buyers.*

SNACK PRODUCT TASTE TEST

Hello, I'm from _____ and we are conducting a survey among homemakers. May I ask you a few questions?

A. Into which of these age groups do you fall? (HAND CARD.)

Under 18 years   □   END INTERVIEW.

18 to 24 years   10-1

25 to 30 years   2

31 to 49 years   3

50 years and over   4

B. First of all, do you or does someone else in your household work for an advertising agency, the food business, drug company, automotive industry, radio, television, newspapers, magazines or marketing research?

YES   □   ASK Q. C   NO   □   GO TO Q. D

C. Which company/companies would this be?

YES

ADVERTISING AGENCY   □

FOOD BUSINESS   □   END

DRUG COMPANY   □   INTERVIEW.

AUTOMOTIVE INDUSTRY   □   ERASE AND

RADIO   □   CIRCLE IN

TELEVISION   □   TALLY

NEWSPAPERS   □   BOX

MAGAZINES   □   BELOW.

MARKETING RESEARCH   □

FIGURE 7.1. *Questionnaire used in shopping mall survey.*

NONQUALIFIERS:

1	2	3	4	5	6	7	8	9	10	11-
11	12	13	14	15	16	17	18	19	20	12-

D. Do you live in the local telephone calling area?

Yes ☐   No ☐ END INTERVIEW. ERASE AND CIRCLE IN TALLY BOX BELOW.

E. Are you going on vacation or do you expect to be away from home for the next couple of weeks?

Yes ☐ END INTERVIEW. ERASE AND CIRCLE IN TALLY BOX BELOW.   No ☐

NONQUALIFIERS:

1	2	3	4	5	6	7	8	9	10	13-
11	12	13	14	15	16	17	18	19	20	14-

1. Have you purchased dip chips such as Hostess Dip Chips, Humpty Dumpty Dip Chips, or Ruffles within the past month?

Yes ☐   No ☐ END INTERVIEW. ERASE AND CIRCLE IN TALLY BOX BELOW.

NONQUALIFIERS:

1	2	3	4	5	6	7	8	9	10	15-
11	12	13	14	15	16	17	18	19	20	16-

2. How often would you say you would buy dip chips? (HAND CARD.)

ONCE A WEEK OR MORE OFTEN	17-1
ONCE EVERY 2 WEEKS	2
ONCE EVERY 3 WEEKS	3
ABOUT ONCE A MONTH	4
LESS THAN ONCE A MONTH	☐ END INTERVIEW. ERASE AND CIRCLE IN TALLY BOX BELOW.

NONQUALIFIERS:

1	2	3	4	5	6	7	8	9	10	18-
11	12	13	14	15	16	17	18	19	20	19-

3. Which brand of dip chips would you say you buy most often?

                HOSTESS DIP CHIPS   20-1

            HUMPTY DUMPTY DIP CHIPS   2

              FRITO-LAY RUFFLES   3

            OTHER BRANDS (Specify)   _____

                                        _____

                                        _____

4. How often do you use this type of product with a chip dip?

            ONCE A WEEK OR MORE OFTEN   21-1

              ONCE EVERY 2 WEEKS   2

              ONCE EVERY 3 WEEKS   3

              ABOUT ONCE A MONTH   4

            LESS THAN ONCE A MONTH   5

                        NEVER | 6   GO TO QUESTION 7. |

5. (IF USES CHIPS WITH DIP, ASK:)
    Out of every 10 occasions you use a chip dip, how many do you
    think would be:

        For entertaining guests?   _____ (WRITE IN.) 22-

        For use just by your own family? _____ (WRITE IN.) 23-

share of market you have (this is the proportion of buyers you have in the market). The latter figure is also a description of the size of the potential market you have achieved. Astute marketers keep a sharp eye on their share of market and how it rises or falls. It is a continuing description of how well they are doing in the marketplace.

2. *How do your customers buy?* There are many aspects of the purchasing procedure your customers—and potential customers—follow that may be crucial to figuring out your marketing plans and strategies. You need many types of such information; we mention just two. You should know the type of store in which your customers buy; this will help determine the emphasis of your sales

CONSUMER OPINION CENTER

TESTING INSTRUCTIONS

AND

RESPONDENT'S QUESTIONNAIRE

Please use the product which is marked "TRY FIRST"
and then use the one marked "TRY SECOND".

When you have tested both products, please fill
in this questionnaire and keep it by the phone so it
will be there when the interviewer calls you back.

WILL CALL YOU ON: _____ TIME: _____
A.M.
P.M.
Date

1A. Which product do you prefer overall?

THE ONE TRIED FIRST ☐

THE ONE TRIED SECOND ☐

NO PREFERENCE ☐   GO TO QUESTION 2.

1B. What are all your reasons for preferring that one for
overall flavor? (PLEASE BE SPECIFIC.)

_____

_____

_____

1C. What are your reasons for not preferring the other one?
(PLEASE BE SPECIFIC.)

_____

_____

_____

FIGURE 7.2. *Follow-up survey: snack product taste test.*

		Yes	No

2. Did you use: THE PRODUCT TRIED FIRST WITH A CHIP DIP? ☐ ☐

THE PRODUCT TRIED SECOND WITH A CHIP DIP? ☐ ☐

3A. (IF YOU USED BOTH PRODUCTS WITH A CHIP DIP)
Which product was better for dipping?

THE ONE YOU TRIED FIRST ☐

THE ONE YOU TRIED SECOND ☐

NO PREFERENCE ☐   GO TO QUESTION 4.

3B. (IF YOU HAD A PREFERENCE)
Why did you like that one better for dipping? (PLEASE BE
SPECIFIC.)

_____

_____

_____

4. Now, I want to find out which one you preferred for certain
specific qualities. Which one did you prefer for:

	One tried first	One tried second	No preference
Flavor?	☐	☐	☐
Overall appearance?	☐	☐	☐
Mouth feel?	☐	☐	☐

5. Which of the two do you think is:

	One tried first	One tried second	No difference
Crispier	☐	☐	☐
Greasier	☐	☐	☐
Fresher	☐	☐	☐
Crunchier	☐	☐	☐

6. Now we would like you to rate these Dip Chips on the following qualities:

		Tried first	Tried second
a. SALTINESS			
Is it -	Much too salty	☐	☐
	A little too salty	☐	☐
	Just right amount of salt	☐	☐
	Not quite salty enough	☐	☐
	Not nearly salty enough	☐	☐
b. THICKNESS			
Is it -	Much too thin	☐	☐
	A little too thin	☐	☐
	Just right thickness	☐	☐
	A little too thick	☐	☐
	Much too thick	☐	☐
c. SIZE			
Is it -	Much too big	☐	☐
	A little too big	☐	☐
	Just right size	☐	☐
	A little too small	☐	☐
	Much too small	☐	☐
d. COLOR			
Is it -	Much too dark	☐	☐
	A little too dark	☐	☐
	Just right color	☐	☐
	A little too light	☐	☐
	Much too light	☐	☐

CONSUMER OPINION CENTER

CALLBACK INTERVIEW

Hello, I'm _____ from the Consumer
Opinion Center. We gave you two versions of dip chips to
try. Would you please get the rating sheets that we gave
you.

1A. Referring to question 1A on your rating sheet, which product
do you prefer overall?

        THE ONE TRIED FIRST   32-1

        THE ONE TRIED SECOND   2

            NO PREFERENCE   3   GO TO QUESTION 4.

1B. (IF RESPONDENT HAD A PREFERENCE, ASK:)
What are all the reasons for preferring the one tried
FIRST/SECOND?
(RECORD VERBATIM - PROBE.)   (RESPONDENT'S CHOICE)

_____ 33-

_____ 34-

_____ 35-

1C. What are your reasons for not preferring the other one?
(RECORD VERBATIM - PROBE.)

_____ 36-

_____ 37-

_____ 38-

FIGURE 7.3. *Telephone call-back interview form.*

2. Did you use: THE PRODUCT TRIED FIRST WITH A CHIP DIP?   <u>Yes</u> <u>No</u>
                                                                             39-1   2

                    THE PRODUCT TRIED SECOND WITH A CHIP DIP?   4   5

3A. (IF BOTH PRODUCTS USED WITH A CHIP DIP, ASK:)
Which product was better for dipping?

        ONE TRIED FIRST   40-1

        ONE TRIED SECOND   2

        NO PREFERENCE | 3 GO TO QUESTION 4. |

3B. (IF RESPONDENT HAD A PREFERENCE, ASK:)
Why did you like that one better for dipping? (RECORD
VERBATIM - PROBE.)

_____ 41-

_____ 42-

_____ 43-

4. Now, I want to find out which one you preferred for certain
specific qualities. Which one did you prefer for:

	ONE TRIED FIRST	ONE TRIED SECOND	NO PREFERENCE
Flavor?	44-1	2	3
Overall appearance?	45-1	2	3
Mouthfeel?	46-1	2	3

5. Which of the two do you think is:

	ONE TRIED FIRST	ONE TRIED SECOND	NO DIFFERENCE
Crispier	47-1	2	3
Greasier	48-1	2	3
Fresher	49-1	2	3
Crunchier	50-1	2	3

6. Now we would like you to rate these dip chips on the following qualities:

	TRIED FIRST	TRIED SECOND
a. SALTINESS		
Is it - Much too salty	51-1	55-1
A little too salty	2	2
Just right amount of salt	3	3
Not quite salty enough	4	4
Not nearly salty enough	5	5
b. THICKNESS		
Is it - Much too thin	52-1	56-1
A little too thin	2	2
Just right thickness	3	3
A little too thick	4	4
Much too thick	5	5

		TRIED FIRST	TRIED SECOND

c. SIZE

	TRIED FIRST	TRIED SECOND
Is it - Much too big	53-1	57-1
A little too big	2	2
Just right size	3	3
A little too small	4	4
Much too small	5	5

d. COLOR

	TRIED FIRST	TRIED SECOND
Is it - Much too dark	54-1	58-1
A little too dark	2	2
Just right color	3	3
A little too light	4	4
Much too light	5	5

7A. Finally, did you think that one product had more broken pieces in the bag than the other?

NO	59-1
YES	☐

7B. Which one had more broken pieces?

ONE TRIED FIRST	2
ONE TRIED SECOND	3

Thank you very much for your cooperation.

1-   2-   3-   4-

TELEPHONE STUDY—CUSTOMER SERVICE

Hello, I am _____ representing _____ ,
a national marketing research company. We are conducting a survey on
automotive service. Registration records show that someone in your
household owns a 19__ Mercedes-Benz. Is that correct?

   YES [ ]   NO [ ] (TERMINATE.)

May I speak to the person responsible for having maintenance and repair
work done on the car? Are you he (she)?

   YES [ ]   NO [ ] (ASK TO SPEAK TO THAT PERSON.
                                      REPEAT INTRODUCTION IF
                                      NECESSARY.)

1. Is your Mercedes-Benz a gasoline or diesel powered model?

    GASOLINE [ ] 7-1   DIESEL [ ] -2

2a. When it comes time to replace your Mercedes-Benz with another car,
    how likely will it be with another Mercedes-Benz product? Would you
    say: (READ CHOICES ALOUD AND CHECK ONE BOX.)

        DEFINITELY   [ ]8-1 ⎤
        VERY LIKELY   [ ] -2 ⎥(ASK 2b, THEN SKIP TO 3a.)
        SOMEWHAT LIKELY   [ ] -3 ⎦

        NOT VERY LIKELY   [ ] -4 ⎤
        DEFINITELY NOT   [ ] -5 ⎦(SKIP TO 2c.)

  b. Would you use the same dealer from whom you purchased your present
     car?

     YES [ ] 9-1   NO [ ] -2

  c. What are the most important reasons why you are unlikely to purchase
     another Mercedes-Benz? (PROBE FOR SPECIFIC REASONS.)   10-
     _____ 11-
     _____ 12-
     _____ 13-
     _____ 14-
     _____ 15-
     _____ 16-

FIGURE 7.4. *A telephone survey.*

d. What make and model series do you think you would most likely buy?

17-

MAKE: _____ SERIES: _____

18-
19-
20-
21-

3a. Considering all aspects of ownership of your Mercedes-Benz, how would you describe your overall satisfaction with the car? Would you say you were: (READ CHOICES AND CHECK ONE BOX.)

COMPLETELY SATISFIED   [ ] 22-1 (SKIP TO 4a.)

VERY SATISFIED   [ ] -2
FAIRLY WELL SATISFIED   [ ] -3
SOMEWHAT DISSATISFIED   [ ] -4 ⎤(ASK PART b.)
VERY DISSATISFIED   [ ] -5

b. You indicate that you are less than completely satisfied with your Mercedes-Benz. What do you feel should be necessary to have you completely or 100 percent satisfied with this car? (PROBE: Anything else?)

23-
24-
25-
_____ 26-
_____ 27-
_____ 28-
_____ 29-
_____ 30-

4a. How would you rate the service department at the dealership where you bought your car? Would you rate it: (READ CHOICES AND CHECK ONE BOX.)

EXCEL-   VERY
  LENT [ ] 31-1   GOOD [ ] -2 GOOD [ ] -3 FAIR [ ] -4 POOR [ ] -5

b. Why did you give the dealer's service department this rating? (PROBE FOR SPECIFIC REASONS.)

_____ 32-
_____ 33-
_____ 34-
_____ 35-
_____ 36-

5. Based on your experience, how would you rate the dealership which sold you your Mercedes-Benz on (ITEM CHECKED AT LEFT)? Would you say Excellent, Very Good, Good, Fair, or Poor? (REPEAT FOR REST OF ITEMS. CONTINUE TO BOTTOM, THEN RETURN TO TOP AND FINISH. CHECK ONE BOX IN EACH ROW.)

	Excellent	Very good	Good	Fair	Poor
[ ] THEIR ABILITY TO GET WORK DONE ON TIME	[ ] 37-1	[ ] -2	[ ] -3	[ ] -4	[ ] -5
[ ] THEIR EFFORTS TO MAKE IT AS CONVENIENT FOR CUSTOMER AS POSSIBLE IN GETTING NECESSARY REPAIRS	[ ] 38-1	[ ] -2	[ ] -3	[ ] -4	[ ] -5
[ ] FAIRNESS OF PRICES FOR SERVICE	[ ] 39-1	[ ] -2	[ ] -3	[ ] -4	[ ] -5
[ ] OVERALL QUALITY OF REPAIR WORK	[ ] 40-1	[ ] -2	[ ] -3	[ ] -4	[ ] -5
[ ] THE WAY THEY TREAT THEIR CUSTOMERS	[ ] 41-1	[ ] -2	[ ] -3	[ ] -4	[ ] -5
[ ] THE JOB THEY ARE DOING TO IMPROVE THE QUALITY OF SERVICE AND REPAIR WORK WITHIN THE DEALERSHIP	[ ] 42-1	[ ] -2	[ ] -3	[ ] -4	[ ] -5
[ ] APPEARANCE OF SERVICE FACILITIES	[ ] 43-1	[ ] -2	[ ] -3	[ ] -4	[ ] -5

44-
45-

6. Thinking only about repairs you paid for yourself, not including routine maintenance such as oil changes or lubrication, how long has it been since you had work done on this car? (CHECK ONE BOX.)

UP TO 3 MONTHS AGO   [ ] 46-1

3 BUT LESS THAN 6 MONTHS   [ ] -2

6 MONTHS BUT LESS THAN 1 YEAR [ ] -3

1 YEAR BUT LESS THAN 2 YEARS [ ] -4

NEVER   [ ] -5 (SKIP TO QUESTION 10.)

7a. Think about the most recent time you had service or repair work done on this car which you paid for yourself. Not counting oil changes or lubrications, where did you go to obtain this service or repair work? (CHECK ONE BOX.)

A MERCEDES-BENZ DEALER   [ ] 47-1 (ASK PART b.)

GASOLINE STATION   [ ]   -2

INDEPENDENT GARAGE   [ ]   -3

DEPARTMENT OR CHAIN STORE
(SEARS, PENNEY'S, ETC.)   [ ]   -4   —(SKIP TO QUESTION 8.)

SPECIALTY SHOP (MIDAS,
AAMCO, ETC.)   [ ]   -5

OTHER (PLEASE DESCRIBE): _____

DID IT YOURSELF   [ ]   -6   (SKIP TO QUESTION 10a.)

47-

b. Was this work done at the same dealership where you bought this car?

YES [ ] 48-1   NO [ ] -2

8. With regard to this most recent service visit, how satisfied were you with _____? Would you say Completely Satisfied, Very Satisfied, Fairly Well Satisfied, Somewhat Dissatisfied, or Very Dissatisfied. (REPEAT FOR OTHER ITEMS. CHECK ONE BOX IN EACH ROW.)

	Com-pletely satis-fied	Very satis-fied	Fairly well satis-fied	Some-what dis-satis-fied	Very dis-satis-fied
a. OVERALL QUALITY OF REPAIR WORK	[ ] 49-1	[ ] -2	[ ] -3	[ ] -4	[ ] -5
b. OVERALL CONVENIENCE FOR YOU IN OBTAINING THE SERVICE	[ ] 50-1	[ ] -2	[ ] -3	[ ] -4	[ ] -5

c. TREATMENT OF YOU AS A
   CUSTOMER   [ ] 51-1 [ ] -2 [ ] -3 [ ] -4 [ ] -5

d. FAIRNESS OF PRICES FOR
   SERVICE   [ ] 52-1 [ ] -2 [ ] -3 [ ] -4 [ ] -5

e. ALL THINGS CONSIDERED,
   YOUR OVERALL
   IMPRESSION   [ ] 53-1 [ ] -2 [ ] -3 [ ] -4 [ ] -5

                                                               54-
                                                               55-

9. For this most recent service work:

                                                       Yes   No

a. Were all repairs performed that you requested? [ ]56-1   [ ]-2

b. Was the car ready when promised?   [ ]57-1   [ ]-2

c. Did you receive an estimate of cost before
   work was begun?   [ ]58-1   [ ]-2

d. Did you receive a follow-up contact by phone,
   mail, or in person inquiring as to your
   satisfaction with the repair work?   [ ]59-1   [ ]-2

e. Was there a guarantee on the service or
   repair work?   [ ]60-1   [ ]-2

10a. Have you been contacted by your Mercedes-Benz dealership's service
     department within the past 6 months or so, either by phone, mail,
     or in person for purposes of service reminder or otherwise asking
     for your service business?

          YES [ ] 61-1   NO [ ] -2

  b. Is the dealer from whom you purchased your Mercedes-Benz
     exclusively a Mercedes-Benz dealer, or does he handle other makes
     of new cars through that same dealership?

          EXCLUSIVE [ ] 62-1   HANDLES OTHER MAKES
                                      OF NEW CARS   [ ] -2

11a. Think about the most recent time you had routine maintenance done
     on your Mercedes-Benz such as oil changes, lubrication, filter,
     and so forth. Where did you go to obtain this routine maintenance?
     (CHECK ONE BOX.)

     A MERCEDES-BENZ DEALER   [ ]63-1 (ASK PART b.)

     GASOLINE STATION   [ ] -2

     INDEPENDENT GARAGE   [ ] -3

     DEPARTMENT OR CHAIN STORE
     (SEARS, PENNEY'S, ETC.)   [ ] -4 ──(SKIP TO
                                                  QUESTION 12a.)
     SPECIALTY SHOP (MIDAS,
     AAMCO, ETC.)   [ ] -5

     OTHER (PLEASE DESCRIBE):

     DID IT YOURSELF   [ ] -6

   b. Was this work done at the same dealership where you bought this
      car?

          YES [ ] 64-1   NO [ ] -2

12a. In addition to your Mercedes-Benz, are there other cars in your
     immediate household?

          YES [ ] 65-1 (ASK PART b.)   NO [ ] -2 (SKIP TO QUESTION 13.)

   b. Would you please tell me the make, series, and model year of each
      of these other cars. (ASK FOR EACH.) Was it bought new or used?
      (RECORD ANSWERS IN GRID.)

                                                    Bought
      Make   Series   Model year   New   Used

   _____ _____ _____   [ ]   [ ]

   _____ _____ _____   [ ]   [ ]

   _____ _____ _____   [ ]   [ ]

13. Finally, a few questions about you, to classify the sample. How
    old are you?

                                       66-
                          _____
                          (Age in years) 67-

14. What was the last grade you attended in school?

NO SCHOOLING   [ ]68-1   FINISHED HIGH SCHOOL   [ ] -5

SOME GRADE SCHOOL   [ ] -2   SOME COLLEGE   [ ] -6

FINISHED GRADE SCHOOL   [ ] -3   GRADUATED COLLEGE OR MORE [ ] -7

SOME HIGH SCHOOL   [ ] -4   POSTGRADUATE WORK   [ ] -8

15. And finally, is your total annual family income under $40,000 or $40,000 and over?

Under $40,000   [ ] $40,000 and over   [ ]

   (ASK.)   (ASK.)

Is that under $25,000 [ ]   Is that under $50,000   [ ]

      or   or

$25,000 and over   [ ] $50,000 and over   [ ] 69-

16. May I have your name please?   (OBTAIN FULL NAME—PRINT.)

_____
Mr./Mrs./Ms.   First name   Last name

House no. and street:_____   70-

City:_____ State and zip code:_____   71-

Telephone no.:_____   72-

                                  Time
Interviewer's name:_____ Date:_____ finished:_____

Validated by:_____ Date:_____

                                                    _____
                                                    Card 2

5-   8-   11-   14-   17-   20 -   23-

6-   9-   12-   15-   18-   21-   24-

7-   10-   13-   16-   19-   22-   25-

efforts. You will also want to know the timing of purchases. Is there a seasonal pattern? How about frequency of purchase?

3. *What is your customer profile?* Another important information area is the nature of your customers. For total understanding, you also should know the customer profile for your major competitors; it gives you a real insight into how you are serving the market versus each of your competitors. There are two aspects of such profiles: demographics and psychographics.

Demographics are objective population characteristics typically provided by censuses, such as geographic area, sex, age, income level, education, family size, and dwelling type. *Psychographics* are psychological characteristics, measured far less tangibly, according to procedures independently defined by whatever research firm undertakes the study. This does not make the idea less useful than demographics; it simply means that such measurements are far less standardized. This is likely as it should be, for the nature of useful psychographics will vary considerably depending on the sort of study you are doing.

Psychographics include measurements such as the person's lifestyle, his or her self-image, and how he or she wants to appear to other people (see Chapter 8).

Lifestyle is the way a person lives and what he or she sees as important in that style. Is the person a sit-at-home in the evening, watching TV, perhaps with beer? Is the person a do-it-yourselfer on home projects? Does the person go for lawn care and gardening? Is the person a hobbyist (if so, of what nature)? Is the person a socializer, frequently going out with others or entertaining at home regularly? Is the person an outdoor type, stressing barbecue living during warm-weather months?

Lifestyle is the way a person lives and what he or she sees as important in that style.

Lifestyle can be measured by asking about the behavior of the person, in terms of both nature and frequency (Figure 7.5). The type of lifestyle questions you want to ask will be dictated by the nature of your product (service) and problem. If you manufacture outdoor barbecues, your approach will be far different from that of a travel agency.

Product Promotion

"Promotion," as marketers use the word, includes all marketing activities concerning informing and influencing the consumer's purchase decision. This covers a lot of territory. However, we shall limit ourselves here to the testing of two major promotional tools: the product "wrap," as we call it, and advertising.

You immediately understand the term *advertising*. Since product "wrap" is of our own coinage, we had better define it at once. We mean the brand name, the logo, and the specific package. All of these, when well designed, are powerful promotional tools, and so we consider them quite separately from advertising.

Testing Product "Wrap"

In this sort of test, you may simply present your customers (or potential customers) with the proposed brand name, the logo, or package and ask whether they like it or not. This is a straight voting deal.

In association testing, you ask what things a person associates with each potential name.

LIFE-STYLE QUESTIONS (Belden)

1. Have you gone to any local supper clubs that feature live entertainment in the past 6 months?

2. How many times have you dined out in the evening during the past 6 months, not counting business dinners?

3. During the past 6 months, how many times has your family purchased food or eaten at a drive-in or take-out restaurant?

4. During the past 6 months, about how many times have you traveled on commercial airlines, considering round-trip flights as 2 trips?

    a. The last time you made a flight, did you travel first-class or tourist?

    b. Were any of these flights to places outside of the United States?

5. During the past 6 months have you taken any trips by boat?

6. Do you have a passport? (IF NOT) Have you ever had one?

7. During the past 6 months have you: (READ EACH)

    Called someone long-distance other than for business?
    Written a letter to the editor of a newspaper?
    Ridden in a taxicab other than for business?
    Attended a zoning hearing?
    Ridden in a local transit bus?
    Ridden in a long-distance bus?
    Attended a PTA meeting?
    Cooked out?
    Done gourmet cooking?
    Done any outside painting of your own?
    Done any inside painting of your own?
    Painted or sketched a picture?

FIGURE 7.5. *Lifestyle questions seek information to guide editors and advertisers.*
(Courtesy of Belden Associates.)

PERSONAL VALUES (Belden)

Some of the cards in this deck describe things that you might
consider very important in your own life. Other cards might
describe things which are not too important. Using the 0 to 5
point scale on each card, 5 meaning "very important" and 0
meaning "not at all important," please tell me how important
each of these is to your personal happiness and satisfaction
with life.

Civic Involvement, Privatism

a. Getting to know my neighbors

b. Being active in charity work or other community affairs

c. Being active in church or synagogue work

d. Being active in politics

e. Working with youth in organizations such as B'nai B'rith,
   Boy Scouts, Camp Fire Girls, YMCA, YMHA

f. Working with the local schools through the PTA or other
   organizations

g. Belonging to a fraternal organization such as American
   Legion, Elks, Masons, Hadassah, Knights of Columbus

h. Belonging to a civic organization such as Lions Club or
   Rotary

"In the Know," "Not in the Know"

i. Being well-informed about what is happening in other countries

j. Being well-informed about what is happening in the United States

k. Being well-informed about what is happening in the state

l. Being well-informed about what is happening in my community

<u>Self-Improvement, Self-Satisfaction</u>

m. Becoming a leader

n. Being better than others in such things as education, work, or sports

<u>Role of Women</u>

o. Women staying home and devoting full time to their families

<u>Traditional, Nontraditional Values</u>

p. Getting it all together for myself and letting the rest of the world go by

q. Having a personal relationship with someone I love, even if it means sacrificing some of my freedom

r. Obeying the laws of a religious faith

s. Being strongly patriotic

t. Having strict moral standards

u. Discouraging sexual relationships before marriage

It is dangerous. Reactions in the marketplace are far more subtle. The respondent may give you what he or she regards as an "acceptable" answer. Do you think Tussy would have been a preferred cosmetic brand name if it didn't rhyme with "Hussy"? Tussy, in a direct-question test, would almost surely have lost to "Angel."

An indirect approach is far better. For name testing, one such approach is the *association test,* where you ask what things a person associates with each potential name, without even revealing the product category (although you have certainly got to qualify each respondent, to ensure that each person questioned fairly represents your actual or potential market).

The Name Test. The name-test questionnaire for an automobile (Figure 7.6) is an example. Question 1 covers word association. Question 2 associates car qualities with each name, and question 3 concerns suitability of each name for the particular car type. The parts of question 4 are direct questions. But if they are

HOW TARGET GROUP INDEX DEFINES PSYCHOGRAPHIC CLASSIFICATIONS

Self-concept

Classifications of self-concept are based on self-ratings with respect to groups of adjectives on a 5-point scale.

1. Agree a lot
2. Agree a little
3. Neither agree nor disagree
4. Disagree a little
5. Disagree a lot

The adjectives and the scale points that define the classifications in each case are:

AFFECTIONATE, passionate, loving romantic
AMICABLE, amiable, affable, benevolent
AWKWARD, absent-minded, forgetful, careless
BRAVE, courageous, daring, adventuresome
BROAD-MINDED, open-minded, liberal, tolerant
CREATIVE, inventive, imaginative, artistic
DOMINATING, authoritarian, demanding, aggressive
EFFICIENT, organized, diligent, thorough
EGOCENTRIC, vain, self-centered, narcissistic
FRANK, straightforward, outspoken, candid
FUNNY, humorous, amusing, witty
INTELLIGENT, smart, bright, well-informed
KIND, good-hearted, warm-hearted, sincere
REFINED, gracious, sophisticated, dignified
RESERVED, conservative, quiet, conventional
SELF-ASSURED, confident, self-sufficient, secure
SOCIABLE, friendly, cheerful, likeable
STUBBORN, hardheaded, headstrong, obstinate
TENSE, nervous, high-strung, excitable
TRUSTWORTHY, competent, reliable, responsible

Buying style

Classifications of buying style are based on agreement or disagreement with the following statements on the same 5-point scale used for self-concept.

Brand Loyal
I always look for the name of the manufacturer on the package.
Cautious
I do not buy unknown brands merely to save money.
Conformist
I prefer to buy things that my friends or neighbors would approve of.
Ecologist
All products that pollute the environment should be banned.
Economy-minded
I shop around a lot to take advantage of specials or bargains.
Experimenter
I like to change brands often for the sake of variety and novelty.
Impulsive
When in the store, I often buy an item on the spur of the moment.
Persuasible
In general, advertising presents a true picture of the products of well-known companies.
Planner
I generally plan far ahead to buy expensive items such as automobiles.
Style-conscious
I try to keep abreast of changes in styles and fashions.

```
┌─────────────┐
│  NAME TEST  │
│  INTERVIEW  │
└─────────────┘
```

1. I am going to read you a list of words. As I read each one, I would like
   you to tell me the first thing that comes to mind.

   (START WITH NAME MARKED WITH X. RECORD RESPONSES VERBATIM—CLARIFYING ONLY.
   CONTINUE UNTIL ALL NAMES HAVE BEEN READ.)

( ) VECTOR _____   35-
          _____   36-
          _____   37-
          _____
          _____
          _____

( ) MIRADA _____   38-
           _____   39-
           _____   40-
           _____
           _____
           _____

( ) ALPIN _____   41-
          _____   42-
          _____   43
          _____
          _____
          _____

( ) OZ _____   44-
       _____   45-
       _____   46
       _____
       _____
       _____

(X) ARCHER _____   47-
             _____   48-
             _____   49-
             _____
             _____
             _____

( ) ACE _____   50-
        _____   51-
        _____   52-
        _____
        _____
        _____

FIGURE 7.6. *Example of a name-association test.*

2. (HAND NAME CARD)

These names are being considered for a new car. I'm going to read a series
of car descriptions to see whether or not a particular description would
apply to or fit <u>one or more</u> cars with those names. First of all, which names
would seem to fit with the description:

(READ LIST. START WITH DESCRIPTION MARKED WITH X.)

Description	VECTOR	MIRADA	ALPIN	OZ	ARCHER	ACE	
( ) Solid and well built	1	2	3	4	5	6	55-
( ) Fun to drive	1	2	3	4	5	6	56-
( ) Economical to operate	1	2	3	4	5	6	57-
( ) Fully equipped	1	2	3	4	5	6	58-
( ) Sporty-looking	1	2	3	4	5	6	59-
( ) Stable on the highway	1	2	3	4	5	6	60-
(X) Modern-styled	1	2	3	4	5	6	61-
( ) Different and interesting	1	2	3	4	5	6	62-

3. These names are being considered for a new economy, small, 2-door, sporty car.
How suitable would you say each name is for that type of car?

(READ NAMES IN ORDER LISTED.)

	Very suitable	Somewhat suitable	Not very suitable	Not at all suitable	
VECTOR	1	2	3	4	63-
MIRADA	1	2	3	4	64-
ALPIN	1	2	3	4	65-
OZ	1	2	3	4	66-
ARCHER	1	2	3	4	67-
ACE	1	2	3	4	68

(TAKE BACK NAME CARD.)

4a. Of these various names, which one do you like <u>best</u> as the name for a car?

b. Which one do you like <u>second</u> best?

c. Which one do you like <u>least</u> as the name for a car?

	Q.4a like <u>best</u> <u>69</u>	Q.4b like <u>second</u> <u>70</u>	Q.4c like <u>least</u> <u>71</u>
VECTOR	1	1	1
MIRADA	2	2	2
ALPIN	3	3	3
OZ	4	4	4
ARCHER	5	5	5
ACE	6	6	6

5. Which name, as a name, best fits or goes with the <u>Dodge</u> name?
(RECORD BELOW.)

6. Which name, as a name, best fits or goes with the <u>Plymouth</u> name?
(RECORD BELOW.)

	<u>72</u> Q.5 <u>Dodge</u>	<u>73</u> Q.6 <u>Plymouth</u>
VECTOR	1	1
MIRADA	2	2
ALPIN	3	3
OZ	4	4
ARCHER	5	5
ACE	6	6

7. What is your age, please? (READ LIST IF NECESSARY.)

Under 20	1	74-
20-24	2	
25-34	3	
35-44	4	
45-54	5	
55 and over	6	
Refused	7	

8. Sex:

Male   1   Female   2   75-

Name: _____ Phone: _____ 76-

Address: _____ City/state/zip: _____ 77-
                                                        78-
Interviewer: _____ Date: _____ 79-

80-

used with the indirect approach, they are likely appropriate. Questions 5 and 6 ask about the suitability of each name for Dodge, on the one hand, and Plymouth, on the other.

Another indirect approach to measuring response to name—or package—is the "phony" product test. No real choice is given the consumer, although he or she does not realize it. The person is presented with two—or more—"wraps" of the identical product, although the tester has no way of knowing that the products are identical. An example will make it clear.

We did a study in Canada for a distiller considering four different brand names for a particular whiskey: Carrington, Alberta, Grey Cup, and Rocky Mount. Carrington is a prestigious British family name. Alberta is a stolid, usually prosperous, grain-growing Canadian province. Grey Cup is the championship game of the Canadian Football League. The celebrations typically begin the morning of the event, ending only in the early hours of the following morning, and are somewhat analogous—on a less formal side—to Mardi Gras in New Orleans. Rocky Mount needs no explanation.

A group of male whiskey drinkers was invited to a central location. Each person was given four different jiggers of the same whiskey, all from the same bottle, although they did not know this. Each jigger was stationed on a tray just in back of a gummed label on the tray with one of the names of the label. The men were asked to sip and compare the brands and to state which they preferred and why.

Carrington was the overwhelming winner. It was seen as smooth and expensive. Alberta was described as bland; Rocky Mount was seen as harsh and raw. Grey Cup was said to be too high in alcoholic content and for the masses.

The Package Test. The possible procedures are much the same as those with the name test, but the study is far more complicated to carry out. For one thing, there is the problem—and cost—of producing several packaging forms. Then there is the question of how to present them.

If it *is* possible to create good finished package forms, there is then the question of the form and circumstances under which to present them to your consumers. Since, as a reader of this book, you are likely a marketing research user with a limited budget, we give ideas about an approach you may be able to afford.

Your in-house commercial artist, an outside commercial artist, or your advertising agency can prepare a "rough" of each proposed package.

Have your in-house commercial artist, an outside commercial artist, or your advertising agency prepare a "rough" of each proposed package. You have the option of making individual prints or putting them onto slides for presentation to groups. You can then use these in the procedure described earlier in this chapter as the "concept test," or you can offer each unidentified product as a no-charge choice.

If you can afford the proposed new packages in quantity, you have additional options. You can put together—with the help of a research firm having its own mall facilities—a simulated retail shelf display with your proposed new package displayed against that of your competition without drawing any special attention from the person asked to do "shopping" off the shelf. With a controlled design, you can measure "pull" of the new package versus your current one. You also can ask follow-up questions, once the choice has been made, about the shopper's reactions to the package.

There is another option. Following the sort of procedure described for consumer product tests, you can conduct a study based on home use, with dependable results. Depending on the nature of the package changes, you can ask about convenience of storage and of use. Or, if it is largely a cosmetic change (in the sense of labeling), you can measure *brand image*—the perceptions people have of your brand.

Some of these package studies get pretty complicated. Unless you feel absolutely sure of what you are doing, we recommend that you go to a consultant for advice and possible study design and perhaps to a research firm to handle the study for you. You will want to digest the material in Chapter 16 before deciding.

Advertising: Development and Testing Before Use (Pretesting)

Developing Advertising Ideas. Although there are several methods you can use to help you develop advertising, the simplest—and perhaps the most effective—is the focus group interview (described in Chapter 11). The big advantages are that you can, with skilled use of the technique, measure in depth what seems to appeal to those in your market, and you also can get the benefits of interacting ideas—ideas that develop through mutual exchange in discussion.

To create good advertising ideas through use of this tool, you must learn as much as you can about why people buy the product or service and what they look for in making their choice. You will need a skilled moderator, for we cannot tailor a content outline in advance. The moderator will have to structure the session during the meeting, depending on the direction that responses to the open-ended questioning take.

The focus group interview may aid you in developing advertising ideas, but you are not yet home free. Now you need to find out which of several alternative ideas that you or your people have devised is the best one to use. One possible way is the *shuffle-card test*. In this procedure, each of the several themes is listed on a separate card. Each is shown to the respondent, who is asked which one is most appealing or likely to make him or her want to buy. This is a dreadful method, and we list it only so that if someone suggests it, you understand that. It assumes that the person can really give a valid reply to such questions. People do not react that consciously to advertising themes.

Your starting point in pretesting advertising (before its widespread use) is to decide what you are trying to achieve with your advertising. In what way or ways do you hope to influence those exposed to your advertising? If this sounds like a foolish question, consider that (1) some advertising is aimed at making people aware of your brand, (2) some attempts to get people interested in your brand or enterprise, (3) some tries to make them want what you are offering for sale, (4) some attempts to get them to buy, and (5) some aims at achieving all four of the preceding.

If you are an insurance company (we include national service firms as manufacturers), you do not expect your advertising to make the sale for you, but you do want people to be aware of what you have to offer, perhaps even to send in a coupon which you may use as a sales lead for your agents. (We do *not* condone pretending with consumers that you are doing research when you really are after sales leads, but use of coupons does not do this.) If you specialize in infant wear, you need to get the attention and interest of prospective mothers, so that close to the time of "the event" they will be knocking on your door. If you run a telephone-answering service, you must convince people they have a need for you. Only then is there a chance of making the sale. Few ads can complete the sale. Only in the case of direct-mail and telephone ordering does this take place. Most sales are completed in the retail marketplace.

There are five methods for pretesting advertising: direct questioning about the person's reactions, indirect questioning, memory tests, SELECTOR (one particular "branded" method that includes both recall and persuasion), and mixed testing methods.

In what way or ways do you wish to influence those exposed to your advertising.

1. *Direct questioning about a person's feelings.* Here you ask direct questions about a person's reactions to one or more proposed advertisements after these are shown or played. Sometimes the questioning follows a pattern of asking how likely the ad is to make the person buy. We cannot recommend this kind of questioning. As in the shuffle-card test, people cannot really tell you that. An annoying ad may be effective, but this sort of questioning would never show that.

The respondents felt negatively toward a man who was apparently quite willing to interrupt romping with his son to take a business call.

Direct questioning can be helpful for getting other kinds of information. You can measure the comprehension the ad provides by asking such questions as "What did the ad say?" "What points did it make?" or "What message or messages did you get from the ad?" You can ask direct questions about the believability of each point.

2. *Indirect questioning.* This procedure uses the focus group interview. A particular advertisement is exposed. In the physical environment of the group it is easy to show print or television ads or radio commercials. The moderator then asks the general question: "What do you think of this ad?" This procedure will not tell you which ad is going to be most effective, any more than direct questioning can. What it can do is to spot weaknesses in an ad.

In one case, a particular telephone print ad was trying to sell the idea of extension telephones in the home. The very attractive ad showed an illustration of a man on the floor in his living room. He had been playing with his very young son, but at the moment he was taking a business call. The living room was expensively and beautifully furnished, with a deep-pile rug and other luxurious appointments. Reaction to the ad was strongly negative. The group agreed that they could not identify at all with the ad. None had such luxury in their homes. They would not want to know a man like that—one who apparently quite willingly would interrupt romping with his son to take a business call.

In a proposed television commercial for a refrigerator, the test commercial showed an immaculate woman announcer standing in front of an opened refrigerator full of food. She was talking about the merits of the machine. The women in the group got little or none of the message. They simply did not listen. They found the announcer unbelievable. She did not look like she had ever been close to a kitchen. They were appalled that the announcer would leave the door open all that time.

3. *Memory tests.* If you want to test memorability of your proposed advertisements, there are at least two alternatives, one basically for print ads and the other for broadcast. For a print ad, place your proposed ad in a series of perhaps six advertisements, all in the same product category. In a personal interview, show the person each ad and allow the person to examine each ad as long as he or she wishes. Then remove the ads and ask two questions: "What brands were mentioned in these advertisements?" And for each brand named, "Will you tell me everything you can remember about what the ad said or showed?" Make sure that the order of ads is rotated in each successive interview, so that each brand gets the same equal average position. If the same brand is always in last place, it will get higher recall than it should.

A similar procedure can be used with broadcast media, although it is difficult and expensive to do this in a face-to-face situation except in a central location such as a mall, where the particular research firm has its own facilities for handling such a study.

More common in memory testing of broadcast commercials is *day-after recall* (DAR). You air the commercial you are testing, and the next day you locate people who were tuned to the particular radio or television station during the program period when your commercial was aired. After making certain that the person was really tuned to that station at that time, you ask a number of questions about recall of your message. The questionnaire shown in Figure 7.7 is used by Burke Marketing Research (a national firm headquartered in Cincinnati, Ohio), which originated the technique back in the 1950s and probably does more DAR testing than any other research firm around.

You will see that there are several steps. First, as mentioned, there is the screening test to determine whether or not the person was exposed to the test program. Second, there is a measurement of claimed recall, determining whether or not the person remembers being exposed to the test commercial. Third, as Burke puts it, there is related recall, measurement of any details about the test commercial. You must be careful, if you use this method, to make sure that you get not only those exposed to the program, but those who were in the room where the set was located at the time of the commercial. Otherwise you will be unfairly overstating the number of those exposed to the commercial and will end up with underestimates of recall levels for your commercial.

Burke average recall scores for selected product categories are reproduced in Figure 7.8. The results reflect 30-second TV commercials separately for women and for men. If you use the Burke DAR method and follow it strictly with extremely well-trained interviewers, this figure can help you interpret the results you get.

In related recall, make sure that you get not only those exposed to the program but also those who were in the room where the set was located at the time of the commercial.

4. *SELECTOR.* Burke, in 1983, combined DAR with a follow-up procedure that measures persuasion. Termed *SELECTOR,* it starts with a DAR among a recruited audience (the standard DAR uses unrecruited audiences). The first step is to recruit people (by telephone) to view a particular show (with an explanation that their views are being sought for aid in planning a future production of the show). Those who agree are sent a packet by mail, scheduled to arrive at the home the day of airing.

The respondent fills in a preprogram questionnaire one-half hour before airing of the show. While this questionnaire covers a lot of material, the key element for the persuasion measure is an expression of brand preference for a product, to be used in a drawing, should the person win it.

Immediately following the show, the respondent completes a postprogram questionnaire. While this, too, covers a lot of territory, there is also a second measurement of brand listing for another drawing. Between the preprogram and the postprogram questionnaires, therefore, there is a measurement of any shift in brand preference.

The day following exposure, the usual DAR questions are asked. The combination of procedures provides the usual DAR material plus pre-post commercial persuasiveness (measured by the change in pre-post brand choice).

If you are a relatively small business, chances are you cannot afford to buy this sort of Burke study—even the least expensive study (costs vary by nature of the sample needed) will run you some $8,500, including media charges. But we describe the procedure because we think it is about the best advertising testing procedure around.

```
DARTS 1Q-P1      DAR QUESTIONNAIRE     CITY _____ BMR# _____

        This is_____ from Burke Marketing Research.
        We're doing a study on television viewing.

    1A.  Are you/may I speak with the lady/man of the house?

             No (MAY I SPEAK WITH HER/HIM?)
             Not available (EXPLAIN/DISC/RECORD COL. 4)
             Yes (Q.___)

       1B.  Today we are speaking with _____.
            Are you/may I speak with _____?

S            No (MAY I SPEAK WITH_____?)
C            Not available (EXPLAIN/DISC/RECORD COL.___)
R            Yes (Q. 2 or Q. 1C IF NECESSARY.)
E
E      1C.  Today we are speaking with women/men 18-49 years of
N           age.  Are you 18-49 years of age, or not?
I
N            18-49 (Q. 2)
G            50+   (REF. - DISC/RECORD COL.___)

    2.   Last night _____ was shown on Channel___
         between_____ and_____ P.M.  Did you, yourself, see
         any part of (the ___1/2 hour of)_____
         last night, or not?

             Watched test program (Q. 3)
             Not watched test program (DISC/RECORD COL.___)

       2X.  By chance, did you watch any part of_____
            on Channel ____ , from _____ , or not?

             No (Q. 3)
             Yes (DISC/RECORD COL.___)
```

FIGURE 7.7. A day-after recall questionnaire. (Courtesy of Burke Marketing Research, Inc.)

    5. *Other mixed testing methods.* Sometimes less sophisticated combination procedures are used. The potato chips communications questionnaire is an example (Figure 7.9). The questionnaire was administered in a mall, where the research firm had interior facilities. Note that there are measurements of recall as well as direct questioning about the individual's reaction to the proposed commercial.

<table>
<tr><td>P
R
O
D
U
C
T</td><td>

3. While watching _____ last night,
   did you see a commercial for any _____, or not?

   No/DK (Q. 4)
   Yes (WHAT BRAND WAS IT? WHAT OTHER BRANDS?) | Acceptable Vols.

        Correct brand (Q. 5)
        Incorrect brand (WHAT OTHER BRANDS?)
        DK brand (Q. 4)
</td></tr>
</table>

P
R
O
D
U
C
T

3. While watching _____ last night,
   did you see a commercial for any _____, or not?

   No/DK (Q. 4)
   Yes (WHAT BRAND WAS IT? WHAT OTHER BRANDS?) | Acceptable Vols.

     Correct brand (Q. 5)
     Incorrect brand (WHAT OTHER BRANDS?)
     DK brand (Q. 4)

B
R
A
N
D

4. While watching _____ last night,
   did you see a commercial for _____, or not?

     Yes (Q. 5)
     No (Q.___)
     DK (I HAVE A YES OR NO TO MARK. WHICH WOULD YOU
       HAVE ME MARK?)

          Yes (Q. 5)
          No/DK (Q.___)

S
P

  4X. While watching _____ last night,
     did you see a commercial for _____, or not?

       Yes (Q. 5)
       No (Q. 6)

C
U
E

  5A. Now, please tell me anything at all you remember about the
     _____ commercial you saw last night.
     What else can you remember about last night's commercial?
     (UNTIL UNPRODUCTIVE.)

  5B. What did the commercial <u>look like</u>; what did you <u>see</u> in the
     commercial for _____ last night?
     What else did the commercial <u>show</u> about _____ last
     night? (UNTIL UNPRODUCTIVE)

Advertising: Testing Following Use (Posttesting)

The key question here is how successful the particular advertising campaign has been. As in testing advertising before its use, you must define the goals of the campaign before you design a study to measure how well your advertising has performed.

If you define the goal as sales, you might question right off whether this

5C. What did the commercial <u>say</u> about _____ last night?
What else did the commercial <u>say</u> about _____ last night?
(AS WRITTEN)

5D. What <u>ideas</u> about _____ were brought out in the commercial last night?
What <u>other ideas</u> were brought out in the commercial last night? (AS WRITTEN)

_____

(ASK OF ALL RESPONDENTS.)

6A. We're also interested in people's television viewing habits. I'm going to tell you about some scenes and commercials from one part of the program. When I stop reading, would you tell me if you remember seeing <u>any</u> part of them?

Do you remember seeing any of the part near the beginning/middle/end of _____ when

A C T I V I T Y

B E F O R E

Just after that, did you see any part of the _____ commercial when

D U R I N G

Just after that, did you see any of the part when

A F T E R

2 or more no answers (GO TO Q. 6B)
Otherwise (GO TO EXTRA QUESTIONS)

6B. You mentioned you didn't see some/any of the parts I just read to you.

During that time, were you out of the room at any time, or not?

Out/DK (ASK EXTRA QUESTIONS/AGE IF NECESSARY, THEN DISC/MARK AS COMP.)
In (GO TO Q. 6C AND Q. 6D)

6C. While you were in the room, what were you doing during that time?

6D. Did you change channels during that time, or not?

_____

E
X
T
R
A

Q
U
E
S
T
I
O
N
S

_____

(ASK OF ALL NOT DISCONTINUED AT Q. 6.)
These last questions are just to help us divide our interviews into groups.

D
E
M
O
G
R
A
P
H
I
C
S

VV. Last night, did you, yourself, watch_____on a color or black-and-white television set?

WW. Are you, yourself, employed outside the home, or not? (IF YES): Is that full-time or part-time? (IF NO): Are you a student?

XX. What is your age, please?

YY. What was the last grade of school you, yourself, completed?

GS - Grade school (0-8)	-1
SHS - Some high school (9-11)	-2
HSG - High school graduate (12)	-3
SC - Some college (13-15)	-4
CG - College graduate (16+)	-5
Refused	-0

ZZ.

so-called posttesting of advertising is really necessary. Can't you use sales as a measure of the advertising impact? Strong answer: No! There are too many other factors that affect sales. We mention only three. If your competition comes in with heavy advertising, your sales may be affected regardless of how good your advertising is. An unexpected new product introduction may make a major difference. If the economy takes a sudden downswing, its impact on sales will be greater than that of your advertising. Even weather, for some products or services, can play a major role in sales. About the only situation where you can directly evaluate advertising from sales results is in direct mail. Over a period of time, if you use approximately similar mailing lists, you can determine which advertising produces the best results for you.

But let's say you have determined the aims of the advertising and have designed a research study to measure these. How do you decide what results indicate success? You have to state these as part of each goal statement in advance of the campaign. What proportion of your potential public do you want to be

WOMEN
BY PRODUCT CATEGORY
30-SECOND COMMERCIALS

All commercials	24%	1692	0–57%
Beverages	22%	123	4–46%
Branded food products	26%	558	3–57%
Housekeeping cleaning aids	26%	384	5–53%
Oral dental breath care products	20%	43	7–51%
OTC drugs/ proprietary medicines	21%	175	2–53%
Personal accessories	22%	32	5–41%
Services	20%	100	0–44%
Toiletries/cosmetics	22%	185	3–48%
Wearing apparel	24%	41	9–41%

0   25   50   75   100

FIGURE 7.8. *Average recall scores for 30-second TV commercials.*

Data from standard 30-second tests conducted January 1, 1975, through December 31, 1977. Product categories do not add to the total because 51 tests were classified into product categories consisting of fewer than 25 tests. This "all other" category has a mean of 21 percent and a range of 3 to 53 percent.

MEN
BY PRODUCT CATEGORY
30-SECOND COMMERCIALS

	%	Tests	Range
All commercials	21%	320	1–60%
Automotive products	27%	39	6–49%
OTC drugs/proprietary medicines	17%	43	4–35%
Personal accessories	23%	39	4–44%
Services	22%	100	1–60%
Toiletries/cosmetics	15%	37	5–29%

0   25   50   75   100

Data from standard 30-second tests conducted January 1, 1975, through December 31, 1977. Product categories do not add to the total because 62 tests were classified into product categories consisting of fewer than 25 tests. This "all other" category has a mean of 21 percent and a range of 3 to 53 percent.

aware of your product or service? During the campaign, how often do you want to reach the average person? What levels of knowledge of major advertising aspects are you aiming for? What proportion do you want to try your product or service? What levels of favorable attitude do you want to attain by your advertising?

If you are planning a one-time measurement of a single campaign, you must set these numerical goals ahead of time. Otherwise you—and your associates—will have an impossible task in interpreting your numerical results. It is the first time around that is tough, when you have to start with completely estimated achievement levels.

Once the first such study has been completed, you have some basic levels as rough guides, and from there on, successive studies of following campaigns can use—at least in part, as long as the basic objectives remain the same—standards set by the earlier study or studies. Whatever the method of setting these numerical objectives, they should be stated in advance of the campaign, so that there can be no disagreement later on how to interpret results of your study.

Brand Awareness.   There are three types of measurements of brand awareness. In *unaided recall,* the person is asked to name the first brand in the product category that comes to mind. This is sometimes called "top of mind" recall. The top-of-mind figure has been found to be a predictor of future buying. In the second type, the person is asked to name all (other) brands that come to mind. This is sometimes called "share of mind." *Aided recall* is the third type of brand

Even weather, for some products or services, can play a major role in sales.

POTATO CHIPS COMMUNICATION CHECK

(SHOW COMMERCIAL.)

1. What was the name of the product being advertised?

2. Besides trying to persuade you to buy it, what was the main point the commercial was trying to make about the product?

3. What else was the commercial trying to say about the product?

(SHOW COMMERCIAL AGAIN.)

4. Now that you have seen the commercial again, was it trying to say anything else about the product?

5. I am going to read out a number of statements that could describe the commercial. Using the words on the card, please tell me how much you agree or disagree with each.

	Agree completely	Probably agree	Agree somewhat	Don't know	Disagree somewhat	Probably disagree	Disagree completely
Very interesting	☐	☐	☐	☐	☐	☐	☐
Irritating	☐	☐	☐	☐	☐	☐	☐
One I wouldn't mind seeing again	☐	☐	☐	☐	☐	☐	☐
Believable	☐	☐	☐	☐	☐	☐	☐
Difficult to understand	☐	☐	☐	☐	☐	☐	☐
Meaningful to me	☐	☐	☐	☐	☐	☐	☐

6. (IF IRRITATING) What did you find irritating about the commercial?

7. (IF NOT BELIEVABLE) What did you find unbelievable about the commercial?

8. Would you say you liked or disliked the music in the commercial?

        Liked   (Q. 9a) ☐
        Disliked   (Q. 9b) ☐
        Did not notice (END)   ☐

9a. What did you particularly like about the music?

9b. What did you particularly dislike about the music?

10. Would you tell me if you think each of the following words decribes the music?

    (READ ONE AT A TIME)

	Yes	No	Don't know
Catchy	☐	☐	☐
Lively	☐	☐	☐
Dull	☐	☐	☐
Out of place	☐	☐	☐
Suitable	☐	☐	☐
Repetitious	☐	☐	☐

FIGURE 7.9. *A shopping mall questionnaire using mixed testing methods.*

awareness. The person is presented with a list of brands or makes and reports which brands he or she recognizes. This sort of measurement is not of too much use. Only the real "dogs" will not be recognized. Unless your brand is in this category or is a new brand, we do not think the question has too much use for you.

You will want to ask questions about advertising. It is likely you will need to learn what brands the person has seen or heard advertised within some stated time period.

Details of Advertising Content Recalled.   For each brand you may want to know details of the advertising for the brand recalled, as described earlier in the pretesting discussion.

Advertising Media Recalled.   You also may decide to ask about the medium where the person was exposed to the brand's advertising. Be careful here; television is almost always overstated. Even when a brand has not used TV, it is likely to get reports that this was the medium.

Purchase Behavior.   Typically, you will also want to measure purchase behavior. Build in questions that show purchase and repurchase of your brand versus those of the competition. But be sure to limit the time period you use in such measurement, since people's memories are just not that good.

Brand Image.   You may—depending on the nature of your advertising—want to measure brand image. Brand image is the perceptions people have about your product. We are not talking about reactions to physical attributes, such as shape, size, or flavor. Instead, we refer to perceptions of intangible aspects of your brand or make, such as quality, dependability, and prestige.

These intangibles of brand image should be important to you. You may offer the best product in your category, but unless your product has a good image, the product will not make it. The intangibles of brand image are produced by your advertising and by word-of-mouth discussion.

Chapter 8 talks more specifically about image measurement, and you may want to look at that discussion now if you think your advertising study requires a measurement of brand image. If you *are* considering brand image as one of your campaign aims and measurements, it will require some imaginative thinking about your advertising objectives. Do you want your product to be seen as for teenagers, at one extreme, or for retirees, at the other? Is it to be basically oriented to males, females, or both? If you are in apparel, is it intended to be high-fashion or economy? If you are a bakery with a broad product line, do you want to be seen as basically American, French, Italian, German, or something else?

Brand image is the perception people have of intangible aspects of your brand or make, such as quality, dependability, and prestige.

Many postadvertising studies take the form of tracking studies.   Instead of a one-shot study, the *tracking study* is a series of timed studies through the course

```
┌─────────────────────────────────────────────────────────────────┐
│              TRACKING STUDY QUESTIONNAIRE                          │
│                                                                   │
│                                                                   │
│  Hello!  I'm _____ , from _____ Research.  We're │
│  doing a study, and there are a few questions I'd like to ask you.│
│                                                                   │
│  This happens to be about _____ (product field).        │
│                                                                   │
│                                                                   │
│  1. First, when you think of _____ (product field), what is │
│     the first name that comes to your mind?                       │
│                                                                   │
│  2. What other names come to mind?  (PROBE)  Are there any others?│
│                                                                   │
│  3. What brand of_____ have you seen or heard advertised in │
│     the past 30 days?                                             │
│                                                                   │
│  4. (FOR EACH ONE MENTIONED)  What did this advertising say or show?│
│     (PROBE)  Was there anything else?                             │
│                                                                   │
│  5. What brand, if any, of_____ (product category) have you │
│     bought within the past 30 days?                              │
│                                                                   │
└─────────────────────────────────────────────────────────────────┘
```

FIGURE 7.10. *A tracking study questionnaire used to determine continuing attitudes and purchases.*

of a campaign, with a largely identical questionnaire used on each successive study and a comparable sample of respondents on each wave.

The tracking study measures progress as the campaign proceeds. It may enable you to modify the advertising program as you go, to try to correct for those objectives not being attained. If you are not getting sufficient trial of the product and there is low brand recall, it may be that your advertising is not attention-getting. For all its advantages, the tracking study may not be for you. Despite its many advantages, only you can decide whether your firm can afford the expense.

A copy of a questionnaire used in one tracking study is provided in Figure 7.10. It covers only recall and purchase, but it provides a basic idea of what a tracking study is all about.

Media research is survey material that will help the advertising medium. It will be of benefit to management of the medium, to advertisers or potential advertisers, or to both. In short, an advertising medium can use research either for its own guidance or in a promotional way.

We shall start with an explanation of the major ways in which survey research can be useful to a medium. Table 8.1 shows the major types of research and whether each is chiefly management-oriented (for your own guidance in making management decisions), for promotion (customers or potential customers), or both.

All these types of study are of interest to your market and potential market; two are also of specific interest in making management decisions.

Audience research and potential audience research measure the group you reach and the group you could potentially reach. The former is basically more important as a sales tool, although your management had better be quite aware of the latter as well.

Reading habits are important for media management to help design a better product, but your media promotion people will also want to know a lot about reading habits to sell your medium more effectively. (We omit broadcast media here only because these are in a time frame. Typical viewers or listeners tend to stay a while with the same channel or station, whereas readers of a particular issue of a publication tend to be far more selective about the items they decide to examine, where they begin, and what they read.)

Audience involvement with your medium is important. How closely does your audience identify with you? To what degree do they depend on you for information (news, entertainment, and so on)? Are you a source of shopping and buying information?

Then there is the area of imagery. What do people think of your product—your medium? Here the study design depends primarily on whether you are doing it primarily for management or as a promotional tool. More about this later.

We shall spell out some of the specifics of these areas in this chapter. This is the way the chapter is organized, to make it easy for you to concentrate on the areas of your primary concern.

There is a basic distinction that should be made in the role of promotional research for broadcast versus print media. It has been said that broadcast media are bought, while print media are sold. This means that broadcast research tends to concentrate on the "hard" data of audience (ratings). Print media, on the other hand, must make considerably more use of surveys of all types as selling tools. This has a significant impact on the kinds of research used by each.

Both broadcast and print media depend heavily on the "hard" data from audience studies (both size and nature) and buying habits. Broadcast media, when doing "qualitative" studies such as audience involvement with the medium and imagery, are more likely to depend on the less expensive and less definitive focus group studies than they are to go to quantitative studies. Print media, to make the results "stick" with advertisers, may have to take the route of the quantitative approach—outlined in this chapter.

eight

How Marketing Research Can Help the Advertising Medium

Audience research and potential audience research measure the group you reach and the group you could potentially reach.

Table 8.1 Major Types of Research

	Type of media study by primary user	
Type of research	Media management	Advertisers, potential advertisers
Audience, potential audience		X
Reading habits	X	X
Audience involvement with medium		X
Buying habits		X
Image	X	X

Before we outline the specific research methods for these various areas, we must guide you in a preliminary but basic step. You must define your *market area*. You have to put definite boundaries on the market area you cover or intend to cover. Only then can you determine the population group (the statisticians call it the "universe") you need for the particular study.

There are three standards for defining media marketing areas, each set up by a different group.

1. The first is the *government-defined area*. The most commonly used definition of the marketing area for an advertising medium seems to be the SMSA (Standard Metropolitan Statistical Area). This is a *Census Bureau* term. The SMSA puts boundaries on an area where there is a dominant city of 50,000 people or more, surrounded by a less densely populated area socially and economically integrated with that city. Another definition following governmental lines is the use of local government boundaries. The local government you select may be your county, your city, or—particularly in the case of a small community newspaper—your school district.

2. Second are *broadcast media research firm areas*. One is the ADI (area of dominant influence). This defines the media area as all counties where the dominant share of TV viewing hours is spent with "home" stations. Another such definition is TSA (total survey area). This includes all counties where the net weekly audience of "home market" stations occurs.

3. There is the possibility of *your own definition of market area*. It is possible that none of the preceding definitions may meet your needs. You may serve a geographic group that overlaps or does not include any of the preceding definitions. Your publication—or broadcast medium (now particularly cable TV)—may be aimed at particular professionals, businesspeople, or some other specialized group (those interested in health, religion, or whatever).

Audience

As we have said, you have to decide, before you try to design a survey, whether you are interested in your present audience or, beyond that, in your potential

You have to put definite boundaries on the market area you cover or intend to cover.

audience as well. As you read this section of the chapter, keep in mind which way your needs run. We are going to talk about two aspects of audience measurement: size and nature.

Audience Size. If you are in the publishing business, you almost surely know about the Audit Bureau of Circulation (ABC). It makes periodic checks on circulation data for its members. Only periodicals with 70 percent or more paid circulation are eligible, and ABC checks the quantity and nature (mail, hand-delivered, newsstand) of distribution. If yours is a highly specialized or controlled (free) circulation medium, check your professional or trade association for sources of parallel audits.

If you are in broadcasting, you already know about Arbitron. This firm conducts periodic local surveys on TV viewing in all major areas of the country. Its figures are used by advertisers in determining their media purchases. You have to know and understand it to compete for the advertising dollar.

Perhaps none of these services can provide your particular measurement. You may have to design and conduct your own study. So what do you do?

Your starting point is to determine just what you want to measure. What is a member of the audience, for instance? If you are a publisher, how often does a person have to read your publication to qualify as a reader? If you are a broadcaster, you will have to set up a definition for a viewer of a particular program.

The nature of your audience may be more important than its size.

Audience Nature. The nature of your audience may be more important than its size. A Florida radio station claiming to appeal to the retired must be able to demonstrate that it delivers such an audience. Whether it is an affluent audience or teenagers you aim for, you must show that this is what you deliver.

These descriptions are *demographics*—hard statistics about people. Almost as important—some would say more so—are *psychographics*—psychological characteristics (including lifestyle). They describe the individual in terms of his or her opinions, activities, interests, buying behavior, and the like. Most successful advertisers have some idea of the psychographics of their target market. A store featuring wickerware will want to reach those with a psychological need for it, perhaps because they do much outdoor living or dream of it. A suburban newspaper will hope to show that its subscribers do more spending in local stores than in the big city to which they commute.

Reading Habits

This section applies to publications rather than to broadcast media.

Frequency of Reading. This tells you and your advertisers how loyal your readers are, how much your readers really "go" for you in terms of behavior. However, if you opt for this sort of measurement, do your questioning well. Avoid asking a vague question about reading "regularly" or "occasionally." Ask about behavior. If you are a weekly, ask how many of the past four issues the individual

Pyschographics describes the individual in terms of his or her opinions, activities, interests, and buying behavior.

has looked at. Ask about the reading—in the last issue—of each area of the paper, so that you can report not only generalizations, but specifics.

Kinds of Items Read. This sort of study is aimed at helping you improve your product by tailoring it to what your audience (or potential audience) reports about their reading behavior. Start by delineating your editorial areas and potential areas. In the questionnaire of the Suburban Newspapers of America in Figure 8.1, the first step makes sure that the person is a reader. Then the questionnaire goes on to measure, for each section, its readership, its importance, and its value. Then the reader is asked about how the content should be modified and about reactions to many specifics. (A set of interviewer instructions is also provided.)

Pattern of Reading. How does a person read a periodical? Where does he or she start? What path does he or she follow? Do most male readers begin with the sports section, going only afterward to the first page? Do most women start with what used to be called the "women's page," then moving to other sections? Both you and your advertisers need to know these answers.

Audience Involvement with the Medium

This measurement shows the dependence of your audience on your medium. It is a statement of how closely that member of your audience identifies with you. There are at least two areas you might want to measure.

Your Medium as a Source of "Editorial" Content. You will want to learn the degree to which members of your audience depend on each kind of editorial (as opposed to advertising) content. With publications, the distinction is clear. With broadcast media, it concerns reports and opinions expressed.

You need to find out the faith and dependence the person places on the various kinds of editorial content, perhaps the degree to which that item is anticipated, and the credence placed in it.

Your Medium as a Source of "Advertising" Content. Here the purpose is different. You want to do one or more of three things: help your advertisers get better results from advertising with you, get additional advertisers, or change your medium to attract new advertisers. The real issue is the degree to which your audience depends on your medium as a source of advertising and a basis for buying.

The questionnaire shown in Figure 8.2—a do-it-yourself form from Suburban Newspapers of America—shows one way of doing this. First, make sure that the person is a member of your audience. Then find out what advertising the person looks at, whether he or she is a purchasing decision maker in the product area, whether he or she would use you for information about where to shop, and how helpful he or she feels you are in assisting the buying decision. The remainder of the questionnaire provides demographics and psychographics.

The real issue is the degree to which your audience depends on your medium as a source of advertising and a basis for buying.

NEWS READERSHIP QUESTIONNAIRE

INTRODUCTION. Hello. I am _____, representing the Suburban Newspaper Advertising Bureau. We are making a study of newspaper reading habits. In your household I am to talk with adult (male, female) head of the family. (GET TO TALK TO DESIGNATED PERSON BEFORE PROCEEDING.)

1. Which of these newspapers come into your house regularly, or is read regularly by someone when he is outside the home? (READ EACH NEWSPAPER NAME. RECORD RESPONSE BELOW.)

2. Which of these newspapers do you, yourself, usually read? (READ EACH NEWSPAPER NAME. RECORD RESPONSE BELOW. TERMINATE INTERVIEW IF RESPONDENT DOES NOT READ YOUR LOCAL NEWSPAPER.)

(LIST NAMES OF NEWSPAPERS.)	Question 1		Question 2	
	Regularly in home or outside	Not regularly in home or outside	Read	Do not read
_____	( )	( )	( )	( )
_____	( )	( )	( )	( )
_____	( )	( )	( )	( )

3. Now let's talk about_____(YOUR OWN NEWSPAPER NAME). First, who is responsible for having the newspaper in your home?

Male head of house	( )	Other adult	( )
Female head of house	( )	Child	( )

4. Now I'd like to talk about the various sections of the paper. As I mention each one, please tell me whether you usually read this section. (READ EACH SECTION NAME BELOW SEPARATELY AND RECORD RESPONSE. SPECIAL FEATURES CAN BE ADDED TO COVER YOUR NEWSPAPER IF DESIRED.)

5. Now I'd like to go back over the list. As I read each item this time, please tell me how important this section is to you. If it is about as important as it could be to you, you'd mention number 5. If it is about as unimportant as it could be to you, you'd mention number 1. Here we go. (READ EACH SECTION NAME BELOW SEPARATELY AND RECORD RESPONSE.)

6. Now I would like to get your response on how good each of these parts of the paper is. We'll use the 5-to-1 scale again. If it is just about as good as possible, please mention number 5. If it is as poor as it could be, you'd mention number 1. Here we go.

FIGURE 8.1. *A questionnaire for a study of what people read in newspapers. (Courtesy of Suburban Newspaper Advertising Bureau.)*

	Question 4		Question 5	Question 6
(LIST SECTIONS OR AREAS OF READER INTEREST IN YOUR NEWSPAPERS.)	Read	Do not read		
(MEN ONLY) Sports	( )	( )		
(WOMEN ONLY) Women's section	( )	( )	_____	_____
(MEN ONLY) Business news	( )	( )	_____	_____
Society	( )	( )	_____	_____
Births and deaths	( )	( )	_____	_____
Editorials	( )	( )	_____	_____
Letters to the editor	( )		_____	_____
Village/town government	( )	( )	_____	_____
Front-page stories	( )	( )	_____	_____
Amusement section	( )	( )	_____	_____
School news	( )	( )	_____	_____
(Up to 6 regular features can go in here)	( )	( )	_____	_____

7a. Do you enjoy features about individual people?

Yes ( )   No ( )
(ASK REST OF Q. 7)   (GO TO Q. 8)

7b. Should such stories include write-ups mainly of:

    People who are an important part of the local scene—in the news, in
    government, etc.?   ( )
    "Little" people who are interesting?   ( )
    Both about equally?   ( )

7c. Should there be:

    Many such stories, with just a short bit on each person?   ( )
    Or a few of these, with a lot about each person?   ( )
    A mix of the two?   ( )

8. Now I'd like to get your opinion as to how important each of several other aspects of the paper is to you. Let's use the 5-to-1 scale again. If the particular feature is of the greatest possible importance to you, rate it as 5. If it is of the least possible importance to you rate it as 1. (READ EACH ASPECT BELOW AND RECORD REPLY.)

9. Now, as we go through this list again, please rate each aspect in terms of how good (YOUR LOCAL NEWSPAPER NAME) is, from 5 down to 1.

	Question 8	Question 9
Ease of reading the material	—————	—————
Titles given to stories and articles	—————	—————
Accuracy of the stories	—————	—————
Completeness of the stories	—————	—————
Lack of bias in reporting	—————	—————
General style of writing	—————	—————
Appearance of the photographs	—————	—————
General appearance of the paper	—————	—————
Size of the page	—————	—————
Number of pages	—————	‖‖‖‖‖
Size of the print	—————	—————
Clarity of the print	—————	—————

10a. Is it important for you to be able to locate easily and quickly the particular features you are interested in?

Yes ( )   No ( )
(ASK Q. 10b) (GO TO Q. 11)

10b. Can you find your particular interest sections reasonably easily in (NAME OF LOCAL NEWSPAPER)?

Yes ( )   No ( )

11. On the scale of 5 for the most, 1 for the least, how much do you look forward to seeing (YOUR NEWSPAPER NAME)? (RECORD BELOW.)

12. On the same scale, how enthusiastic are you about it?

13. How much do you get "wrapped up" in an issue?

Q. 11 ——— Q. 12 ——— Q. 13 ———

14. Would you say that you read (YOUR NEWSPAPER NAME) primarily for the advertising content or for the news content?

Advertising ( )   News ( )

15. Do you feel you are getting your money's worth from (YOUR NEWSPAPER NAME)?

Yes ( )   No ( )

16. How often do you pick up the paper during the week?

Once ( )   Twice ( )   Three or more times ( )

17. How do you read the paper? Front to back ( ) Back to front ( )
                             Go to specific section ( )

18. What age group should I put you in? (READ EACH GROUP UNTIL RESPONDENT REPLIES)

Under 30 ( )   40-49   ( )
30-39   ( )   50 or over ( )

19. Which is the occupation of the head of the house? (READ EACH ONE AND CHECK WHICH)

Managerial   ( )   Unemployed   ( )
Blue collar ( )   Wife   ( )
Student   ( )   White collar ( )
Professional ( )   Retired   ( )

20. What was the name of the last school attended by the head of the house? How far did he or she go? (CHECK ONLY TOP CATEGORY)

	Some	Graduated
Elementary school (grades 1-8)	( )	( )
High school (grades 9-12, including technical or vocational school)	( )	( )
College (through bachelor's degree)	( )	( )
Postgraduate (toward master's, doctorate)	( )	( )

21. Please stop me when I read the group which includes your family's total annual income—including all family members and all sources of income. (READ LIST)

Under $5000   ( ) $15,000-24,999 ( )
$5000-7999   ( )   25,000-29,999 ( )
$8000-9999   ( )   30,000-49,999 ( )
$10,000-14, 999 ( )   50,000 or more ( )

22. Do you own or rent your home?   Own ( )   Rent ( )

23. (INTERVIEWER, PLEASE RECORD) Sex of respondent: Male ( ) Female ( )

Respondent name: _____

Telephone number: _____

Date of call: _____

Interviewer signature: _____

Buying Habits

If you can show advertisers (and potential advertisers) that the buying habits of your audience are closely related to their needs, your chances of selling advertising are increased. An automobile dealer welcomes evidence that shows that your audience looks to your medium before deciding where to look for a new or used car. If you analyze your findings by demographics and psychographics (see Chapter 7), you can suggest to your advertisers how to slant their advertising to make it more effective. For example, if your audience is retired and likely conservative and old-fashioned, you can advise your advertisers to push traditional products and advertising approaches in your medium.

In general, you will be able to give your advertisers knowledge that will help them, even if it is unrelated to your medium. If you do a particular survey, you will be able to tell them how and where shopping occurs in their particular field.

Take a look at the shopping habits questionnaire developed by Suburban Newspapers of America (Figure 8.3). As always in media studies, the first thing is to make sure the person is really a member of your audience. This is what the first two questions do. Then there is a question about frequency of shopping. It is based on behavior, not a guesstimate or generalization (see Chapter 13). Questions are then asked about shopping areas visited during the time period and then about shopping areas visited when the person is shopping for particular kinds of products.

Image

What does your audience really think of you? We are not talking about reactions to specific columnists, your editorial policies, or your program content. We are talking about how people *generalize* their feelings about your particular medium. What are the *total* feelings and impressions they have about you? What is their mental picture of you? If you were a person, how would they describe you?

Do they think of you as honest, sensational, thorough, dependable, influential? Do they see you as demeaning, oversexualized, overfrank?

Image measurement is important to you in terms of your particular target audience. If you do not meet their needs, you will not make it. And you need an image statement as well as an image measurement to make the right appeal to your advertisers.

How do you design an image study? The problem is that an image of anything—a friend, a product, or a company—is usually vague and undefined. If you were asked to describe your impressions of your good friend Bill, it would likely take you quite a while to come up with all you felt about him.

The starting point is the *focus group interview,* described in Chapter 11. Assemble either audience or nonaudience members, depending on your needs, but do not mix them together, for it will kill your session. There will be so much debate between viewers and nonviewers of a specific program that you will end up nowhere. We do not go into the details of the focus group interview here,

What does your audience really think of you?

<u>QUESTIONNAIRE</u>

<u>Introduction</u>. Hello, I am _____, representing the _____ We are making a study in this area, and I would like to ask a few questions. Now in this household I am to talk to an adult (male, female) of the family. (BE SURE TO TALK TO DESIGNATED PERSON BEFORE PROCEEDING.)

1. (HAND CARD A) Here is a list of products. As I mention each one, will you please tell me whether you personally either buy this, or play a part in selecting it? (READ EACH ITEM SEPARATELY AND RECORD REPLY IN ANSWER SPACE AT TOP OF SECOND QUESTIONNAIRE PAGE. IF NONE IN Q. 1, MARK "NONE" BOX AND GO ON TO BASIC DATA.)

2. (HAND CARD B. ASK FOR EACH ITEM NAMED IN Q. 1.) At which of these locations are you most likely to shop for or buy _____? (RECORD REPLY IN ANSWER SPACE AT TOP OF SECOND QUESTIONNAIRE PAGE.)

3. Which of these newspapers do you see regularly? (READ EACH ONE AND RECORD REPLY IN ANSWER SPACE BELOW.)

   a. (PAPER 1) See regularly ( ) Do not see regularly ( )

   b. (PAPER 2) See regularly ( ) Do not see regularly ( )

   c. (PAPER 3) See regularly ( ) Do not see regularly ( )

   (IF NONE IN Q. 3, GO ON TO BASIC DATA.)

4. (ASK APPROPRIATE PART FOR EACH PAPER REPORTED AS SEEN REGULARLY IN Q. 3.)

   a. (FOR PAPER 1) Now please think about the <u>last 4 weeks</u>. <u>During the past 4 weeks</u>, did you happen to read or look into a copy of the (name of paper)? (CIRCLE THE "1" OR "2" ANSWER IN THE SPACE AT TOP OF SECOND QUESTIONNAIRE PAGE.)

   b. (FOR PAPER 2) Since last _____(NAME DAY OF WEEK INTERVIEW IS BEING CONDUCTED) did you happen to read or look into a <u>weekday</u> copy -- that is, a Monday to Friday issue of _____ _____? (CIRCLE THE "1" OR "2" ANSWER IN THE SPACE AT TOP OF SECOND QUESTIONNAIRE PAGE.)

   c. (FOR PAPER 3) Since last _____(NAME DAY OF WEEK THIS INTERVIEW IS BEING CONDUCTED) did you happen to read or look into a weekday copy -- that is, a Monday to Friday issue of _____? (CIRCLE THE "1" OR "2" ANSWER IN THE SPACE AT TOP OF SECOND QUESTIONNAIRE PAGE.)

   (IF NONE IN Q. 4, GO ON TO BASIC DATA.)

5. (ASK FOR EACH ITEM NAMED IN Q. 1.) When you are thinking of buying _____, which of these papers (THOSE SEEN IN Q. 4), if any, do you consult? Do you consult _____ (NAME EACH PAPER SEEN IN Q. 4, AND RECORD REPLY IN ANSWER SPACE AT TOP OF SECOND QUESTIONNAIRE PAGE.)

FIGURE 8.2. *A questionnaire for a study of advertising readership. (Courtesy of Suburban Newspaper Advertising Bureau.)*

RECORDING SPACE FOR QUESTIONS 1, 2, 4, and 5

Item on Card A	Q. 1 Personally buys/helps		Q. 2 Shopping area					Q. 4						Q. 5 Paper number		
	Does	Does not	1	2	3	4	5	a Paper 1 Yes / No		b Paper 2 Yes / No		c Paper 3 Yes / No		1	2	3
	1	2	1	2	3	4	5	1	2	1	2	1	2	1	2	3
1 Groceries	1	2	1	2	3	4	5							1	2	3
2 Drugs	1	2	1	2	3	4	5							1	2	3
3 Laundry	1	2	1	2	3	4	5							1	2	3
4 Restaurant meal	1	2	1	2	3	4	5							1	2	3
5 Toys	1	2	1	2	3	4	5							1	2	3
6 Home furnishings	1	2	1	2	3	4	5							1	2	3
7 Men's wear	1	2	1	2	3	4	5							1	2	3
8 Women's wear	1	2	1	2	3	4	5							1	2	3
9 Children's wear	1	2	1	2	3	4	5							1	2	3
10 Shoes	1	2	1	2	3	4	5							1	2	3
11 Fabrics	1	2	1	2	3	4	5							1	2	3
12 Large appliances	1	2	1	2	3	4	5							1	2	3
13 Small appliances	1	2	1	2	3	4	5							1	2	3
14 Music/stereo	1	2	1	2	3	4	5							1	2	3
15 Jewelry	1	2	1	2	3	4	5							1	2	3
16 Liquor	1	2	1	2	3	4	5							1	2	3
17 Autos, new	1	2	1	2	3	4	5							1	2	3
18 Auto supplies	1	2	1	2	3	4	5							1	2	3
19 Auto repairs	1	2	1	2	3	4	5							1	2	3
20 Hardware	1	2	1	2	3	4	5							1	2	3
21 Building materials	1	2	1	2	3	4	5							1	2	3
22 Garden supplies	1	2	1	2	3	4	5							1	2	3
23 Sporting goods	1	2	1	2	3	4	5							1	2	3
24 Recreation equipment	1	2	1	2	3	4	5							1	2	3
25 Real estate	1	2	1	2	3	4	5							1	2	3
26 Insurance	1	2	1	2	3	4	5							1	2	3
27 Banks, small and large	1	2	1	2	3	4	5							1	2	3

None ( )   None ( )

6a. Now I'd like to talk about classified advertising in (MENTION NEWSPAPERS NAMED AS BEING READ IN Q. 4)_____. Some people like to read classified ads, whether or not they're ready to make a purchase. Some read only when they're in the market. Which of these classified sections have you read in the past month in (NAME PAPER OR PAPERS)_____? None ( ) _____

	Paper 1	Paper 2	Paper 3
1 Apartment rentals	1	2	3
2 Real estate	1	2	3
3 Help wanted	1	2	3
4 Business services	1	2	3
5 Merchandise	1	2	3
6 Pets	1	2	3
7 Automobiles	1	2	3
8 (Add your own)	1	2	3
9 (Add your own)	1	2	3

6b. During the past month, have you or a member of your family, as a member of the general public, placed an ad in the classified section of any of these 3 newspapers? (IF NO, DO NOT RECORD. IF YES) In which paper or papers? No ( )

	Paper 1	Paper 2	Paper 3
	1	2	3

OPTIONAL QUESTIONS

In general, do you prefer advertising in your newspaper to be by business firms spread over a broad geographic area, or do you prefer the advertising to be mainly by business firms located within a relatively small area?

Broad area ( ) 1   Small area ( ) 2   No preference ( ) 3

In general, do you prefer the size, form, and content of [YOUR PAPER] or that of [LOCAL SHOPPER]?

[Suburban] ( ) 1   [Shopper] ( ) 2   No preference ( ) 3

BASIC DATA

7. (HAND CARD C) What age group should I put you in?

18-29 ( ) 1   40-49 ( ) 3
30-39 ( ) 2   50 or over ( ) 4

8. (HAND CARD D) What is the occupation of the head of the house? (READ EACH ONE AND CHECK WHICH)

Managerial ( ) 1   Unemployed ( ) 5
Blue collar ( ) 2   Wife ( ) 6
Student ( ) 3   White collar ( ) 7
Professional ( ) 4   Retired ( ) 8

9. What was the name of the last school attended by the head of the house? Did he or she graduate?
(CIRCLE ONLY TOP CATEGORY)

	Some	Graduated
Elementary school (grades 1-8)	1	2
High school (grades 9-12, including technical school)	3	4
College (through bachelor's degree)	5	6
Postgraduate (toward master's, doctorate)	7	8

10. (HAND CARD E) Into which of these groups does the total family income fall? All I need is the letter of the group.

A. Under $5000   ( ) 1   D. $15,000-$19,999 ( ) 4
B. $5000-$9999   ( ) 2   E. $20,000-$24,999 ( ) 5
C. $10,000-$14,999 ( ) 3   F. $25,000-over   ( ) 6

11. Do you own or rent your home?   Own 1   Rent 2

(OBSERVE AND RECORD. DO NOT ASK.)

12. SEX: Male 1   Female 2

13. TYPE OF DWELLING: Single or semidetached   1   Row   2
                       Duplex, triplex, quadruplex 3   Apartment   4

Respondent name: _____   Address: _____

City and zip code: _____   Phone: _____

Date of call: _____   Hour at end of call: _____

Interviewer signature: _____

SHOPPING HABITS QUESTIONAIRE

INTRODUCTION. Hello. I am _____ , representing the Suburban
Newspaper Advertising Bureau. We are making a study of newspaper reading and
shopping habits. In your household I am to talk with the adult female head of the
family. (GET TO TALK TO DESIGNATED PERSON BEFORE PROCEEDING.)

1. Which of these newspapers comes into your home regularly or is read regularly
    by someone when he or she is outside the house? (READ EACH NEWSPAPER NAME.
    RECORD RESPONSE BELOW.)

2. Which of these newspapers do you, yourself, usually read? (READ EACH NEWS-
    PAPER NAME. RECORD RESPONSE BELOW. TERMINATE INTERVIEW IF RESPONDENT DOES
    NOT READ YOUR LOCAL NEWSPAPER.)

	Question 1		Question 2	
	Regularly in home or outside	Not regularly in home or outside	Read	Do not read
_____	( )	( )	( )	( )
_____	( )	( )	( )	( )
_____	( )	( )	( )	( )

3. About how many times did you go shopping in the past 7 days, not counting
    today?
    0 ( )   4 ( )
    1 ( )   5 ( )
    2 ( )   6 ( )
    3 ( )   7 ( )

4a. Which of these shopping areas did you visit in those trips? (READ LIST AND
    CHECK WHICH.)
        Shopping center A ( )
        Shopping center B ( )
        Shopping center C ( )

4b. Did you shop anywhere else? (WRITE IN.)

5. Which shopping areas do you visit when you are shopping or buying? (READ EACH
    ITEM SEPARATELY AND CHECK REPLY.)

	Shopping center A	Shopping center B	Shopping center C
Groceries	( )	( )	( )
Furniture	( )	( )	( )
Small appliances (toaster, radio, etc.)	( )	( )	( )
Major appliances (TV, washing machine, etc.)	( )	( )	( )
Women's clothing	( )	( )	( )
Children's clothing	( )	( )	( )
Hardware	( )	( )	( )
Drugs and toiletries	( )	( )	( )

FIGURE 8.3. *A questionnaire for a study of newspaper readers' shopping habits.*
(Courtesy of Suburban Newspaper Advertising Bureau.)

6. In general, which shopping area do you believe offers: (READ EACH ITEM. RECORD REPLY TO EACH.)

	Shopping center A	Shopping center B	Shopping center (or retail area) C
The best parking	( )	( )	( )
The greatest selection of merchandise	( )	( )	( )
The nearest location to you	( )	( )	( )
The best quality of stores	( )	( )	( )
The nicest atmosphere	( )	( )	( )

7. When you shop for_____(READ EACH ITEM), about how many stores do you visit? groceries_____furniture_____small appliances_____major appliances_____ women's clothing_____children's clothing_____hardware_____drugs and_____ toiletries_____

8. Which of these items is your family planning to buy during the next 12 months? (READ EACH ITEM AND CHECK RESPONSE.)

Washing machine or dryer	Yes ( )	No ( )	Not sure ( )
Dishwasher	Yes ( )	No ( )	Not sure ( )
Refrigerator or freezer	Yes ( )	No ( )	Not sure ( )
Gas or electric range	Yes ( )	No ( )	Not sure ( )
Power mower	Yes ( )	No ( )	Not sure ( )
Television set	Yes ( )	No ( )	Not sure ( )
Stereo equipment	Yes ( )	No ( )	Not sure ( )
Luggage	Yes ( )	No ( )	Not sure ( )
Outdoor furniture	Yes ( )	No ( )	Not sure ( )
Home furniture	Yes ( )	No ( )	Not sure ( )

9. Up to now, we've been talking about your shopping habits. Now I'd like to ask you some questions about some of your other attitudes and activities.

Generally, do you consider yourself as someone who: (READ BOTH CHOICES BEFORE ACCEPTING ANSWER.)

Likes to try new products soon after
they come on the market   ( )

Or prefers to wait until the new
products have proven themselves
before trying   ( )

10. During the past 4 weeks, about how many times, if any, have you entertained a group of 4 or more people in your home?

                                        Number of times _____

11. To which of these types of groups or clubs do you belong?

	Yes	No
School PTA	( )	( )
Local political club or group	( )	( )
Volunteer fireman or policeman	( )	( )
Volunteer charitable or fund-raising group	( )	( )
Church group	( )	( )
Sports club	( )	( )

12. What age group should I put you in? (READ EACH GROUP UNTIL RESPONDENT REPLIES.)

            Under 30 ( )   40-49   ( )
            30-39   ( )   50 or over   ( )

13. What is the occupation of the head of the house? (READ EACH ONE AND CHECK WHICH.)

            Managerial   ( )   Unemployed   ( )
            Blue collar ( )   Wife   ( )
            Student   ( )   White collar ( )
            Professional ( )   Retired   ( )

14. What was the name of the last school attended by the head of the house? How far did he or she go? (CHECK ONLY TOP CATEGORY.)

	Some	Graduated
Elementary school (grades 1-8)	( )	( )
High school (grades 9-12, including technical or vocational school)	( )	( )
College (through bachelor's degree)	( )	( )
Postgraduate (toward master's/doctorate)	( )	( )

15. Please stop me when I read the group which includes your family's total annual income—including all family members and all sources of income. (READ LIST.)

            Under $5000   ( ) $15,000-24,999   ( )
            $5000-7999   ( )   25,000-29,999   ( )
            8000-9999   ( )   30,000-49,999   ( )
            10,000-14,999   ( )   50,000 or more   ( )

16. Do you own or rent your home?
                        Own ( )   Rent ( )

17. Do you, yourself, have a car available to go shopping? Yes ( )   No ( )

18. Which of these types of credit card, if any, do you, personally, carry?
(READ EACH ONE AND RECORD REPLY.)

	Carry	Do not carry
Bank card (Visa, etc.)	( )	( )
Gasoline	( )	( )
Department store (including mail order)	( )	( )
Hotel	( )	( )
A fee card (such as American Express, Diner's Club)	( )	( )

19. Do you have a check-cashing card, such as the ones sometimes offered by grocery stores?

Yes ( )   No ( )

20. (INTERVIEWER, PLEASE RECORD.) Sex of respondent? Male ( )   Female ( )

Respondent name: _____

Telephone number: _____

Date of call: _____

Interviewer signature: _____

however, because it is only the starting point of what we see as the basis for a quantitative study, to determine the areas of questioning in such a study.

In the focus group interview, you can ask such questions as "What comes to mind when you hear the name of [*the medium*]?" Then let the participants go at it. You will quickly learn the major and positive elements they associate with you. If you are in a position to make a quantitative study, the focus group interview provides a basis for a questionnaire.

There are three different aspects of image measurement: personality image, product image, and advertising image.

Personality Image. Just as you have distinct concepts of the personalities of your friends and associates, people have images of media. One is seen as "warm"; another is seen as "cold." There is one that is "dependable"; another is "sensational and unreliable." People and media can be categorized as "liberal" or "conservative."

In asking these personality-image questions, you may want to cover one or more of your competitive media. You also might want to ask about what the "ideal" medium should be like to help you understand where you stand against the ideal. In image measurement, you want to find out your audiences gut feelings about your personality, product, or advertising image.

In image measurement, you want to find out your audience's gut feelings about your personality, product, or advertising image.

Product Image. The product image for an advertising medium concerns what people think of the product (the particular publication or broadcast medium) and covers aspects such as general quality, completeness of coverage, quality of photography, ease of understanding, and the like.

Advertising Image. What message do people get from your advertising? In a study one of the authors conducted in Canada, a magazine (to remain nameless) carrying lurid, sensational content was found to have an image of its advertising along the same lines.

You might want to think about other aspects as well, such as whether your medium carries ads that are prestigious, convincing, or attractive. You can think of many more good possibilities.

nine

How Retailers and Consumer Service Firms Can Use Marketing Research

For many small stores and consumer service firms, marketing research probably should not come first when there are obvious business problems. Self-analysis, definition of goals, and determination of present position all take priority over marketing research studies. Such analyses will be better if they are put on paper. A completed, written scrutiny of the present and probable future position of the firm would work wonders in clearing the minds of the owners.

It is well known that approximately 50 percent of small retailers and consumer service firms fail during their first 2 years in business. Among the reasons for such failure is the inability or unwillingness of the owners and managers to use information readily available from a number of sources (see Chapters 4 and 5). Too often the sorry tale is one of hope, some funds, a grand opening, a slow downhill ride, and a final tragedy of selling out or bankruptcy.

This chapter concerns mostly new businesses, prospective new businesses, and businesses that are dissatisfied with their sales and profits and really want to do something about it. Before undertaking marketing research, certain matters should be well thought out long before consideration of market research. Two major forces that can hurt a small retailer or service firm are

1. Unwillingness of the entrepreneur to admit that his or her knowledge about the business is probably limited. Sometimes it almost appears to be a genetically based drive that pushes a new firm into decisions that would be much safer if based on better knowledge of the product or service.

2. Unwillingness to seek advice from persons or firms which could be of help.

It is unfortunate that even now many men and women will choose a location and open a business with no more reason than "people will always have to eat" or "there is a real trend toward gourmet cooking." But these gourmets do not have to buy their supplies in *your* store. Women may not choose to buy their clothing from your establishment, no matter how attractive you make your store atmosphere. They may be unwilling to pay the prices you will have to charge for your better merchandise or service. They *should,* you think, but perhaps they will continue to go elsewhere. It is possible, then, that you have made a mistake which could have been prevented by more forethought and some better marketing research.

Even retail stores or service firms which have done well in one location and seek to enlarge their sales by opening in another area have been known to find disaster. Small restaurants which have done so well that they enlarged their premises sometimes wonder where all the customers have gone. Again, more forethought and better market knowledge could make a difference.

Clear Reasons for Most Failures Among Small Retail and Service Enterprises

The major reasons for business failure have been cited so often by other sources that we hesitate to list them again. However, the Old and New Testaments have

Self-analysis, definition of goals, and determination of present position all take priority over marketing research studies.

It is possible that you have made a mistake which could have been prevented by more forethought and some better marketing research.

Marketing research can be useless if there is not enough money available to carry out its recommendations.

been read for almost 2,000 years without fundamentally changing our ways. Perhaps one more repetition can save a few eager new businesspersons from an otherwise steady march to bankruptcy.

Inadequate Capital. Marketing research can be useless if there is not enough money available to carry out its recommendations. There is no rule for how much capital is needed to open and continue a retail establishment, but it can be safely said that it will probably take more capital than at first thought. It is often said that a new enterprise cannot hope for a satisfactory cash flow or profit (if any) for some time. This is not always true, of course—some stores are "gold mines" from their first days—but it would be much safer to anticipate a time gap before an adequate cash flow is realized or profit is turned. So—is there enough money available to keep the place running and without profit for 3 years?

Lack of Management Expertise. Here we mean, for the small retailer and service establishment, lack of expertise in merchandising. There are ways of bringing customers into your place of business, keeping them there, and sending them out happy enough to return another day. This is partly a matter of the personality of the owner and crew and partly a matter of experience in such things as product display, ambience, and so on. Without some experience, the odds are against a bright-eyed store starter. At one time one of the authors thought it would be nice to open a bookstore which would be ready for his retirement years. A little research in the field proved that he would be smart to work for a year or so in a small bookstore where he could gain knowledge about buying and selling. Obvious it may have been, but it took several friendly bookstore owners to prove to him the wisdom of actual experience. Since he had a full-time job and many years before retirement, gaining this experience was impossible, and the dream of peddling literature faded away.

Lack of Knowledge of the Merchandise or Service to Be Sold. All business owners learn "on the job." Learning goes on continuously and endlessly, but—obvious again—the more the entrepreneur knows about his or her merchandise (and the service that will be expected by customers), the more healthy is the business. It is up to the store owner to be completely honest with himself or herself about the adequacy of his or her product knowledge.

A Real Dislike of the Business by the Owner. A small town had a jewelry store, inherited by a man who really preferred another career. He "hated" jewelry. Research for a store that is hated by its owner is useless.

What Prospective Store and Service Establishment Owners Should Consider Before Taking Any Further Major Action

What will be the "competitive advantage" of your outlet or branch over others? Why would anyone buy from you? Would *you*, if you were not connected with this establishment? Can you, after the most rigorous thought, find good reasons why your market area can support what you propose to do? Marketing research later on can support or deny your conclusions—but thought should come first.

Will your personality and the personalities of those working with you be suitable for this enterprise? Honest self-analysis is required. A service station hires boys who are mostly dropouts from high school. Their intentions are good, but their customer approach is poor and a bit rough. Women customers are especially put off. There is nothing the matter with what is sold; the location is good. The station survives, but it could do better if the owner understood the need for sales training. Since the owner himself does not realize what is needed, he should begin by analyzing himself and his own relations with "the boys." As difficult as it may be, merchants should regularly try to size themselves up. Figure 9.1 helps merchants analyze how they would react to specific problem situations.

What is the target market (economic, social, cultural)? This ties in with what has already been said in this chapter. Do you understand how your market thinks, what your customers want? A new owner of a high-priced, high-fashion women's clothing store has a reputation for being hard-nosed and harsh-spoken. The customers notice this. And the salespeople have been victims. This woman is a good merchant, but her own personality and manner are hurting her business. The customers she "wants" desire better service. In the case of this merchant, these "wanted" customers are available, but they are discouraged by the owner's personality and consequent poor atmosphere in the store. Self-analysis is obviously required. Figure 9.2 illustrates how a large store sought guidance on ways to do a better merchandising job.

Research for a store that is hated by its owner is useless.

Do you really want to be in this particular business or do you merely want to "be in business for myself"? In these days of huge staff cuts in large businesses, many middle managers appear to want to be free to "run their own shop." A good thought, but it should be tempered by good analysis of themselves and their abilities. Success stories for such persons often appear in *Readers Digest*. The many who did not achieve success remain unheralded. A former staff person with a large service business was terminated and decided to fulfill a dream of growing herbs on his own land, packaging them attractively, and living well though his own efforts. He knew nothing about this particular market, however, or about how to sell to distributors, how to price the product, or what competition might do. He failed in just over a year because of inadequate knowledge, inadequate marketing research, and inadequate capital to see him through the early days.

Are your personality and the personalities of those working with you suitable for the enterprise?

What Present Owners Should Consider Before Doing Any Marketing Research

What target markets (kind, type, and social class) is the establishment attracting? What kind should be attracted? Visual inspection of present customers is required. An analysis of charge account customers, if any, will help. Some examination, if possible, of what geographic areas customers are from

October 13, 1986

Dear Store Manager:

Ten years ago, Store Managers and Assistant Store Managers of Department, Specialty and Discount stores in the Cincinnati, Dayton and Indianapolis areas were asked to share their opinions on fourteen store management issues. We, as Marketing faculty at Miami University would like to again ask these same questions to determine if the suggested answers have changed over time. We are also asking our retail students the same questions, and plan on comparing their responses to yours.

The questions will take about ten minutes to answer. All responses are anonymous, and should be returned in the enclosed envelope. We are only sending out a small number of these questionnaires, and therefore your response is very important to us.

Thank you in advance for sharing your expertise.

Respectfully,

Jack Gifford

Dr. Jack Gifford

Donald Norris

Dr. Donald Norris
Professors, Dept. of Marketing
Miami University

cb

Excellence is Our Tradition

FIGURE 9.1. *A thought-provoking questionnaire for store owners and managers. (Courtesy of Drs. Jack Gifford and Donald Norris, Department of Marketing, Miami University, Oxford, Ohio.)*

On the following three pages are fourteen situations which might be faced by a store manager or assistant store manager during her or his career. Please indicate after each how you feel about the action taken. Please check only one space on the answer line.

1. A young man, recently hired as a salesman for a local retail store, has been working very hard to favorably impress his boss with his selling ability. At times, this young man, anxious for an order, has been a little overeager. To get the order, he exaggerates the value of the item or withholds relevant information concerning the product he is trying to sell. No fraud or deceit is intended by his actions; he is simply overeager.

   Action: His boss, the owner of the retail store, is aware of this salesman's actions, but he has done nothing to stop such practice.

   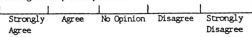

   Strongly Agree   Agree   No Opinion   Disagree   Strongly Disagree

2. A local retailer has a coat with a fur collar that he wants to get rid of. He has tried unsuccessfully for months to sell it for $89.95. He then decides to put it on sale at his approximate cost, $63.95. He still is unable to sell the coat, so he makes a new price tag, listing an original price of $129.95.

   Action: The retailer marks down this price ($129.95) to the sale price ($63.95).

   Strongly Agree   Agree   No Opinion   Disagree   Strongly Disagree

3. A person bought a new car from a franchised automobile dealership (in the local area). Eight months after the car was purchased, he began having problems with the transmission. He took the car back to the dealer, and some minor adjustments were made. During the next few months, he continually had a similar problem with the transmission slipping. Each time the dealer made only minor adjustments on the car. Again, during the 13th month after the car had been bought, the man returned to the dealer because the transmission still was not functioning properly. At this time, the transmission was completely overhauled.

   Action: Since the warranty was for only one year (12 months from date of purchase), the retailer charged full price for parts and labor.

   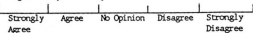

   Strongly Agree   Agree   No Opinion   Disagree   Strongly Disagree

4. A woman purchased a dress from a local retail store. Instructions for washing the dress were attached to the garment by the manufacturer. These instructions were still attached to the dress at the time of the sale and the customer was fully aware of them. After wearing the dress one time she washed it, carefully following the manufacturer's instruction. Much to her dismay, the colors in the dress faded with the washing. Also, the colors ran and made colored streaks in the white collar and cuffs of the dress. She returned to the retail store within three days after the purchase date with the merchandise.

   Action: The retailer refused to refund her money, since the dress had been worn and washed.

   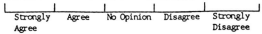

   Strongly Agree   Agree   No Opinion   Disagree   Strongly Disagree

(continued on back)

5. A local retail store ran an ad in the Sunday newspaper, announcing a sale on a well-known brand of high-quality men's slacks. The ad read that a large quantity of these slacks were available in all sizes, colors, fabrics, and styles. Response to this ad was very enthusiastic. After the second day of the sale, only ¼ of the advertised merchandise was still available.

   Action: The retailer continued to run the same ad each day for an entire week (up to and including the following Saturday).

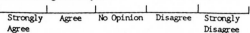

   Strongly Agree   Agree   No Opinion   Disagree   Strongly Disagree

6. Sets of a well-known brand of "good" china dinnerware are advertised on sale at a considerable discount by a local retailer. Several patterns are available from which to choose, each requiring the purchase of a typical 45-piece service for eight. The customer may also buy any "odd" pieces which are available in stock (for instance, a butter dish, gravy bowl, etc.). The ad does not indicate however, that these patterns have been discontinued by the manufacturer.

   Action: The retailer offers this information only if the customer directly asks if the merchandise is discontinued.

   Strongly Agree   Agree   No Opinion   Disagree   Strongly Disagree

7. A retail grocery chain operates several stores throughout the local area, including one in the city's "ghetto" area. Independent studies have shown that prices do tend to be higher and there is less of a selection of products in this particular store than in the other locations.

   Action: On pay day (the day welfare checks are received in this area of the city), the retailer increases prices on all his merchandise.

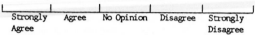

   Strongly Agree   Agree   No Opinion   Disagree   Strongly Disagree

8. Some recent research has shown that many consumers are misusing Product X, a product distributed and sold through local retailers. There is no danger involved in this misuse; the consumers are simply wasting their money by using too much of it at a time. Displays, which actually seem to encourage this misuse, are provided by the manufacturer to each retailer. A certain retailer, Retailer A, is aware that consumers are misusing Product X. He is also aware that the manufacturer's display encourages this misuse.

   Action: The retailer continues to use this display in his store.

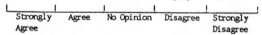

   Strongly Agree   Agree   No Opinion   Disagree   Strongly Disagree

9. According to a local retail store's credit policy, any purchase made before the 10th of the month is included on that billing. Full payment is required on an account within 25 days of this day (usually this is the 5th of the following month). If not paid in full, interest charges are then added to the balance. A person ordered a piece of furniture from this store on May 9, and charged the purchase to his credit account. The particular piece of furniture was not available for immediate delivery. By June 5, the furniture still had not been delivered, so the bill was not paid. The furniture finally arrived on June 7, and a check was then sent to the store for payment in full. The June 10 billing was received the following week.

   Action: On the bill sent by the retailer, interest charges were included since the bill had not been paid by the due date, June 5.

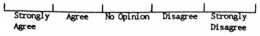

   Strongly Agree   Agree   No Opinion   Disagree   Strongly Disagree

(continued on next page)

10. A customer brings into the store a coffee pot which he explains was a wedding gift. He indicates that he already has a fine coffee pot and would like a cash refund. The pot is carried by the store, but since it was a gift the man has no sales slip. The pot retails at $12.00.

Action: The man should receive a full cash refund.

Strongly Agree	Agree	No Opinion	Disagree	Strongly Disagree

11. A customer purchased a bicycle from a store at a cost of $59.95. A week later the same bicycle is put on sale by that store for $49.00.

Action: The store should refund the customer the difference.

Strongly Agree	Agree	No Opinion	Disagree	Strongly Disagree

12. A customer purchased a foundation garment. A year later the garment was returned, with no sales slip. Since that time styles had changed and the garment had been reduced to half price. The customer requested a full cash refund.

Action: The customer should not receive the full refund but should receive the current selling price.

Strongly Agree	Agree	No Opinion	Disagree	Strongly Disagree

13. A customer calls the retailer to report that her refrigerator purchased two weeks ago is not cooling properly and that all the food has spoiled.

Action: The retailer should repair the refrigerator at no cost.

Strongly Agree	Agree	No Opinion	Disagree	Strongly Disagree

14. A customer calls the retailer to report that her refrigerator purchased two weeks ago is not cooling properly and that all the food has spoiled.

Action: The customer should be reimbursed for the value of the spoiled food.

Strongly Agree	Agree	No Opinion	Disagree	Strongly Disagree

Please indicate below the type of store in which you work.

_____ Department Store

_____ Specialty Store

_____ Discount Store

_____ Other (please specify) _____

PLEASE RETURNED THE COMPLETED QUESTIONNAIRE TODAY IN THE ENCLOSED ENVELOPE.
THANK YOU VERY MUCH FOR YOUR ASSISTANCE!

STEWART DRY GOODS COMPANY
LOUISVILLE, KENTUCKY 40202

JOHN L. HOERNER
CHAIRMAN
CHIEF EXECUTIVE OFFICER

Dear Charge Customer:

We are continually searching for new and better ways to serve
our Stewarts customers. In order to accomplish this more
successfully, I would appreciate your candid comments concerning
some issues which are addressed in the attached questionaire.
These issues deal with merchandise selection, sales personnel,
store appearance, displays, etc.

Enclosed is a discount coupon as a token of our appreciation
for your taking the time to do this.

When you have completed the questionaire, please place it in
the enclosed self-addressed, stamped envelope and drop it in the
mail by February 24.

Your response will help us make a better Stewarts and is very
much appreciated.

Sincerely,

John L. Hoerner

FIGURE 9.2 *How a large department store sought to improve its service. (Courtesy of L. S. Ayres and Company, Indianapolis, Indiana.)*

STEWART'S CREDIT CUSTOMER SURVEY
FEBRUARY, 19

INSTRUCTIONS

The following questions are designed to help us understand how we can better serve our customers. Be sure to check only ONE box out of seven for each question in Section 1. It is important that you answer all the questions in this section so that we know what changes Stewart's should consider making to satisfy your shopping needs.

SECTION 1

In Section 1, you are asked to check the box that best describes your level of satisfaction or dissatisfaction concerning our merchandise selection, pricing, advertising, services, etc. When you are answering these questions, be sure to think of the Stewart's store in which you **most frequently shop**. We will be tabulating the results of this survey by specific store locations, and it is therefore very important to us that your answers reflect your experiences at this particular store. The store **I most frequently shop in** and will reflect in my answers in this section is:

PLEASE CHECK ONLY ONE STORE!!!

[　] DOWNTOWN　　[　] OXMOOR　　[　] SHELBY　　[　] JEFFERSON　　[　] DIXIE MANOR
　　　　　　　　　　　　CENTER　　　　　MALL　　　　　MALL　　　　　　SHOPPING
[　] FAYETTE　[　] EVANSVILLE　　　　　　　　　　　　　　　　　　　　　CENTER
　　　MALL

GENERAL STORE PERSONALITY AND PHYSICAL APPEARANCE

1. CLEAN .... [　] [　] [　] [　] [　] [　] [　] .... DIRTY
   Extremely Quite Fairly So-So Fairly Quite Extremely

2. ATTRACTIVE INTERIOR ... [　] [　] [　] [　] [　] [　] [　] UNATTRACTIVE INTERIOR
   Extremely Quite Fairly So-So Fairly Quite Extremely

3. EASY TO FIND .... [　] [　] [　] [　] [　] [　] [　] .... DIFFICULT TO FIND
   ITEMS I WANT   Extremely Quite Fairly So-So Fairly Quite Extremely   ITEMS I WANT

4. MERCHANDISE IS .... [　] [　] [　] [　] [　] [　] [　] ..... MERCHANDISE IS NOT
   DISPLAYED ATTRACTIVELY   Extremely Quite Fairly So-So Fairly Quite Extremely   DISPLAYED ATTRACTIVELY
   　　　　　　　　　　　　Agree　　Agree　　Agree　　Agree

MERCHANDISE SELECTION

5. WIDE SELECTION .... [　] [　] [　] [　] [　] [　] [　] ...... NARROW SELECTION
   OF MERCHANDISE   Strongly Agree Slightly So-So Slightly Agree Strongly   OF MERCHANDISE
   　　　　　　　　Agree　　　Agree　　Agree　　　Agree

6. ALMOST ALWAYS HAS...... [　] [　] [　] [　] [　] [　] [　] .... RARELY HAS
   WHAT I'M LOOKING FOR   Strongly Agree Slightly So-So Slightly Agree Strongly   WHAT I'M LOOKING FOR
   　　　　　　　　Agree　　　Agree　　Agree　　　Agree

7. FIRST TO SHOW .... [　] [　] [　] [　] [　] [　] [　] .... LAST TO SHOW
   THE NEWEST FASHIONS   Strongly Agree Slightly So-So Slightly Agree Strongly   THE NEWEST FASHIONS
   　　　　　　　　Agree　　　Agree　　Agree　　　Agree

8. ALMOST ALWAYS .... [　] [　] [　] [　] [　] [　] [　] .... OFTEN IS OUT
   HAS MY SIZE   Strongly Agree Slightly So-So Slightly Agree Strongly   OF MY SIZE
   　　　　　　　　Agree　　　Agree　　Agree　　　Agree

9. CARRIES MY .... [　] [　] [　] [　] [　] [　] [　] .... DOES NOT CARRY
   FAVORITE BRANDS   Strongly Agree Slightly So-So Slightly Agree Strongly   MY FAVORITE BRANDS
   　　　　　　　　Agree　　　Agree　　Agree　　　Agree

10. SALES PROVIDE........... [　] [　] [　] [　] [　] [　] [　] ...SALES DO NOT PROVIDE
   GOOD VALUES   Strongly Agree Slightly So-So Slightly Agree Strongly   GOOD VALUES
   　　　　　　　　Agree　　　Agree　　Agree　　　Agree

SALES PERSONNEL

11. FRIENDLY/PLEASANT . . . . [   ] [   ] [   ] [   ] [   ] [   ] [   ]   UNFRIENDLY/UNPLEASANT
Extremely Quite Fairly So-So Fairly Quite Extremely

12. WELL INFORMED ABOUT . . . [   ] [   ] [   ] [   ] [   ] [   ] [   ]   . . . . . NOT WELL INFORMED
THE MERCHANDISE   Extremely Quite Fairly So-So Fairly Quite Extremely   ABOUT THE MERCHANDISE

13. ARE ALWAYS AVAILABLE . . . . . [   ] [   ] [   ] [   ] [   ] [   ] [   ]   . . . . ARE RARELY AVAILABLE
WHEN I NEED THEM   Strongly Agree Slightly So-So Slightly Agree Strongly   WHEN I NEED THEM
Agree   Agree   Agree   Agree

14. ARE HELPFUL WHEN . . . . [   ] [   ] [   ] [   ] [   ] [   ] [   ]   . . . . . . ARE NOT HELPFUL IN
SELECTING MERCHANDISE   Strongly Agree Slightly So-So Slightly Agree Strongly   SELECTING MERCHANDISE
Agree   Agree   Agree   Agree

PRICES OF MERCHANDISE

15. ALWAYS RECEIVE A . . . . [   ] [   ] [   ] [   ] [   ] [   ] [   ]   . . . . RARELY RECEIVE
GOOD VALUE   Strongly Agree Slightly So-So Slightly Agree Strongly   A GOOD VALUE
FOR THE PRICE   Agree   Agree   Agree   Agree   FOR THE PRICE

16. PRICES ARE LIKELY . . . . [   ] [   ] [   ] [   ] [   ] [   ] [   ]   . . . . PRICES ARE LIKELY
TO BE LOWER THAN   Strongly Agree Slightly So-So Slightly Agree Strongly   TO BE HIGHER THAN
OTHER DEPARTMENT   Agree   Agree   Agree   Agree   OTHER DEPARTMENT
STORES   STORES

ADVERTISING

17. INFORMATIVE . . . . [   ] [   ] [   ] [   ] [   ] [   ] [   ]   . . . . UNINFORMATIVE
Extremely Quite Fairly So-So Fairly Quite Extremely

18. BELIEVABLE. . . . . [   ] [   ] [   ] [   ] [   ] [   ] [   ]   . . . . UNBELIEVABLE
Extremely Quite Fairly So-So Fairly Quite Extremely

19. HELPFUL IN PLANNING . . . . . [   ] [   ] [   ] [   ] [   ] [   ] [   ]   NOT HELPFUL IN PLANNING
SHOPPING TRIPS   Extremely Quite Fairly So-So Fairly Quite Extremely   SHOPPING TRIPS

20. ADVERTISING . . . . [   ] [   ] [   ] [   ] [   ] [   ] [   ]   ADVERTISING DOES NOT
ACCURATELY REFLECTS   Strongly Agree Slightly So-So Slightly Agree Strongly   ACCURATELY REFLECT
THE MERCHANDISE FOUND   Agree   Agree   Agree   Agree   THE MERCHANDISE
IN THE STORE   IN THE STORE

21. MORE ATTRACTIVE THAN . [   ] [   ] [   ] [   ] [   ] [   ] [   ]   . . LESS ATTRACTIVE THAN
MOST OTHER AREA   Strongly Agree Slightly So-So Slightly Agree Strongly   MOST OTHER
DEPARTMENT STORE   Agree   Agree   Agree   Agree   AREA DEPARTMENT STORE
ADVERTISEMENTS   ADVERTISEMENTS

SECTION 2

22. What changes would you like to see Stewart's make in order to serve you better?

(PLEASE CONTINUE ON THE BACK PAGE)

23. Are there any changes that Stewart's has made in the past year or so which you feel make Stewart's a **MORE** desirable place to shop?

24. Are there any changes that Stewart's has made in the past year or so which you feel make Stewart's a **LESS** desirable place to shop?

25. Are there any other comments that you would like to share with the management of Stewart's which might help us serve you better?

26. Are you aware that Stewart's has merged with L.S. Ayres, a leading department store principally located in Indianapolis and Cincinnati?   [   ] YES   [   ] NO

SECTION 3

The following questions are optional. However, your responses would be very helpful. They will allow us to determine if we need to do a better job in serving men, women, small families, women who wear petite sizes, etc.

27. Sex: [   ] Female   [   ] Male
28. Age: [   ] Under 18   [   ] 18-24   [   ] 25-34   [   ] 35-44   [   ] 45-54   [   ] 55-64   [   ] 65-74   [   ] over 74
29. What was the last grade completed in school? [   ] Grade school or less   [   ] Some high school   [   ] Graduated from HS   [   ] Some college   [   ] Graduated from College   [   ] Post graduate work
30. What is your marital status? [   ] Single (never married)   [   ] Married   [   ] Widowed   [   ] Divorced or separated
31. What size do you most often purchase (women only)? [   ] Petite   [   ] Junior   [   ] Misses   [   ] Women's (large sizes)
32. Please enter your Zip Code in the following boxes. [   ][   ][   ][   ][   ]
33. How many persons including yourself are in your household?
    [   ] One   [   ] Two   [   ] Three   [   ] Four   [   ] Five   [   ] Six or more
34. Approximately how often have you shopped at Stewart's in the past 6 months?
    [   ] 0   [   ] 1-3   [   ] 4-6   [   ] 7-9   [   ] 10-12   [   ] More than 12 times
35. To which of the employment groups do you belong?
    [   ] Not employed outside the household for pay or retired   [   ] Employed part time for pay (less than 30 hours)
    [   ] Employed full time (30 hours or more)   [   ] Temporarily laid off
36. Please indicate your approximate total annual family income before taxes:
    [   ] Under $10,000   [   ] $10,000-$14,999   [   ] $15,000-$19,999   [   ] $20,000-$24,999   [   ] $25,000-$29,999
    [   ] $30,000-$34,999   [   ] $35,000-$39,999   [   ] $40,000-$49,999   [   ] $50,000-$70,000   [   ] Over $70,000

THANK YOU VERY MUCH FOR YOUR INTEREST AND COOPERATION!!

Are the people attracted to your place of business the type you want?

would help. It is not difficult to find out the kinds of people attracted to your place of business. Are they the type you want? If not, what can you do to change the circumstances? For more on how to do this, read about suggested market studies in later pages. You may be surprised at the business you are missing, the geographic areas not covered. One of the largest grocery chains recently had an interviewer ask customers in one store where they lived. After each interview, the worker marked a city map. After only 2 days of work, it was clear where a large percentage of the store's business originated. The store is slated to be rebuilt. The map shows a probable need for rebuilding in a different place. This is good, simple research which, if enlarged by census information about tract and block statistics (see Chapter 4), can provide guidance for rebuilding and relocation.

What "competitive advantage" does the store or service establishment have? Even establishments in business for some time should constantly be appraised to determine this competitive advantage. Large chains know this well and constantly work on it. The advantage need not be just price—that may be the weak way to go. Location, appearance, types of products or services offered, and all the other matters covered so far in this chapter enter into the analysis. Why *should* anyone buy from your store? Would you? What do you think your customers (and you) would like to have? All this can be submitted to marketing research, but thinking should precede that activity. Marketing research is useless if not preceded by good thinking.

Does your establishment say "welcome"?

Does the establishment say "welcome"? What do your customers really think of you? It is so easy to forget customer thinking. One large discount store greeted its customers with a sign saying the store reserved the right to examine all bundles being brought in. The store manager was afraid of pilfering. However, the manager also was saying that each person entering the door was suspected of being a thief. Not the best atmosphere. In addition, salespeople, if found at all, appeared to lack any desire to help find wanted goods. After a few years, the store closed its doors. Soon the whole chain of discount stores went out of business.

We will never forget an incident of several years ago in an Eastern city. A man in his fifties was sitting in the sun in front of his hardware store. Inside were no lights. Only the open door gave any hint of expected business. During a chat with the store owner (who did not offer the visitor a chair), the owner commented that his business was being "stolen" by Sears, Roebuck and the little man had no chance against such a giant. There was no use arguing. A few months later, the store was closed for good. Where the man and his rocking chair went is not known. We can safely presume that Sears did not hire him. An exaggerated instance, but this is typical of the thinking of some merchants. In many cities, the hardware store has survived and prospered. It survived, however, because it changed with the times, perhaps joined cooperatively with other stores and wholesalers or altered its merchandise offerings. The owner thought rather than rocked.

More often than owners or managers of small establishments realize, their success depends on what customers think of them. Quickly the word spreads that

Mr. or Ms. X is a friendly, knowledgeable person always willing to help. A friendly, helpful owner almost certainly will have similar employees. Research can provide answers to the question of what customers think.

What kinds of promotions are being used? Have you determined their effectiveness in any adequate way? Have you set up any consistent ways of determining whether your promotion techniques are paying off in sales and profits? This is a difficult thing to do, but it is worth trying. Many businesses are afraid to spend money on promotion and just as afraid *not* to. Before doing the simple kinds of research that could give some measure of promotion results, give careful thought to whatever evidence is at hand. Do you keep a running record of promotion costs and subsequent sales? Even though other factors such as weather enter in, a consistent and constant recording of these matters can give you guidance for future efforts. Large stores and chains do this; small stores and small chains are likely not to do it in a consistent fashion.

Specifically, an ad for one or two items can be measured by sales results over the next few days. Or a coupon included in the ad can yield measurable results. By using keyed ads and coupons in competing media, it is possible to determine which "pulled" the best. This is easy to do and very important to start!

What kinds of promotions are being used? Have you determined their effectiveness in any adequate way?

Before Research: Statement of Purpose and Objectives of the Establishment

Get it into writing. The best road to clear thought is the written word. Every store owner thinks about these things, but few go to the trouble of making a written credo.

Sales Volume to Make the Firm Profitable. Considering salaries and wages, rent, cost of goods, taxes, and all other costs, what sales volume and markup will be required to break even? Is that sales volume a reasonable hope?

One interesting thing about so many businesses is their unwillingness or inability to die. People's lives are invested in their businesses. Next year will be "better." We will do this or that to change our fortunes. And for many companies, the road continues downhill. Certainly any store or service establishment would be smart to make a cold, glinty-eyed calculation of what the future is likely to be. Large corporations make 5-year business projections, with listed actions to get there. So should small businesses, no matter what other important matters must be attended to. And certainly this should be done before a new business is started. Research can help and should be a part of planning.

Return on Investment to Make the Enterprise Worth Doing. After all costs, including salaries of the owners, will there likely be a sufficient return on investment to warrant the venture? A reason for going into a small business may be the strong need for "being in business for myself." This is a psychological need; beyond this, a reasonable return on money put into the business should be

Few store owners go to the trouble of making a written credo.

in sight. Moreover, if an establishment presently operating cannot see such a return in the near future, continuation of the business may be questionable. Before reaching this decision, though, some do-it-yourself marketing research may be in order—to clear the owners' minds about the probable future as well as the present.

Is there enough capital to wait out the interval between an unsatisfactory present to a well-thought-out future? A $50,000 a year man or woman may dream of driving a Rolls Royce, but unless a rich uncle dies, there is little prospect of enough capital to fulfill the dream. Visible sources of money must come before serious planning—which includes market research.

Questions that Can Be Answered Through Marketing Research

We cannot list them all. Here is a sample of kinds of important information which a store or service establishment should have—and which marketing research can help find answers to:

1. Where do my customers live? Or where would customers of a proposed outlet live?

2. In the light of the preceding, what are the demographics (economic and social circumstances) of these people? How would this knowledge affect my plans for pricing, inventory, types of products or services, and so on?

3. Can my sales goals come from an enlarged territory? Or from a branch in another area? Where?

4. How do my customers really rate my establishment in comparison with my competitors?

5. What age group should I target? Is this age group available, and just what products or services should I offer them?

6. What is the best location for a new outlet or a better location for my present establishment? Or a branch?

7. How can customers and prospective customers best be "reached" by advertisements and other promotions?

Kinds of Appropriate Research

Specific types of research are covered in depth in other chapters. Use of presently available information sources is covered in Chapter 4. To whet your appetite for fact finding, however, here is a partial list of the kinds of jobs that research can do for you.

Where do my customers live? What is my territory? There are several ways of getting the answers to these questions:

Where do your customers live? What is your territory?

1. It is possible to map the home addresses of charge account customers. This is at least a start. Frequency of purchase can be indicated on the map by some coding device, so that your map will clearly show those areas which are giving you most of your regular charge business.

2. Many stores do not have charge accounts or their charge business may be only a fraction of total sales. To find where your cash customers live is a bit more difficult.

You can offer a questionnaire to be completed on the premises and deposited before the customer leaves. Or you can slip a questionnaire into a sample of bundles or bags, along with a stamped return envelope. By using such a questionnaire at different times of the day and the week, a fairly objective sample can be obtained. There is no harm in urging people to fill out and return an *unsigned* questionnaire. You will not get a great many returns, human nature being what it is, but the ones you do get should be helpful. Chapters 10 and 12 tell you how to handle this.

Certain ethnic groups may be less likely to answer questionnaires—partly because of difficulty with the English language. Knowing this, you can allow for low returns from certain parts of your territory. You might consider some sort of incentive for returns, but we think this would cause more trouble than it is worth.

A simple means of passing out questionnaires is often used in restaurants, motels, and hotels. The customer is asked to deposit his or her completed questionnaire on the table or at the desk. Another approach is business reply postcards which ask about service, courtesy, quality of merchandise, and so on. Not a great many of these will come back—far fewer than when questionnaires with stamped return envelopes are included in bundles. The business reply postcard, however, seems to play a part in building goodwill. The proprietors are saying that they are interested in the welfare of their customers and want to know their complaints, if any, so that management can improve performance.

3. Another method of determining home addresses of customers is to interview outside your establishment, even in the shopping mall (if the mall management allows it). You can use people from a local research firm or hire people yourself. Follow the guidance in Chapter 10 on how to do interviewing. Researchers can find out where people live. They also can ask other questions, such as the degree of satisfaction with the merchandise and services received, where else the respondents shop, and what stores they shop at regularly. Perhaps you may even get some idea of *why* people shop at certain stores.

4. Another device is to take license numbers from cars parked in the lot. Here, as with the interviewing mentioned earlier, it is vital to space the work over a period of time in order to get the Saturday shopper, the Monday shopper, working people, and so on. Refer to Chapter 5 on how to spot locations from license numbers.

To do the best job, repeat these checks throughout the year at regular intervals to catch seasonal shoppers who may come to you in good driving weather but not in the winter. The cost of such interviewing or of reading license plates is minor compared to the possible benefits if the information is acted on. In addition—if allowed—the expense can be spread among all stores, thus amounting to a very small sum for any particular store.

Now that I know where the customers live, what do I do about it? If you have plotted your customers on a map—both cash and charge—and indicated by some code which are the regular, loyal customers and which are only occasional visitors, you are in a position to find out a great deal about these people. Now is the time to turn to some of the *Department of Commerce* publications described in Chapter 4. City statistics, tract statistics, and block statistics may be available. You can learn a great deal about demographics (average income, number of children, size of families, and much more). You suddenly have a wonderful guide: an accurate description of the people you would like to have as customers, where they live and who they are, and some indication of how to reach them.

What do customers really think of my establishment? An independent (and high-priced) grocery may succeed because of the personality of the proprietor and because the right types of customers are handy. Quality goods, higher-than-average prices, an excellent inventory of specialty goods, and a well-liked proprietor in the right neighborhood may pay off.

A business, even though high-priced, may succeed because of the personality of the proprietor and because the right kinds of customers are handy.

We know an independent grocery only a half mile from an excellent, clean, well-stocked unit of a nationally known chain. The chain has few customers; the independent is busy. The local store has personality; the other does not. The local store fits its home town perfectly.

Other competitive stores are within easy driving distance. How could you discover their positions in the eyes of potential customers? A telephone survey, conducted by a local research firm with central telephone facilities and good supervision, is a possibility. The identity of the sponsor can be hidden, and questions can be asked about the strengths and weaknesses of the important stores in the minds of an adequate sample of those who live in the trading area. A telephone survey in this town would be difficult, however, since we have recently been barraged by pseudosurveys that ended up with pitches for the sale of aluminum siding.

Another possibility is with *intercept interviewing,* in which people are stopped in a store or in a mall. A sample of people can be picked over a period of hours and days so that a good representation of all types of customers can be questioned. Such interviews go further than just finding out where people live. We give hints on how to achieve the cooperation of potential respondents in Chapter 10.

The types of questions must fit the particular circumstances. In both telephone and personal interviews, customers can be asked what is their *favorite* store and why, what is their next favorite, and so on. They also can be asked for negative comments on each store in which they indicate they have shopped recently. Respondents can be invited to comment on the parking situation for each store and on the friendliness of the salespeople or checkout-counter workers. Breadth of inventory, pricing policies, brands carried, and other such matters can be subjects for inquiry. Personal interviews can be a little longer than telephone interviews. Once a respondent has been stopped, the researcher can usually hold him or her for a sufficient time to learn a great many things.

The questions should be worked out ahead of time. Do some practice (test) interviews and then revise the questions and the procedure, if necessary. See Chapter 13 on these points.

Rarely do noncompeting stores work together in a fact-finding mission, and we do not know why. Costs can be shared among a group of stores that have the same general problems and purposes. Such an arrangement probably takes more leadership than most merchants have been willing to give; it can be hoped that the retailer reading this chapter will assume the leadership role.

Mail questionnaires typically have a very low return percentage. Effective ways to get a good return are explained in Chapter 12. The best method is probably the personal intercept interview at the shopping site. Next would be a telephone survey, but this would run into some opposition and might create more ill will than local retailers want to incur.

For intercept interviewing—as for all other forms—if interviewers are hired, they should be carefully selected. They should not be local people who may know too many customers. Interviewers should be aware that shoppers cannot be interviewed properly if they are carrying large bags of groceries. Interviewers must be closely supervised to ensure this and that they are not interviewing only the nice-looking, well-dressed people.

At the same time your research people are asking questions, they can learn something about where the shoppers read store advertising: "What grocery ad do you remember reading last?" "Do you remember anything that was advertised?" "What price was advertised for that item?" These sorts of questions can be asked for most types of outlets that do any advertising at all. By combining answers about what ads people last saw, you can begin to get some definitive notion of which advertising medium is doing the best job. The reason for asking respondents to name a specific ad is to avoid general answers that may or may not be factual. Both questions can be asked, if you wish: "Where do you generally expect to see grocery advertisements?" and "What grocery ad do you remember seeing last, and where was it (newspaper, TV, or where)?"

People also can be asked what brought them to this shopping area today. Was there a specific item (or items) they wanted? Were they successful in obtaining what they wanted? If not, why not? Where else will they go if they were not successful?

Since the interviews cannot be indefinitely long, include only those vital questions which can lead to action. There is reason to doubt the wisdom of continuing to advertise in a medium which no one mentions having seen. A great many remarks about surly cashiers should lead to an immediate training program in courtesy. If a large number of people say they were unsuccessful in finding what they wanted (and some say that they can "never find anything in that store"), the need for a good look at stocking policies is apparent.

Interviewers must be closely supervised to make sure they are not interviewing only the nice-looking, well-dressed people.

Other Types of Research

Group interviews were already mentioned in earlier chapters. The detailed procedure is discussed in Chapter 11. Getting the right groups is not difficult, but it requires thought and planning. Those selected must be persons who are able to offer useful and knowledgeable answers to particular problems. A group of entrepreneurs would be unlikely to have useful ideas about kitchen utensils. A group of young wives living in new homes would be a good source of ideas about how new houses should be built. More on this in Chapter 12. Such sessions, on a continuing basis, can provide a sort of early warning system to let you know of impending trouble. Traffic and parking may be getting worse, and shoppers may be beginning to avoid your area because they cannot find a place to stop. Or the new shopping center in the next town may be beginning to eat into your trade more than you know.

In-store interviews offer the advantage of having the respondents right on the premises. The customers are there because they want to be there, and they are probably a little biased in favor of your store. However, there are things that can be learned at a front-door exit interview. Did the customer get what he or she came for? Is the customer happy with the treatment he or she got? Some sort of randomness can be practiced, taking every fifth person or something of the sort. Once again, interviewers should be cautioned not to avoid anyone; you really want a good random sample of your customers. People will generally be honest in their answers if they are told that honesty is what you *really* want.

There are other things that can be done, but if most merchants even did a *part* of the preceding, they would be far better off. In one Eastern city, a large department store under new management started to become a hard-hitting, price-minded, aggressive firm. It lost many of the old and loyal customers who had been the backbone of its existence for a great many years. The gut feeling of the new management was incorrect. The store lost its old customers and did not win a profitable new trade. Now it is beginning to try to return to what it used to be. Research of the types mentioned in this chapter might well have told management it was on the wrong track, but the "bottom line" was what rang the warning bell. By that time, a dangerous situation had been created. It will take some years to recover what was lost.

So, small merchant, do not think you are alone. The whole retail trade needs more and better marketing research. Computers and gut feelings cannot substitute for factual knowledge of the market or for good, solid planning.

Some sort of randomness can be practiced, taking every fifth person or something of the sort.

Site Selection

This section of the chapter is addressed to (1) retailers who feel they should move, after conducting research in their present markets; (2) those who want to start a new store and (3) those who want to start a branch operation. The principles are the same. We are going to try to cover the various questions that should be given consideration topic by topic.

Site selection is at best a pseudoscience. There are consulting firms specializing in this type of research and advice. For the most part, such firms offer a great deal of experience, but they have no greater information than is available to you with a little effort. We cannot give you the experience, but we can suggest some of the problems that need consideration.

Customer Traffic versus Rent.   This is a balance that must be achieved in terms of the kind of establishment. The worst mistake of all is to seek low rents when you really need a great deal of customer traffic. With very few exceptions, low rents for a showroom mean fewer people going by and fewer people being attracted to the area. You cannot sell something to nobody.

Some kinds of retail establishments can thrive in out-of-the-way places. Shops selling high-quality antiques or home furnishings may give up a major traffic location for the sake of more room. Other factors will be sufficient draw.

For every such store, however, there are 10 bookstores, for example, that start business in a location that is entirely wrong, apparently in the belief that culture and the love of knowledge will attract enough trade to the "wrong side of the street" or to a back location away from the major retail trade.

Site selection is at best a pseudoscience.

This can be suicide, as many a bookstore or card shop has found to its sorrow. A healthy rent may be the cheapest thing of all to pay, because it is perfectly logical that rent should be viewed only as a percentage of sales. A rent of several thousand dollars a month can be perfectly acceptable if it amounts to only 5 or 6 percent of sales. A rent of several hundred dollars a month is completely unacceptable if it amounts to 20 percent of sales. The big question is *customer traffic.*

Patterns of automobile movement and public transportation are something you must study yourself. Of course, the first thing to do is to study a map of the city to see where the major arteries are. Where are the wealthier suburbs? Where do these people come to shop? How do they get to where they want to go? Your knowledge of your own city will be a big help.

There are other things that you can do. You can get information on traffic movements from the state highway department and the city highway people. Traffic flow at different hours of the day will give you clues to when you can expect shoppers and how many will be going by or stopping.

The state and city highway departments and the state and city planners (whatever they call themselves where you live) also can give you some idea of future plans. If a new highway is scheduled to bypass the location you are looking at, you had better know about it in advance. New streets, new parking garages, new parking regulations—all these things are important, and all are more or less available from public planning authorities.

What sales per month do you need to survive? What percentage of customer traffic can be converted into sales in your store? There is no scientific way to answer these questions, but you do have to make an estimate if you are to choose a location wisely.

Customer Traffic in Light of the Kinds of People You Want.   If you are starting a new store or thinking about moving from your present store, your possible choices of location are limited. Even if there is the possibility of building a new structure, you still have to face zoning regulations. In other words, the places you can go are more scarce than you might like.

We assume that you have some experience in the *kind* of store you are planning. You know something about hardware, shoes, or whatever you plan to sell. You know enough to be able to make some judgment concerning the kinds of people you will need as customers if you are to be successful. Your own judgment, therefore, will eliminate many of the locations available.

There are so many factors to be considered that this chapter cannot begin to cover them all. Your town may have shopping centers of various sizes and ages, but not all will have vacancies of the size you need. These centers may have done some good basic site research but not necessarily enough for your own store. Smaller shopping areas are in the better suburbs (the word "better" implies no moral measurement; it simply means more money is there), and these will or will not have a space that you would consider. Please refer to special censuses as reported in Chapter 4.

You will prefer a place within reasonable traveling distance of your own home and probably within reasonable traveling distance of people you know, the kinds of people with whom you get along best. Once again, you have eliminated more possible spots.

If you are picking a spot for a new store or service establishment or preparing yourself for a move, the number of possible places that are worth further consideration is rather severely limited. Some of the judgments you have made during the elimination process are irrational in the sense that they cannot be based on wholly reasonable results from unbiased research. These irrational reasons include the choice of a spot not too far from your home and your friends.

It would be good now to do some of the things talked about in the beginning of this chapter. Write your own plan for the *kind* of store or service firm you want and for the kind of policy you believe you are best suited to follow successfully. For this type of business, then, you can do a little accounting in advance. From your own experience, from associations, and sometimes from wholesalers, you can get average or typical figures for rent, employee cost, heat and light, and so on as a percentage of sales. What do you expect to take out of the store if you are the prospective owner? What will you have to pay the manager if you are considering a possible new branch? An analysis of cash flow from the very start of the new enterprise is vital. It is worth the time to make out a list of minimums that will have to be met if your new store is to succeed.

Will sufficient customer traffic be available at these new locations? Will it be the right kind of traffic for the person you are and for the store you want to operate? These are very basic questions that clearly are not asked often enough, or even at all in many cases, judging from the number of empty stores that are so often visible.

How will you find out whether you have the needed customer traffic of the right quality? Once again, you can go back to the research methods discussed earlier: noting license plates of people who are patronizing nearby establishments, conducting interviews, setting up a few group-interview sessions. The interviews and the license plates will give you a good idea where the shoppers

What ways of life have these people chosen? Are they sports-minded? Culture-minded?

live. Census data can tell you what kinds of people these are. Do they seem to be of sufficient affluence to patronize your store and its kind of merchandise? What are the ways of life these people have chosen? Are they sports-minded? Culture-minded? All sorts of knowledge may be obtained through one or more of these research methods and from secondary data.

It is vital to make the best decision possible, also, on what the business trend will be at each possible site. Much of the answer will come from state and city planning departments and from opinions of the people interviewed. Visual inspection of the shopping area is just as necessary as more formal research. Even an inexperienced eye can spot decay or changing ethnic groups—possibly even a trend away from the use of structures as homes to their use by small businesses. Law offices may be replacing family dwellings.

How to Use Scanners, if Available

Most of us are by now familiar with the device called a *scanner* which reads information from a universal bar code as the merchandise is passed across a screen at the checkout counter. Scanners now offer much quicker and more accurate price checkouts. They are still rarely used by other than supermarkets, but it is said that growth into other types of stores will certainly occur.

One store manager told why she liked the scanner as it is now set up in her establishment. Scanners make the pricing task much easier. No longer does she put price tags on each item. Instead, the prices are put on shelf tags which are presumed to be easily read by customers. (She admits that at present price tags on bottom shelves are very difficult for older customers to see.) Nevertheless, when it comes time to change prices, the new prices can be altered on the store computer and on the shelf tags, and no other effort need be made.

This manager uses a hand-held computer to take inventory. Down the road, her scanner and computer will yield inventories by item and price.

Some stores have already begun experimenting with new uses of the scanners. Safeway Stores has developed the use of optical scanners to help their manufacturing suppliers evaluate promotions and find new markets. The scanners can be used to measure the effectiveness of end-aisle displays. They can measure the sales differences between displays, couponing, or best locations for various types of merchandise.

Scanners make the task of pricing much easier.

Safeway says that its scanner techniques can answer such questions as

1. Effect of sampling in stores

2. Effect on unit sales when prices are changed

3. Effect of in-store displays

We cannot go deeply into how scanners are now used or what their future will be. One manufacturer told us that the uses are growing rapidly. Even small chains of only two stores are using them effectively. Retailers of suitable merchandise should contact one of the manufacturers such as NCR to find out whether scanners can be used on a cost-effective basis.

Summary

None of the approaches discussed in this chapter is difficult. All can be done by retailers who make up their minds to take the trouble. The government departments are ready and willing to help. Group and individual interviewing can be organized. City maps are almost always available, even for the smallest towns. Customer locations can be plotted, as well as roads where major automobile traffic flows. If you know which neighborhoods you wish to appeal to, the map can help you determine whether it is feasible for these people to reach your proposed locations. It is all so simple that we cannot help wondering why so few establishments ever bother. It is a rare outlet that has made any effort to research even its own charge customers. Almost always the refrain is, "We certainly should know more, and I guess we should do it . . . one of these days." Why not *now*?

How to Build
Your Own Research Study

This chapter is by no means a textbook in research. It assumes no previous ability or knowledge. It simply tells you the various ways of communicating with people who know collectively what you need to hear.

Marketing research is communicating. It uses the very few methods available to us to receive valuable information and guidance from all potential customers or, much more frequently, from a sample of persons and companies which we hope will become or remain our customers. Perhaps we hope to learn how they can become even better customers. The "bottom line" is sales and profits.

Our ways of communicating with our primary sources of fact and opinion are mail, telephone, interview, group interview, and observation. Almost all of you who read this book and want to do some research of your own must choose one or more of these methods. The questions you must ask yourself are: What answer can I get in advance from already-available printed sources such as described in Chapter 4? How much time and money do I need to spend on any particular question to get a reliable and useful answer? We have covered these matters in earlier chapters, but they need repeating here. Another repetition: In many cases a little research, if done well, is better than no research at all. As someone once said, the beginning of wisdom for all of us is the willingness to admit that we do not know everything and that we can benefit from the knowledge of others—if we but try. This and subsequent chapters are about that *trying*.

The basic ways of first-hand communicating in marketing research can be summarized like this:

I. Nonpersonal
   A. Mail surveys
   B. Other types of self-administered surveys (we will not put much emphasis on these for the purpose of this book)
II. Face-to-face (personal)
   A. Telephone studies
   B. Personal interviewing
      ▪ In-home
      ▪ At business
      ▪ Mall
      ▪ Trade shows, meetings, conventions
      ▪ Focus groups

We will cover each of these in some detail in this and subsequent chapters so that you can quickly learn how to do your own surveys. See Chapters 11, 12, and 13 for information about how to choose a "sample" to work with and how to put your results together to be of most use to you.

Nonpersonal: Mail Surveys

What the Method Is. Mail questionnaires have fallen into some disrepute in recent years. They were overused, frequently by people who did not know how

There are many questions you must ask yourself.

to use them. It became harder and harder to get a satisfactory return percentage. Some mail questionnaires have been deliberately biased and have become completely unscientific. Politicians have used such questions as these: "Don't you think that Senator Jones is on the right track when he opposes further expensive aid to [whatever]?" Yes ____ No ____ "Do you share our opinion that President Jones is doing a good job with the budget?" Yes ____ No ____

We use these exaggerated instances to show how bias can creep into questions when the person who creates the survey wants *his* or *her* side of the argument to win. You must be careful in how you word your questions to eliminate any chance that you are leading your respondents toward answers that you consider to be "right."

A typical questionnaire includes the questionnaire itself, a cover letter explaining what the study is about, and a stamped, self-addressed reply envelope. It is hoped that the combination will appear so interesting and attractive that the recipient will answer the questions and return the questionnaire promptly. The approach will almost never achieve 100 percent returns. The trick is to get the return percentage as high as possible. This may not happen without special effort (outlined later). See Chapter 13 for ideas on building a questionnaire.

Strengths and Weaknesses of the Method. Let us face a few hard truths. Except with one or more careful follow-up checks, it is impossible to be sure that those who do *not* answer your questionnaire are the same kinds of people as those who *do*. Perhaps the people who like your product or company answer the questionnaire. Those who have had trouble with your product or company throw the questionnaire away. The reverse may well be true; mostly the complainers will answer. Busy, important executives may not answer, whereas less busy, less important people have the time to answer. (Sometimes this is a blessing in disguise, since lower-echelon people may be more prone to "spill the beans" than the more experienced and more careful top people.)

You will not know for sure why these things happen unless and until you do a careful follow-up of those who did not respond together with some effort to find out why they refused. For small studies where time is critical and money is scarce, this expensive checking cannot be done. Sending out the first mailing, plus a reminder a few days later, is about all you can do. With this in mind, you can see why it is so important to have a good questionnaire, a good cover letter, a stamped return envelope, and so on—anything at all that will boost your returns. All these factors are discussed below and in subsequent chapters in more detail.

However, mail questionnaires have an important role in do-it-yourself marketing research, as well as in large professional studies. Figure 10.1 shows a mail questionnaire—a satisfaction study for physicians. Mail questionnaires are ordinarily the least expensive technique and can produce more respondents quickly. The larger the return percentage, as we said, the surer you can be that you have something approaching the "right" answer to your problem. If your return percentage is reasonably high, if the answers are borne out by your own experience and knowledge, if the consistency of results remains about the same from day to day as new batches of questionnaires come back, and finally, if the

Mail questionnaires have fallen into some disrepute in recent years.

PHYSICIAN SATISFACTION SURVEY

Dear Doctor:

The Administration of XYZ Hospital is concerned about your satisfaction with how services are provided -- both to you and your patients. Please tell us what you really think. Your individual answers will never be seen by the XYZ Administration -- only combined responses will be reviewed.

I. **NURSING STAFF:**

A. Please evaluate each of the following components of physician satisfaction using a rating scale where "5" means **"Very Satisfied"** and "1" means **"Not At All Satisfied"**. You may circle any number from "5" to "1". If you don't know the answer to a question, please circle the "DK" (Don't Know). Please begin by thinking about your level of satisfaction with the **NURSING STAFF...**

	XYZ RATINGS Very Satisfied . . . Not At All Satisfied
1. CARING ATTITUDE toward patients	5 . 4 . 3 . 2 . 1 . DK
2. COURTESY to patients	5 . 4 . 3 . 2 . 1 . DK
3. RESPONSIVENESS to patient preferences and needs............................	5 . 4 . 3 . 2 . 1 . DK
4. TECHNICAL SKILLS of nursing staff	5 . 4 . 3 . 2 . 1 . DK
5. Reaction to "PRIMARY CARE NURSING"	5 . 4 . 3 . 2 . 1 . DK
6. OVERALL SATISFACTION with nursing care ..	5 . 4 . 3 . 2 . 1 . DK

B. What is the single most important thing related to **PATIENT CARE** that XYZ Hospital could do to improve your satisfaction with the hospital?

____ (11)___

____ (12)___

C. Is there a specific nursing unit at XYZ which does an **ESPECIALLY GOOD** job of providing high quality patient care?

Yes .... 1 ---> **Please identify the unit number:** ___
No 2
Don't Know... 3

D. Is there a specific nursing unit at XYZ which **NEEDS SPECIAL ATTENTION TO IMPROVE** its ability to provide high quality patient care?

Yes .... 1 ---> **Please identify the unit number:** ___
No 2
Don't Know... 3

FIGURE 10.1. *Physician satisfaction survey. (Courtesy of Product Acceptance and Research.)*

E. How useful do you find **XYZ NURSE CLINICIANS** to your practice at the hospital? (Please circle one number below.)

Very Useful 5 .. 4 .. 3 .. 2 .. 1 Not At All Useful

II. **OPERATIONS/CLINICAL AREAS:**

XYZ   RATINGS

	Very Satisfied				Not At All Satisfied	

A. **Key Clinical Areas:**

1. Inpatient Admitting:

    a.   Scheduling .... 5 . 4 . 3 . 2 . 1 . DK
    b.   Room Assignments .... 5 . 4 . 3 . 2 . 1 . DK
    c.   Staff Performance................... 5 . 4 . 3 . 2 . 1 . DK

2. Surgery/Operating Room:

    a.   Scheduling .... 5 . 4 . 3 . 2 . 1 . DK
    b.   Anesthesia Services .... 5 . 4 . 3 . 2 . 1 . DK
    c.   Staff Performance................... 5 . 4 . 3 . 2 . 1 . DK

3. Same Day Surgery:

    a.   Scheduling .... 5 . 4 . 3 . 2 . 1 . DK
    b.   Overall Patient Care .... 5 . 4 . 3 . 2 . 1 . DK

4. Emergency Room:

    a.   Physicians' Attitudes and Cooperation 5 . 4 . 3 . 2 . 1 . DK
    b.   Quality of Services Provided .... 5 . 4 . 3 . 2 . 1 . DK
    c.   Nursing and Ancillary Care .... 5 . 4 . 3 . 2 . 1 . DK

5. Radiology Department:

    a.   Physicians' Attitudes and Cooperation 5 . 4 . 3 . 2 . 1 . DK
    b.   Quality of Services Provided .... 5 . 4 . 3 . 2 . 1 . DK
    c.   Technologists' Support .... 5 . 4 . 3 . 2 . 1 . DK

6. Laboratory/Pathology:

    a.   Physicians' Attitudes and Cooperation 5 . 4 . 3 . 2 . 1 . DK
    b.   Quality of Services Provided .... 5 . 4 . 3 . 2 . 1 . DK

```
                                          XYZ   RATINGS
                                    _____
                                    Very              Not At All
                                    Satisfied         Satisfied
                                    _____       _____

B.   Other Clinical Areas and Departments:
     (Overall)

     1. Respiratory Care ....................... 5 . 4 . 3 . 2 . 1 . DK
     2. Pharmacy ............................... 5 . 4 . 3 . 2 . 1 . DK
     3. Physical Medicine ...................... 5 . 4 . 3 . 2 . 1 . DK
     4. CareUnit (Substance Abuse) ............. 5 . 4 . 3 . 2 . 1 . DK

     5. Radiation Therapy ...................... 5 . 4 . 3 . 2 . 1 . DK
     6. Inpatient Rehabilitation ............... 5 . 4 . 3 . 2 . 1 . DK
     7. Social Services ........................ 5 . 4 . 3 . 2 . 1 . DK
     8. Home Care .............................. 5 . 4 . 3 . 2 . 1 . DK

     9. Medical Records ........................ 5 . 4 . 3 . 2 . 1 . DK
    10. Pediatrics (3100) ...................... 5 . 4 . 3 . 2 . 1 . DK
    11. Maternity ............................... 5 . 4 . 3 . 2 . 1 . DK
    12. Dietetics .............................. 5 . 4 . 3 . 2 . 1 . DK
    13. Family Practice Residency .............. 5 . 4 . 3 . 2 . 1 . DK

C.   Please state additional comments regarding any clinical areas or
     departments:

     _____ (53)____

     _____ (54)____
```

III. ADMINISTRATION/MEDICAL STAFF RELATIONS:

This portion of the questionnaire deals with relations between XYZ
Hospital and the Medical Staff. Please indicate your views by
circling the answer which best represents your opinion.

A.   Generally speaking, I feel that Hospital Administration is genuinely
     interested in and receptive to the needs of the Medical Staff.

     STRONGLY AGREE   5 ... 4 ... 3 ... 2 ... 1   **STRONGLY DISAGREE**

B.   Generally speaking, I feel the President of XYZ Hospital is responsive
     to the needs of the Medical Staff.

     STRONGLY AGREE   5 ... 4 ... 3 ... 2 ... 1   **STRONGLY DISAGREE**

C.   Generally speaking, I feel the Nursing Management is genuinely
     interested in and receptive to the needs of the Medical Staff.

     STRONGLY AGREE   5 ... 4 ... 3 ... 2 ... 1   **STRONGLY DISAGREE**

III. ADMINISTRATION/MEDICAL STAFF RELATIONS (Continued):

D. There is sufficient communication and contact between the Administration and the Medical Staff.

   STRONGLY AGREE   5 ... 4 ... 3 ... 2 ... 1   STRONGLY DISAGREE

E. The Medical Staff Director plays an important role in facilitating Administration/Medical Staff relations.

   STRONGLY AGREE   5 ... 4 ... 3 ... 2 ... 1   STRONGLY DISAGREE

F. What needs to be done to improve Administration/Medical Staff relations?

   _____ (60)____

   _____ (61)____

IV. OVERALL COMPARISON: XYZ vs. ABC:

Recognizing that a large number of physicians who practice at XYZ also admit patients to ABC, we would like you to rate your satisfaction level for each of the two hospitals on the following points. (If you are not familiar with ABC, please complete the XYZ ratings only.)

	XYZ RATINGS		ABC RATINGS	
	Very Satisfied	Not At All Satisfied	Very Satisfied	Not At All Satisfied
A. Overall Nursing Care..	5 . 4 . 3 . 2 . 1 . DK		5 . 4 . 3 . 2 . 1 . DK	
B. Projecting a Caring Attitude	5 . 4 . 3 . 2 . 1 . DK		5 . 4 . 3 . 2 . 1 . DK	
C. Overall Facilities/ Technology	5 . 4 . 3 . 2 . 1 . DK		5 . 4 . 3 . 2 . 1 . DK	
D. Administration (Daily Operations) ...	5 . 4 . 3 . 2 . 1 . DK		5 . 4 . 3 . 2 . 1 . DK	
E. Administration Leadership (Addressing the Future)	5 . 4 . 3 . 2 . 1 . DK		5 . 4 . 3 . 2 . 1 . DK	

V. PRIVATE PRACTICE OF PHYSICIANS:

A. Thinking of your current practice level, would you describe your capacity as...

   100% capacity 1
   90% capacity 2
   80% capacity 3
   70% capacity 4
   60% capacity or less 5

V.   PRIVATE PRACTICE OF PHYSICIANS (Cont.):

B.   Do you expect that your practice level will increase, decrease, or
remain about the same in the next 12 months?

                         Increase 1
                         Decrease 2
                         Remain about the same 3

C.   Approximately what percent of your patients do you refer to area
hospitals? (total should equal 100%)

        XYZ: _____ %   ABC: _____ %   QRS: _____ %   Other: _____%

D.   Do you anticipate the need for the addition of a partner in the next
2 - 3 years?

    Yes .... 1 ---> Would you welcome assistance from
    No 2   XYZ in recruiting a partner at
    Don't Know 3   the appropriate time?   Yes 1
                                                       No 2
                                                       Don't Know. 3

E.   Is it appropriate for hospitals to work with physicians to further
develop their practices (ie., assistance with office automation,
purchasing, promotional efforts)?

         Yes 1   No 2   Don't Know 3

F.   Do you feel there is value in promoting the medical staff and the
hospital to the public?

         Yes 1   No 2   Don't Know 3

VI.   MISCELLANEOUS ISSUES:

A.   What is the single greatest **WEAKNESS** of XYZ Hospital?

    _____ (11)___

    _____ (12)___

B.   What is the single greatest **STRENGTH** of XYZ Hospital?

    _____ (13)___

    _____ (14)___

C.   What is the single most important thing XYZ could do to improve your
satisfaction with the hospital?

    _____ (15)___

    _____ (16)___

mail questionnaire bears out findings from some other work such as group interviews, you can tell your coworkers that you have dependable results. However, we are talking about small studies made by the do-it-yourselfer. If your research project is a new cereal that will sell by thousands of cases per day, get a professional to do the research. Too much money is at stake.

Where Mail Studies Can Best Be Used

1. Where there is a small, homogeneous universe. The word "universe" means all the people who would have useful information for your purposes. Examples are packaging engineers of manufacturing companies, maintenance supervisors for chain grocery stores, and shipping supervisors for carpet manufacturers in the south. Or people who buy canned soups or television sets.

2. Where the same problem faces all these people and can be expressed simply and understandably.

3. In the case of studies among business firms where the particular people, although perhaps competitors, have a feeling of kinship with their counterparts in other companies.

4. Where a wholesaler or retailer may want to question his or her own customers about faults and merits.

5. Preferably where a mailing list of names and titles can somehow be obtained. Many stores have charge account names, but using these will only tell you what charge account people think. Some way may have to be found to sample cash customers.

Mail questionnaires are ordinarily the least expensive technique and can produce more respondents quickly.

We do not want to imply that these are the only places where mail questionnaires can be used. We simply say that when these conditions exist, a higher return percentage is likely. With a higher percentage you can feel more secure about the correctness of your findings.

Nonpersonal: Other Types

Warranty Cards.   One close relative of the mail questionnaire is the *warranty card* so often packed with higher-priced items sold through the retail trade. Using the implied threat that the guarantee will be worthless unless the card is returned, immediate information flows back to the manufacturer from the ultimate customers. Even here return percentages are low. One very large company reports that its warranty card return never runs over 10 percent. It considers the resulting information useful, but it cannot feel that this is a true sample of all customers. This company has made no effort to validate the returned cards to see how they vary from a true sample of *all* customers. However, the company believes that the person who fills out a warranty card, stamps it, and mails it must be different from the person who does not. Whether this difference implies a corresponding difference in buying habits for this company's products is not known.

We have said that mail questionnaires are most likely to be successful if the group being sampled is relatively small and homogeneous, if it has a certain identity (even though its individual members may be competitors), if the questions can be made to appear relevant and important to this group, and if the questions can be simply stated for easy understanding and answering. See Chapter 13 for specific guidance on constructing good questionnaires.

Distributing Questionnaires on the Premises.   Distributing questionnaires on the premises is often done by some types of business. Restaurants, motels, hotels, and others do it this way. Like the in-product questionnaires, these do not provide a true sample. However, they can lead to the discovery of certain bad practices that otherwise might have remained unknown. A large motel in Colorado placed its sign on an interstate highway in such a way that motorists are past the correct exit before they can read it. The result is a 10-mile detour. Figure 10.2 is an example of an on-the-premises questionnaire for a major motel. Figure 10.3 shows a similar survey aimed at cruise-ship vacationers.

Trade Shows.   Trade shows can be used for marketing research, but they rarely provide dependable answers. The mood at these shows is not conducive to serious answers to questions, no matter if they are posed orally or appear on hand-out questionnaires. In neither case can one count on a true sample of the "universe" in question.

Trade shows may provide a vehicle for collecting complaints about service or price. For this reason, they may have value beyond the prime purpose of a show—to exhibit goods.

We attempted market research face to face with wholesale attendees at a trade show. A new item was shown, and opinions were sought. The reaction was very good and the item was put into production. We are convinced that all those with

The mood at trade shows is not conducive to serious answers to questions, no matter if they are posed orally or appear on hand-out questionnaires.

"Will you let me know?"

Welcome to our hotel. We are pleased to have you stay with us.

It's very important to us that we do things right for you. That means . . .

Reservations should be easy to make

- Quick, hassle-free check-ins
- Rooms that are pleasant, immaculate
- Restaurants so good that many times they're local favorites
- A staff brimming with vitality—and smiles
- Expertise in handling meetings
- Fast, painless check-outs

You're the one who can tell us whether we have been successful or not. We value your comments and want to hear about the things we do right and the things we need to improve.

Will you let me know?

I have to make *sure* we do things right. After all, it's my name over the door.

President, Marriott Corp.

We need your assistance to help us provide the service you expect.

Will You Let Me Know?

Washington Marriott

‖‖‖

NO POSTAGE
NECESSARY
IF MAILED
IN THE
UNITED STATES

BUSINESS REPLY MAIL
FIRST CLASS   PERMIT NO. 10161   WASHINGTON, D.C.

POSTAGE WILL BE PAID BY ADDRESSEE

**Mr. J. W. Marriott, Jr., President
Marriott Corporation
Marriott Drive
Washington, D.C. 20058**

FIGURE 10.2. *Example of a well-thought-out questionnaire for a hotel's guests.*

Washington Marriott
OCA 770

1. Please indicate where you obtained this Guest Comment Card.
   ☐ In my hotel room
   ☐ With my receipt at check-out (Express Check-Out, Front Desk or Concierge Desk)
   ☐ Other (please explain) _____

2. How would you rate our hotel on an *overall* basis?
   ☐ Excellent ☐ Good ☐ Average ☐ Fair ☐ Poor

3. How was your room reservation made?
   ☐ This hotel's reservation department
   ☐ Toll free 800 number
   ☐ Travel agent
   ☐ Group reservation card
   ☐ Housing bureau
   ☐ Other: _____

4. When you arrived at the hotel, was the information the hotel had concerning your reservation correct?   ☐ Yes ☐ No
   If you answered "NO," please check *all* the information which *was not* correct.
   ☐ Name incorrect
   ☐ Address incorrect
   ☐ Arrival date incorrect
   ☐ Departure date incorrect
   ☐ Type of room requested not available
   ☐ Rate incorrect
   ☐ Party size incorrect
   ☐ No record of reservation
   ☐ Other: _____

5. How would you rate the following?

	Excellent	Good	Average	Fair	Poor
Check-in speed	☐	☐	☐	☐	☐
Cleanliness and servicing of your room during stay	☐	☐	☐	☐	☐
Check-out speed	☐	☐	☐	☐	☐

Value of room for price paid
What was the rate *per night* for your hotel room? _____

6. How would you rate the *attitude* of our staff on an *overall* basis?
   ☐ Excellent ☐ Good ☐ Average ☐ Fair ☐ Poor
   Please rate the following in terms of their friendly services.

	Excellent	Good	Average	Fair	Poor
Reservation staff	☐	☐	☐	☐	☐
Front desk clerk	☐	☐	☐	☐	☐
Bellstaff	☐	☐	☐	☐	☐
Housekeeping staff	☐	☐	☐	☐	☐
Telephone operators	☐	☐	☐	☐	☐
Gift shop staff	☐	☐	☐	☐	☐
Engineering staff	☐	☐	☐	☐	☐
Front desk cashier	☐	☐	☐	☐	☐
Concierge staff:					
Concierge level*	☐	☐	☐	☐	☐
Hotel lobby*	☐	☐	☐	☐	☐

(*Not available at all hotels)

7. Were *all* of the following in your room in working order? (Engineering items)   ☐ Yes ☐ No
   If you indicated "NO," please check *all* which were *not* in working order.
   ☐ Room air conditioning
   ☐ Room heating
   ☐ Bathtub drain
   ☐ Sink drain
   ☐ Water temperature
   ☐ Water pressure
   ☐ Other bathroom plumbing
   ☐ Television set
   ☐ Television reception
   ☐ Heat lamp
   ☐ Door latch
   ☐ Drapes

8. Were *all* of the following in your room in working order? (Other items)   ☐ Yes ☐ No
   If you indicated "NO," please check *all* which were *not* in working order.
   ☐ Light bulbs
   ☐ Clock/Clock radio
   ☐ Other: _____
   ☐ Telephone
   ☐ TV in-room movies

9. Please rate the following which you have used on this visit.
   How would you rate your *dining experience* on an *overall* basis?
   ☐ Excellent ☐ Good ☐ Average ☐ Fair ☐ Poor

A. RESTAURANT
Please indicate name(s) of restaurant(s). _____

☐ Breakfast ☐ Lunch ☐ Dinner

	Yes	No
Were you seated promptly?	☐	☐
Was your order taken promptly?	☐	☐
Was your food served promptly?	☐	☐

	Excellent	Good	Average	Fair	Poor
Friendly service	☐	☐	☐	☐	☐
Quality of food	☐	☐	☐	☐	☐
Menu variety	☐	☐	☐	☐	☐
Value for price paid	☐	☐	☐	☐	☐

B. ROOM SERVICE (Food and beverage)
☐ Breakfast ☐ Lunch ☐ Dinner ☐ Late evening

	Excellent	Good	Average	Fair	Poor
Friendly service	☐	☐	☐	☐	☐
Telephone order taker	☐	☐	☐	☐	☐
Server	☐	☐	☐	☐	☐
Prompt service	☐	☐	☐	☐	☐
Quality of food	☐	☐	☐	☐	☐
Menu variety	☐	☐	☐	☐	☐
Value for price paid	☐	☐	☐	☐	☐

C. COCKTAIL LOUNGE
Please indicate name(s) of lounge(s) _____

☐ 11 am to 5 pm ☐ 5 pm to 8 pm ☐ 8 pm to closing

	Excellent	Good	Average	Fair	Poor
Prompt service	☐	☐	☐	☐	☐
Friendly service	☐	☐	☐	☐	☐
Attentive service	☐	☐	☐	☐	☐
Quality of drinks	☐	☐	☐	☐	☐
Value for price paid	☐	☐	☐	☐	☐

D. BANQUET/CONVENTION EVENT
Please indicate name of event _____

	Excellent	Good	Average	Fair	Poor
Prompt service	☐	☐	☐	☐	☐
Friendly service	☐	☐	☐	☐	☐
Quality of food	☐	☐	☐	☐	☐

If any members of our staff were especially helpful, please let us know who they are and how they were helpful so that we can show them our appreciation.

Name _____

Position/Comments _____

10. What was the primary purpose of your visit?
    ☐ Pleasure ☐ Convention/group meeting/banquet ☐ Business

11. Have you stayed at this hotel previously?   ☐ Yes ☐ No

12. *If in the area again,* would you return to this Marriott?
    ☐ Yes ☐ No
    If you indicated "NO," please check the main reason for not returning.
    ☐ Other hotels more convenient
    ☐ Quality of guest rooms
    ☐ Quality of service
    ☐ Other
    ☐ Quality of restaurants
    ☐ Quality of meeting rooms
    ☐ Price

13. How many overnight business trips have you made during the past 12 months? _____ trips

14. Are you a member of Marriott's Honored Guest Award Program?
    ☐ Yes ☐ No

15. Additional comments concerning your stay: _____

PLEASE PRINT THE FOLLOWING INFORMATION

Arrival date: _____ Departure date: _____

Length of stay: _____ days. Room number: _____

☐ Mr. ☐ Mrs. ☐ Miss ☐ Ms.

Name _____

Address _____

_____ Zip _____

Business
Telephone: Area code _____ Number _____

THANK YOU VERY MUCH FOR YOUR RESPONSE.
YOUR EVALUATION *WILL* MAKE A DIFFERENCE.

Dear Passenger:

Thank you for sailing with us aboard Holland America Line for your cruise vacation.

We'd like you to please take a few minutes to complete this questionnaire about your cruise experience. Your opinions are extremely important because they let us know what you enjoyed the most, as well as areas for improvement.

Please check the responses reflecting your opinions and turn in the questionnaire at the Front Office. All results will be held in strict confidence. Thanks for your assistance in helping us create the best possible holiday for you. I hope we have the pleasure of welcoming you back aboard another Holland America Line cruise in the very near future.

Cordially,

Mr. A.K. Lanterman
President

General Instructions

Please complete the survey with a dark pen or pencil by circling the one number, or "X" if Not Applicable (NA), after each question that corresponds to your answer. Disregard the number in (   ). They are for computer use only. Also, we encourage you to give us your written comments at the end of the survey.

Previous Cruise Experience

Is this your first cruise?   (7)

1 Yes

2 No

Were any of your previous cruises with Holland America Line?   (8)

1 Yes

2 No

Holland America Line Evaluation

How do you rate your Holland America Line cruise?   (9)

	Poor								Excel-lent
Overall experience	1	2	3	4	5	6	7	8	9

FIGURE 10.3. *Example of an on-the-premises survey.*

Please rate these general aspects of your cruise:

	Poor								Excellent	NA	
Shore transfers	1	2	3	4	5	6	7	8	9	x	(10)
Baggage handling	1	2	3	4	5	6	7	8	9	x	(11)
Cleanliness of ship	1	2	3	4	5	6	7	8	9	x	(12)
Helpfulness and friendliness of ship's crew	1	2	3	4	5	6	7	8	9	x	(13)

Please rate the food in the different ship locations:

In Dining Room	Poor								Excellent	NA	
A. Taste of food	1	2	3	4	5	6	7	8	9	x	(14)
B. Variety of food	1	2	3	4	5	6	7	8	9	x	(15)
C. Presentation of food	1	2	3	4	5	6	7	8	9	x	(16)

In Lido											
A. Taste of food	1	2	3	4	5	6	7	8	9	x	(17)
B. Variety of food	1	2	3	4	5	6	7	8	9	x	(18)
C. Presentation of food	1	2	3	4	5	6	7	8	9	x	(19)

In Cabin											
A. Taste of food	1	2	3	4	5	6	7	8	9	x	(20)
B. Presentation of food	1	2	3	4	5	6	7	8	9	x	(21)

If, in your opinion, one or more of the food and beverage items listed below need improvement, please circle the appropriate number:

1 Appetizers	1 Poultry	(22)
2 Soups	2 Vegetables	
3 Salads	3 Starches	(23)
4 Seafood/Fish	4 Desserts	
5 Beef	5 Coffee	
6 Veal	6 Tea	
7 Pork	7 Juice	
8 Lamb	8 Wine	

Please rate each of the following services:

	Poor								Excel-lent	NA	
Cabin Steward	1	2	3	4	5	6	7	8	9	x	(24)
Dining Room Steward	1	2	3	4	5	6	7	8	9	x	(25)
Deck Stewards	1	2	3	4	5	6	7	8	9	x	(26)
Lounge and Bar Personnel	1	2	3	4	5	6	7	8	9	x	(27)
Wine Steward	1	2	3	4	5	6	7	8	9	x	(28)
Lido Staff	1	2	3	4	5	6	7	8	9	x	(29)
Front Office Staff	1	2	3	4	5	6	7	8	9	x	(30)
Shore Excursion Staff	1	2	3	4	5	6	7	8	9	x	(31)
Laundry and Valet	1	2	3	4	5	6	7	8	9	x	(32)

Please rate the following areas of shipboard entertainment and activities:

	Poor								Excel-lent	NA	
Professional entertainment at shows	1	2	3	4	5	6	7	8	9	x	(33)
Night club/disco	1	2	3	4	5	6	7	8	9	x	(34)
Bridge tournaments/lectures	1	2	3	4	5	6	7	8	9	x	(35)
Religious services	1	2	3	4	5	6	7	8	9	x	(36)

Please rate the Cruise Staff (Cruise Director, Social Hostess, etc.) regarding:

	Poor								Excel-lent	NA	
Organizing and conducting shipboard activities	1	2	3	4	5	6	7	8	9	x	(37)
Helpfulness and friendliness of Cruise Staff	1	2	3	4	5	6	7	8	9	x	(38)

Please rate each of the following facilities:

	Poor								Excel-lent	NA	
Cabin accommodations	1	2	3	4	5	6	7	8	9	x	(39)
Library	1	2	3	4	5	6	7	8	9	x	(40)
Shipboard shops	1	2	3	4	5	6	7	8	9	x	(41)
Photo shop	1	2	3	4	5	6	7	8	9	x	(42)
Casino	1	2	3	4	5	6	7	8	9	x	(43)
Beauty parlor/Barber shop	1	2	3	4	5	6	7	8	9	x	(44)
Gymnasium/Ocean spa	1	2	3	4	5	6	7	8	9	x	(45)
Sauna and massage	1	2	3	4	5	6	7	8	9	x	(46)
Self-service laundromat	1	2	3	4	5	6	7	8	9	x	(47)

Ports of Call and Shore Excursions

Please rate your shore excursion(s) (if applicable):

	Poor								Excel- lent	NA	
Overall Experience	1	2	3	4	5	6	7	8	9	x	(48)

Please rate the information provided during the cruise about ports-of-call and shore excursions:

	Poor								Excel- lent	NA	
Overall experience	1	2	3	4	5	6	7	8	9	x	(49)

About Yourself (for statistical purposes only)

Please indicate your dinner sitting. (Please circle the appropriate number.)

1 First dinner sitting   2 Second dinner sitting   (50)

Table number _____ (51)

Cabin number _____ (52)

In the future, what cruise line will you take?

1 Holland America Line   3 Do not plan another cruise   (53)

2 Another cruise line

Please indicate your age.

1 Under 21   4 50-64   (54)

2 22-34   5 65 and over

3 35-49

Please indicate your sex.

1 Male   (55)

2 Female

Are you:

1 Married   (56)

2 Single (includes divorced, widowed, etc.)

In what region do you live?

1 West (except California)   5 Southeast   (57)

2 California   6 Canada

3 Midwest   7 Other

4 Northeast

favorable attitudes marched down the hall, out the door, and drowned in Lake Michigan. In the next year, few of these men and women actually bought the product, and it was eventually dropped from the line.

Personal interviewing can be extremely valuable and revealing where there is sufficient time and money. For business-to-business studies, personal interviewing is often the best method. Consumer interviews can be done at shopping malls, in homes, at trade shows, and (more frequently in recent years) through group sessions often called "focus groups." All these are covered in the next chapter.

Personal: Telephone Studies

Telephone research is used quite frequently. Some resistance has been built up by the use of the telephone for selling various products. Nevertheless, this is a viable and continuing type of research that has its own place and value.

The *advantages* of using the telephone for research are obvious. Many interviews can be conducted in a relatively short period of time. The cost of research is much lower than traveling. And the cost will compare favorably with mail questionnaires. We did a survey concerning large equipment used in chain supermarkets. Seven companies were contacted by telephone. Because the equipment was expensive and likely to have occasional mechanical trouble, the respondents were eager to talk. Thus the "field work" for the study was completed in just 2 days. Traveling would not have produced any further useful information and would have cost far more.

One great advantage of telephone research for some studies is its flexibility. The researcher can change the course and nature of his or her questions in midstream on the basis of the answers received. A large amount of pertinent and valuable information may be received, information that was unexpected when the study was being planned. Mail questionnaires, of course, do not allow such shifting and therefore may miss opportunities to enrich the study.

The *disadvantages* of telephone research are a mirror-image of the advantages. A wide-scale study requiring a great many interviews may be difficult. And if such a wide-scale study requires interviews in many sections of the country, the expense of using the phone could be prohibitive when compared to mail studies.

A further disadvantage is the probable inability to have a permanent record of each interview. With proper equipment, the conversations can be recorded, but the respondent must know that this is being done. A recorded conversation usually will be transcribed for better analysis. This takes time and money that may not be available.

Telephone research may well take more time than first anticipated. The desired respondents may not be available at all on the first call, or they may answer but be so busy that they cannot spend the time to give the researcher the information desired.

Some telephone surveys can be done by an amateur. The decision depends on the type of study and the kinds of people to be called. Consumers are increasingly unwilling to be bothered by calls from strangers. The rapidly expanding number of unlisted telephone numbers bears witness to this. For a consumer study, therefore, the recommendation must be that you turn to experts in the field of telephone studies.

However, there are some parts of a telephone study that you can and should take part in, even if you do have an outside agency do the actual calling. You can and should plan the study. If possible, you should do a few calls yourself to see how difficult it is to get useful answers to your needs. Most telephone survey companies would rather do the whole study themselves, including writing the final report. However, they can also be persuaded to limit their efforts to the actual telephoning and the tabulation of results. The price is usually not prohibitive.

Consumers are increasingly unwilling to be bothered by calls from strangers.

Types of Studies That Can Be Done by Telephone.   Here is where the telephone technique can be used to advantage:

1. In before-during-after measurements of advertising results.

2. In quick and informal studies of a certain question where wholesalers, retailers, or similar companies may be called for specific (and short) answers to a few questions. The only difference between this and the ordinary calls that have been made for years is your effort to maintain something approaching an unbiased sample and questioning technique.

Using good procedures, small samples are as accurate as—or more accurate than—the large ones of years ago.

3. In short consumer studies where it may be necessary to determine knowledge of a product and preference for a brand.

4. In studies of an industrial field where the total number of respondents is small and where you have reason to believe that these people will answer legitimate inquiries.

5. In certain political polls where a very carefully selected small sample is used. An interesting commentary on how alike we all are in our agreements and disagreements is that just a couple of thousand "votes" in these polls can truly represent the thinking of an entire nation. We cannot go into the selection process used for these polls, and the only reason to mention it here is to emphasize that the very large samples of the early years of marketing research were never really necessary. Lately the trend has been toward smaller, well-chosen samples. Using good procedures, these small samples are as accurate as—or more accurate than—the large ones of years ago.

Basic Strengths and Weaknesses of the Telephone Approach. First the strengths:

1. One of the great strengths of the telephone for marketing research is the ability to get answers quickly. If you want to measure consumer awareness and attitudes toward a product or a store just before and after an advertising campaign, the telephone offers one of the few ways of doing the job before memory loss or extraneous factors such as a competitor's promotions make the results less accurate.

2. A complete territory—the nation, state, or even the area near a shopping center—can often be covered quickly—in 1 or 2 days and evenings of calling in many cases.

3. Telephone calls may be made up to 9 or 9:30 P.M., something that is difficult to do with personal interviewing, especially in city neighborhoods. In addition, few families want to be interrupted by a personal interview when they have just settled in front of the television. A phone call is less objectionable.

4. A telephone interview may produce quick, unrehearsed gut reactions that are very important to hear. Such reactions can be extremely revealing. This sort of reaction might not come out in a personal interview or even in a group interview.

5. Because the respondent cannot see the interviewer and usually never expects to see him or her in the future, just a little flattery can make the respondent "spill the beans." "You are one of a very few people [true] that we are calling in this very important quick survey. We hope that you will take a minute to tell us how you feel about [the product]." Corn is not grown only in Iowa. The ego-building approach still works.

Now the weaknesses:

1. Among consumers there is a growing antagonism toward "nuisance" telephone calls. There have been too many sales campaigns for aluminum siding, roofing, furnaces, and time-sharing condominiums.

2. For calls to consumers, it is wise to use experienced researchers with central telephone facilities and good supervision. They have learned to bore in quickly, to stand up under abuse and rebuffs, and to keep at the job until they get their quota. Using professionals is an added cost over a strictly do-it-yourself approach, but the cost is worthwhile if it means getting the results in time or at all.

3. For calls to businesspeople, whether manufacturers, wholesalers, retailers, or other, you are at the mercy of circumstances. A secretary may refuse to connect you because the person you want is "in conference." If you are put through, you may still be interrupting something important and your call will receive short shrift. Complete and precious truth may suffer a bit in the interest of getting rid of you and your problem.

4. A telephone interview lacks the flexibility of a personal or group interview. Since the respondent cannot be held for long, it is better to have one or two specific things to ask. The opportunity to explore new directions and in depth is usually not present. If you are lucky, you will find exactly what you ask for—but with little chance of getting more. Therefore, it is wise to be well prepared with written questions and a place to put the answers as they are given. It is possible to have your secretary on another extension taking down the respondent's answers in shorthand.

A telephone interview may produce quick, unrehearsed gut reactions that are very important to hear.

The difficulty of doing telephone research yourself may lead you to turn to research firms that have people who are specially trained for the task. They can more than balance the added cost through added productivity.

Moreover, research firms know how to design a questionnaire that will work well by telephone with consumers. They know the kinds of questions that can and cannot be used. Within the general field of what you want to know, it is wise to allow such firms to make out the final questionnaire—subject to your approval, of course.

For industrial and retail calls, it is a toss-up whether you can and want to do it yourself or hire someone else. It does take time; it does tie up WATS lines, if you have them. Even if you are doing only a regional or local survey, it still does tie up the telephones, which are presumably there for regular company business.

The outside company need not disclose your identity, so you can have the added advantage of anonymity, if you wish. For advertising research or for studies of brand recognition and attitude, anonymity is wise in order to avoid bias.

Personal: Face-to-Face Interviewing

Several problems must be decided before active face-to-face interviews are begun:

Questionnaire versus interview guide.

Questionnaire versus Interview Guide.   The word "questionnaire" in this discussion means a formal set of questions which are asked exactly as written. The words "interview guide" mean a written set of topics or subjects to be covered, usually in the same order as they have been set down, but allowing the interviewer to use his or her own words in asking the questions.

The advantages of a *written questionnaire* are

1. Responses are more comparable from one interview to another.

2. Nothing important is forgotten.

3. Personal biases of the interviewer (such as reaction to the respondent or weariness built up during the previous interviews) and biased reactions of the respondent to the interviewer are minimized.

4. Untrained interviewers or interviewers with a minimum knowledge of the subject of the study are less likely to cause trouble through bad interviewing procedure.

5. A questionnaire can be a welcome "crutch" to a new interviewer, making him or her appear more skilled than he or she may really be.

The advantages of an *interview guide* are equally strong. The guide we use is generally 3- by 5-inch cards with just an outline of important points to be covered. Such a guide has two main uses: for business and industrial research and for focus groups (to be covered in the next chapter).

1. In general, the less that comes between the interviewer and the respondent, the better. New interviewers tend to want a clipboard and a pad of paper. While this may appear official, it interferes with the personal rapport necessary to get good information.

2. The interview guide allows for flexibility. Leads may be followed up. The whole interview may take an entirely new but beneficial turn. Many interviews will contain an extremely valuable surprise for the interviewer. Any fixed format can easily kill off opportunities if the interviewer tries to keep the talk "on the track."

3. The guide allows the interview to be as short or as long as necessary. Sometimes the respondent has little to say, because he or she knows almost nothing about the subject. Kindness will dictate making the session as short as possible. On the other hand, sometimes the respondent will, in effect, suggest that you ask about something else. An easy person-to-person atmosphere encourages this cooperative attitude.

4. The interview guide has two main applications: the personal interview (mainly business and industrial) and the focus group (to be covered in the next chapter).

In general, new interviewers in business and industrial research should use questionnaires. More experienced people will move to the guide or simply employ their memory.

Tape Recording versus Note Taking. It is possible in all large cities and many middle-sized ones to rent an adequate tape recorder. Or you may want to own a small, portable model. The cost is usually low compared with the value of the study. Many experienced interviewers use these machines. Other equally experienced persons are opposed to them. Here are the *advantages* of tape recording:

1. It is possible to bring back every word that was said, to analyze at your convenience. You need not depend on your memory. Key people in your firm can listen to the interview and perhaps pick up points and nuances that you have missed.

2. Alternatively, you can use a trained analyst to pick up significant aspects of the responses.

3. Contrary to what you might think, the respondent soon ceases to be aware of the microphone and talks as easily as if it were not there at all. Furthermore, a certain importance may be attached to your obvious desire to record every word.

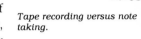

Tape recording versus note taking.

However, there are *disadvantages* concerning tape recording:

1. The respondent may not want his or her every word recorded. There appears to be a loss of confidentiality if the respondent's own voice is carried away.

2. Although it was said that the microphone is soon forgotten, this takes a few minutes, and the first few minutes of an interview may be the most important, establishing the tone of everything that is said later.

3. There is an unavoidable bother about setting up the apparatus. Even a small, battery-operated tape recorder requires some obvious preparatory steps.

4. Tapes have to be run off—taking as much or more time than the interviews themselves. Sometimes they are transcribed, which takes the time of a secretary. It is frequently difficult to follow voices on a tape, separating out people who are talking simultaneously.

5. Less important perhaps, but always present, is the chance that the tape recorder may not work. If no recording was made and no notes taken, important information may be completely lost.

If you or any of your people are doing the interviewing, it is generally unwise to try to hide the name of your company or the purpose of your call. Only in interviews with consumers (whom you will never see again) can you safely hide your identity. If anonymity is necessary, it is wiser to hire an outside research firm to do the work. Often the actual interviewers working for these firms are not told what company they are working for; your identity is absolutely safeguarded. Also, remember that your own people cannot wear two hats. In business research you or your people are likely to be returning to these respondents in the future on another study. Complete honesty in every call is the safest rule.

Some people associate marketing research with trickery. They have had

Only in interviews with consumers whom you will never see again can you safely hide your identity.

experience with the phony fellow who is doing a "heating survey of the neighborhood." The very best approach to an interview is the most honest one. You are calling on this person because he or she knows the answer to a problem that bothers you and your company. No company can afford to make major mistakes, and you hope that this person will help you to avoid making a bad marketing decision. As we said, surveys of consumer products may require concealment of the company doing the research, but no trickery is involved. There will be no speeches about how this research will help the respondents, nothing but the most transparent honesty.

Selecting Those to Do the Interviewing. In large cities, there are experienced interviewers who can be employed on a part-time basis. Such persons can be obtained through one of the well-known temporary help agencies such as Manpower or Kelly Services. With experienced help, it is possible to use an interview guide without fear of losing important information—but choose the people carefully.

Lacking such agencies, it may be necessary to use people from your firm or yourself. Needed will be a strictly controlled training session. If you are going to do the interviewing yourself, think ahead about all the problems that may arise.

How to Train Interviewers. No matter whether you use people from your firm or from some outside agency, it will be necessary to cover the following:

1. Reasons for the survey

2. Whom to approach

3. How to open an interview

4. Ways to interest prospective respondents

5. Ways to allay suspicion—especially in mall, street, or in-store interviewing

6. Ways to get by the secretary—if office interviews are involved

How to Interview. Many marketing research studies involve at least some field interviewing. The interview study shown in Figure 10.4 is an example. Japanese marketing research often utilizes even top corporate executives to visit customers, distributors, and consumers. It is said that a much better "feel" for the market can be obtained in this fashion. Given Japan's business success, it might be wise to follow its lead.

If you are doing a first study and if this study will involve face-to-face meetings, start thinking how interviews can be planned, organized, and controlled. Without planning, you would only be "out talking with the folks."

Certain human reactions characterize all research interviewing, whether talks are held in a shopping center or in a vice president's office. These should be considered before we discuss specific types of interviews.

1. To induce someone to tell you what you want to know requires sales expertise. The respondent is not necessarily antagonistic. A more usual attitude is

RETAILER PANELING

QUESTIONNAIRE

```
Store Name:_____

Location: City_____State_____

Person Completing Interview:_____
_____

Title:_____

Date:_____
```

1. Approximate square feet size of your showroom:
   _____

2. Do you have a special wall paneling section in your store? Yes___ No___. Estimated size of wall paneling section (lineal ft.)_____

3. What paneling producer's products do you regularly carry? (Please check)
   Company A___ Company B___ Company C___ etc.
   Other (please indicate who)_____

4. What percent of your wall paneling (units) would you estimate is sold to:
   a) Do-It-Yourselfers   _____%
   b) Residential remodelers?   _____%
   c) Residential builders?   _____%

FIGURE 10.4. *An interview study among store owners and managers, (names of companies have been omitted). (Courtesy of Ducker Research Company.)*

4. (cont'd)

    d) Commercial builders?   _____ %

    e) Commercial remodelers?   _____ %

    f) Mobile home dealers/owners? _____ %

5. (A) What percent of your total wall paneling sales
(units) now are in the following different
price ranges?

Up to $3.99_____ $4.00-4.99_____ $5.00-5.99_____

$6.00-6.99_____ $7.00-7.99_____ $8.00-8.99_____

$10.00+_____

(B) How many patterns do you presently carry in
each price range?

Up to $3.99_____ $4.00-4.99_____ $5.00-5.99_____

$6.00-6.99 _____ $7.00-7.99_____ $8.00-8.99_____

$10.00+_____

(C) How many patterns should you have in each price
range?

Up to $3.99_____ $4.00-4.99_____ $5.00-5.99_____

$6.00-6.99 _____ $7.00-7.99_____ $8.00-8.99_____

$10.00+_____

(D) If you could add only one more pattern to your
paneling line, which one would do the most to
improve your sales?_____

At what retail price?_____

(E) Would a broad line of panels in the $3.99-8.99
retail range from one supplier in mixed carloads

5. (cont'd)

   help you? Yes___ No___. Comments_____
   _____

6. (A) If you were to guess, how much of your paneling

       sales are: Hardware substrate_____%

       Particleboard substrate_____% Lauan substrate_____%

       Hardboard substrate_____% Plywood substrate_____%

   (B) Would you have difficulty selling a good looking

       3/16"-1/4" vinyl veneer particleboard panel in

       the $6-10 retail price category? Yes_____

       No_____Why?_____

   (C) What product qualities do your customers look

       for in the best selling panels in the $6-10

       retail price range?_____
       _____

7. (A) What were your approximate total wall paneling

       sales units last year? Number of panels?_____

   (B) How are panel sales (units) going this year?

       Up_____%; Approx. the same_____; or Down_____%

8. What percent of total panels sold are decorative____%

   vs. wood grain patterns____%.

9. Are decorative panels increasing in popularity?

   Yes____ No____. What are the best selling patterns?

   Colors?_____
   _____

10. (A) What percent of wood grain sales are now

    lighter? _____% medium?_____% darker·?_____%

    (B) Are lighter_____medium_____darker_____ wood-

    grains becoming more popular? Comments?

    _____

11. What best selling panel patterns represent 20-25%

    of your unit sales? (Please indicate brand names

    also, if possible)

    Manufacturer/Brand/Color   Approx. Retail Price

    _____   _____

    _____   _____

    _____   _____

    _____   _____

12. What percent of your wood grain panels are:

    Standard V-Grooved_____%; Random Board V-Grooved_____%;

    Ungrooved_____%

13. What percent of your total wall paneling sales have:

    Vinyl face____; Paper/Print face____; Plywood face____;

    Other____

14. What manufacturer's paneling do you like to sell

    best? _____

    Why?_____

15. What manufacturers do the best job of providing you

    with sales aids?_____

16. What promotional aids or improved/different product

    offerings would help you to improve your paneling

    sales?_____

    _____

            THANK YOU FOR YOUR HELP!!

neutrality. The respondent is willing to give you a chance, but he or she may or may not give you the needed information. The attitude after the first minute or two is a true function of how good your planning and approach have been. A bad start is not always fatal, but it does eat into the precious short time that this person is willing to give.

2. In spite of what we have said about sales ability, there is one large, important difference between a true selling situation and marketing research. Consciously or unconsciously, by training or by basic personality, a salesperson will usually feel the need to "control" a selling interview, to "lead" a prospect toward a buying decision. In our experience, after first "selling" ourselves as persons who should be helped, our best interviews, either business or consumer, have been those in which we did the least talking. It proved wiser to let the respondent feel that he or she was doing the controlling, the dominating, the impressing— although an occasional question is needed. The logic is obvious. If you want to learn what another person knows, the best thing to do is to let that person talk.

3. A good interview does not produce "tit for tat." If you feel the need to conjure up some artificial reason why these interviews will help the interviewees, the false note may become painfully obvious. If it is honestly true that the interviewee will be *helped,* say so. In consumer interviews it will be clear to the respondent that the research is designed to help develop a better, more salable product for the market.

4. Most people are willing to help you if you approach them honestly and tell them exactly what you want to know and why. It is flattering to be asked for an opinion; few people are immune. The respondent can feel wise—an oracle for the moment. In the hard world that bears down on him or her constantly, you offer the respondent a moment of superiority; his or her opinion is being sought because of its importance. We have seen this reaction from top executives and from average consumers in malls.

If you want to learn what another person knows, the best thing to do is to let that person talk.

Some Special Strengths of Personal Interviewing in Business Offices. Because personal interviewing costs more per received answer than does mail or telephone work, there have to be clear advantages to doing the job in this way before you decide on spending the money on travel and hourly costs. Many times the extra cost is worth it if information and attitudes can be obtained in no other way. Here are some of the advantages of personal interviewing in business research:

1. In many studies, you really do not know the name of the person who has the needed information. This is true all the way up and down the line of distribution from factory to ultimate distributor. You will often find that even the purchasing agent may not have the detailed information you want. Mail or telephone research would simply not be adequate to reach the right person. There is another important aspect. In factory or office research, you often find that the one who is responsible for the specifying and ordering of an item may, in fact, leave the decision to a subordinate. Or to whatever department in the factory uses the

item. A mail questionnaire, even if addressed personally, will be sent on to someone else with a notation such as "Answer if you wish and have the time." This does not lead to accurate or complete results.

2. Depending on the extent to which the personal interview has been structured, conversational leads can be followed up quickly. Lessons learned in one interview can alter and improve the next. It is possible, and happens frequently, that the type of person who was to be sampled turns out to be quite wrong. Some other office or some other title is the direction in which you should be going. A change of plans in midstudy, therefore, should be expected and allowed. The advantage of a fixed list of questions versus the use of a small guide outline has already been discussed. Shopping center personal interviews may be quite structured, with little deviation allowed. Executive interviews can only be free-flowing and in depth.

Types of Business Marketing Research Studies That Can Best Be Done with Personal Interviewing. Personal interviews, as we have said, probably should be a part of most of your planned studies. The best work is often a combination of several research methods. A mail questionnaire plus some personal interviews is a frequent combination. Another is group interviews (discussed in the next chapter) followed by more extensive mail coverage.

The best thing that can be done in preparation for personal interviewing is to write out the specific objectives you hope to accomplish. In exact and specific terms, what knowledge do you want? These specifics are likely to change a bit after your first interviews. You may think you are interested in sales of a certain steel product, but you find that plastic is being introduced. Your specifics will be altered for subsequent interviews.

A decision must be made about the kinds and, if possible, the names of people you want to see. This decision cannot really be separated from your decision about geographic coverage. A degree of judgment is necessary. Newsprint mills will be our example. There are mills scattered around the United States and Canada, but the concentrations are in the Northeast, Southeast, Northwest, and certain provinces of Canada. If your problem concerns the manufacture of newsprint, you can safely decide to visit only those areas of concentration.

In the interest of cost control, you may eliminate more areas. Use of secondary sources will show that a high percentage of Canadian paper is shipped to the United States. Perhaps you can learn all you need to know about Canadian practices from sources in the United States. Is there a difference in practices, however, in the Northeast, Southeast, and Northwest? A few exploratory telephone calls are in order if you are in the east and would prefer not to spend the money and time to fly across the country. Are there differences? Yes, in some details there may be. If you plan to manufacture a certain vital part, you may decide that the cross-country trip is worthwhile. And if you go to Washington and Oregon, you may as well go across the border to see some Canadian mills in British Columbia. We go into such details here to show the kinds of thinking and planning that may be required for so many studies.

For some other product you may find that a week in Chicago will be enough.

Preliminary work may have shown that there are no significant differences between areas and that Chicago offers a good sample of nationwide practices.

Advice from trade associations, some telephone calls to users, and perhaps a call or two to one of the salespeople in a questionable area may save time and travel money. Some purchased mailing lists are fairly good, but some may be out of date, incomplete, or too broad to be useful. As was said earlier, a good source of names is association membership lists. Another is attendance at trade shows. Often a person you call on—if you have gained his or her interest—will volunteer names of people that you "simply must see." If you are told that you can use the recommender's name, you are in luck.

A final bit of preparation is the decision as to how much can be covered in one interview. Although it may seem efficient, it is usually unwise to attempt coverage of more than one topic at an interview. Interest rises, peaks, and then drops. It is practically impossible to rebuild rapport. If two topics must be covered, it would be better to divide respondents into two groups, enlarge the list, and alternate topics as you go along.

Wholesale and Retail Interviewing. Interviewing a wholesaler, a manufacturer's agent, or distributors of various kinds is not essentially different from the business calls described earlier. Calling on retailers, however, has its own special set of problems. These should be read in connection with the procedures already described:

1. Large stores, such as department stores, may be quite dissimilar in their organizations. In some, the department manager or buyer is still king. If it is product information you want, this is the person to see. In other stores, the department manager has little to do with the selction and purchase of goods. He or she is in charge of the sales function and personnel. Purchases are closely supervised. Major decisions are made by the merchandise manager (a person often difficult to see). In still other stores, major purchases are made in a central location, often in another city. These practices vary and may present real problems to a researcher. It would be wise, if department stores are a major factor in the research, to determine in advance the buying practices of the chains you are about to interview. One well-planned interview in New York may give you all you want for all stores around the country.

2. Certain chain and variety stores have definite rules about research interviews in individual store units. You can likely see the person you want to see, but this person may not be allowed to tell you anything. If you are guilty of visiting too many individual chain store units, you may find your company receiving a warning from the chain's top management. You may be asked to visit only the buyers at headquarters. Chain stores and variety stores usually are extremely courteous and cooperative at the head office level. When possible, they will help you—just as long as you do not put too many demands on them.

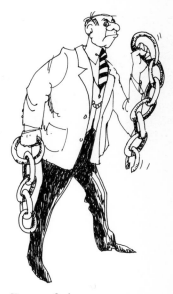

You may find your company receiving a warning from the chain's top management.

3. Ignorance in calling on the retail trade is not a virtue. For example, a bookstore in a shopping center may be a unit of a chain owned by a group of department stores. Any researcher should be aware of this before making a call.

4. Buyers and department heads of local department stores are extremely difficult to pin down. Advance telephoning invites a negative answer, while a personal visit can easily lead to a talk with the right person, an assistant, or even a supervisor.

5. Locally owned stores—the myriad of groceries, hardware stores, flower shops, or whatever—simply require shoe leather and strong leg muscles.

A few hints about local retailers are in order. Do not ever forget that the store's own customers come first. The local store owner buys and may also sell. His or her own business is more important to him or her than anything you have to say. Be courteous, be understanding, and wait as long as needed. Your patience will be appreciated, and in the end, you may get more information than you expected.

All sorts of decisions must be made by a manufacturer or a wholesaler calling on stores for research purposes. You cannot go to *every* city in the country or every store in a sales area. Some choices must be made about what places to sample. For the most part, despite the advanced art of research design, these choices are made from experience, "feel," cost of travel, and the budget for a particular study. To this is added information from secondary sources about the spread in types of employment, average family income, and blue-collar versus white-collar jobs. Size of city and number of possible calls are factors, as is whether the city appears to be a "leading city" of its trading area. A Canadian study may use Montreal, Toronto, Edmonton, Winnipeg, and Vancouver. No one will feel the need to justify such choices; everyone knows that these metropolitan areas must be covered in a nationwide study.

You must go by judgment and common sense. Having chosen the cities that seem to fit your requirements, it is now necessary to lay out a number of calls that appear to cover the territory adequately. For some research, calls on all the important local distributors plus visits to 15 or 20 local retailers will be adequate.

What you will find, in almost all cases, is a repetition that almost becomes boring. The same story is heard again and again. The product in question is not selling, or people do not like it because of certain features. There will not be an even spread among all possible answers. Instead, the picture will become fairly clear early in the game.

At some point in calling on retailers and wholesalers, you will almost be able to predict replies. Research has then fulfilled its function. If the questions have been asked properly, you have not sinned with bias, and you have successfully persuaded the trade to "tell all," then you may assume that no more research is necessary. But one more problem: Sometimes the researcher may feel the need for more interviews just to convince a possibly skeptical management back home.

Shopping Center and Store Interviews with Customers. This section is written especially for suppliers, manufacturers, or distributors who want to make some direct contacts with consumers.

Preparation. Except for a few exhibitionists, most consumers will not allow more than a very few questions. After that they get impatient, so get to the major points quickly.

A show of clipboards and recording sheets is not bad in this kind of interviewing. Anything that makes the interviewer look official will help allay fears and induce cooperation.

One very successful shopping center study used a group of young men dressed in similar sports jackets and wearing large buttons that said "Marketing Research, We Need Your Help." It got results. Another device can be a decorated card table with the products in question laid out on a colored cloth. Curiosity is aroused, and it becomes easier to stop people for a short interview.

Get permission of the store owner, of course, if you are doing in-store interviews, or the management of the shopping center if you want to do work there. In the case of chain stores, your position becomes more difficult. Often there is a company rule against on-premises research. Permission must be obtained from headquarters.

There is a courtesy about field interviewing that your own common sense should dictate. Whether in-store or in a shopping center, customers come first. Interviewing must not interfere with customer traffic flow or customer parking. Moreover, the researcher must be so obviously honest that he or she will not awaken fears in the most timid of people.

A clever little gift can sometimes be used as a reward for an interview. It must be something quite inexpensive, but it should be showy enough to attract attention. Respondents who get the gifts may "advertise" you as they walk to their cars.

If you choose a shopping center, you may find two things standing in your way:

1. The shopping center itself may be a part of a chain of such centers, with the permission-granting central office in some other city. You would have to have some correspondence with this home office in advance.

2. The shopping center management may impose a charge for permission to allow researchers on the property.

When should the interview take place? A moment's thought will tell you that the typical Monday customer is likely to be a different person from the Saturday shopper. The morning customer is different from the evening customer or the afternoon customer. Your interview schedule must cover all these types of people.

There are a variety of shopping center and store interview techniques not discussed in detail here because they are too complex and expensive for the average small study. What we have tried to do in this chapter is to show you how to develop better interviewing practices. Better interviewing means more

A show of clipboards and recording sheets is not bad in this kind of interviewing.

Interviewing must not interfere with customer traffic flow or customer parking.

valuable interviewing that produces worthwhile information. The examples are interview studies that have worked well.

As in the preceding chapter, many illustrations have been reduced to fit book-size pages. Much space has again had to be eliminated—space that would be necessary in a real situation. As before, our only purpose is to show *types* of questions from which you can get ideas for your own needs.

eleven

How to Conduct a Focus Group Interview

Group interviews, often called "focus groups," have increased in popularity and use in recent years. In brief, a *focus group* brings 6 to 15 people together to discuss a topic of mutual concern and interest to each member of the group. A moderator will have a discussion guide sheet. By low-key and relatively infrequent questions to the group, the moderator hopes to bring out attitudes and opinions on the subject at hand. Because the members of the group are urged to talk freely, and because they are also urged to talk among themselves about the subject at hand, a focus group is likely to develop thoughts and ideas that simple questionnaires and personal one-on-one interviews could never do. A researcher seeking depth of thought on a subject or new ideas may profitably turn to focus groups as an ideal vehicle for the study.

Group interviews are often considered almost an art, to be conducted principally by persons well trained in group psychology. But as the Gershwins once said, "It ain't necessarily so." One of the worst group sessions conducted for us was moderated by a well-known New York psychologist. This person did almost all the talking, leaving little time for the group members to voice their knowledge and opinions. Some intelligence and experience are necessary to run a group session, to keep the group members all talking to the point, to draw out the quiet ones, and to produce creative thinking from personal interaction. It is far from impossible, however, and we have conducted such groups many times. So can you.

Types of Studies That Can Best Use This Research Method

Group studies can be used in two ways: alone without any follow-up by other types of research or as a means of discovering how best to plan and carry out other forms of market research. In the latter case, the focus group can help determine the need for further study, help determine more specifically what needs studying, and help narrow the questions down to what specifically needs further research.

Group discussions are used where new, fresh thinking is desired. They can show possible marketing actions or new product lines that deserve further exploration. They have the great advantage of allowing interaction among members of the group—each stimulating the thoughts of the others. They can test understanding, or lack of it, of new advertising themes.

For the retailer, group discussions can be very educational for management by clearly bringing out what customers and noncustomers think about the store. Whereas a mail or telephone questionnaire is most likely to present alternatives to the respondent, asking for his or her choice among them, the group session looks for ideas that may not have occurred to anyone. And, in addition, it allows some measure of the depth and strength of ideas and opinions. Examples:

1. After a few groups have been conducted by a manufacturer, it begins to appear that women like one of the product lines far better than do men.

A focus group brings 6 to 15 people together to discuss a topic of mutual concern and interest.

Discussion groups can develop theories about why this is so and what can be done about it.

Some notions about a wholly new product may begin to appear. "What ifs" you might call them; what if the manufacturer made a product that did this or looked like this or that?

There may be some legal complications here that you would want to talk over with your counsel before beginning group sessions. You do not want a suit brought against the company for "stealing" ideas.

2. A group can discover human buying motivations that may not have been realized. This is much like the preceding, but with the difference that the very "idea" of a present or proposed product can have unexpected connotations. Men may look on a brand, or even its name, as being feminine. In this day of "unisex," it is still important to know about such an attitude. The young man who grows a unisex head of hair also grows a beard in a heroic effort at machismo.

3. A complex of emotions may enter into the simplest of purchases. A hair-down, shoes-off talk fest can sort out some of these emotions and make them useful in merchandising. These are the sorts of motivations almost never obtained from a mail or telephone questionnaire or rarely from face-to-face interviews. To plumb these emotional depths, it is necessary to foster interplay, discussions, and even controlled arguments among the participants. At the point where the group forgets the moderator (except when he or she asks discreet questions to keep the subject on track) and the microphone, the value of the group session begins to appear.

4. A group can bring out product faults or virtues that seem too unimportant for respondents to mention in a mail or telephone study. Yet little things are often the real reason for buying or not buying. A color can be subconsciously repellent to many people on *this* product, even though the same color is perfectly acceptable on some other product.

5. A do-it-yourself product may look "hard to use." The instructions appear difficult to understand, and people impatiently refuse to go beyond the first few sentences. Husbands may want to please their wives with their accomplishments in the garden or home. If they believe that they may fail with a do-it-yourself product, they will not buy the product. A group session can find features that seemed important to the manufacturer but which have no meaning or use at all to the customer. Such features may even be hurting the sale.

6. Retailers can use groups of people to discuss what they are doing right or wrong in the merchandising of fashion goods. What is the real picture of the store in the minds of these persons? Merchants may be shocked to discover what people really think of their stores. A store's patronage may come mostly from customers who want to park in its convenient lot. Such customers hope to find what they want, but they often end up elsewhere because the store is not stocked properly for this type of trade.

7. A group can help determine what kinds of people would most likely buy a new product—or shun it. For the retailer, a group can help guide the formation

You do not want a suit brought against the company for "stealing" ideas.

of a new department or help in the decision to begin stocking a new line of goods. The group also may develop some fresh, new thinking on merchandising in a store. Asking about the quality of salespeople is *guaranteed* to bring about a lively discussion. A woman's group under a good moderator will have many new ideas about how to improve a store. Not all ideas will be workable or affordable, but there will be valuable nuggets among the pebbles.

8. For a manufacturer, a group can bring out hidden fears about a product—fears that may be quite groundless, but exist nevertheless. Unless a manufacturer knows these fears, no correction is possible.

These are just a few ways of using group sessions. You can think of others that would be applicable to your situation. A group can be sort of a "think tank." Its ideas, of course, are not projectable to the whole population. Further research of a different type may be necessary.

Merchants may be shocked to discover what people really think of their stores.

How to Prepare for Group Interview Sessions

Deciding on the Kinds of People You Want.   Finding people who will have useful ideas is an important first task. Clearly, these people must be chosen in light of the problem to be discussed.

You must make a decision about the sex, age, and socioeconomic brackets of people to be chosen. Lifestyle is important: you would not choose a group from big-city apartments to discuss backyard barbecuing. You would not choose country folk to discuss city transportation problems.

Deciding on the Number of Groups.   This is difficult. After three or four groups, it may appear that the same things are being said. A decision may then be made to end the group effort. And you may decide whether more research of a different kind is needed or whether the leads already obtained are sufficient for action.

How Many Locations?   To decide this matter, the researcher will have to consider what regional differences may exist in the use of the product in question. Or a retailer may decide that he or she will need representation from several areas of the city and surrounding areas. Such a retailer may deliberately organize a group from an area that does not shop at the store—to see why.

What Size Group?   The authors have moderated groups of 20 people. Usually this is far too many for open, frank discussion by everyone. Between 10 and 15 people produce the most successful groups. Some experts will say 6 to 10 is the right number to seek. Probably experience will tell you what is the most useful size group that you can handle successfully.

Group interviewing can be relatively inexpensive. If the group is led by a professional, the cost may be as high as $1,500 to $3,000 per session. With proper forethought and preparation, this is one form of research that you can definitely

A group can be sort of a "think tank."

do yourself and save money. By moderating the group yourself, you can get much more out of it than a professional who does not know your company and your problems as well as you do. You can be more flexible, leading the discussion into areas that may have surprised you when they arose, but which are of clear and immediate importance.

Should Group Members Be Paid?   When group sessions are conducted by professional research companies, the group members are usually paid a stipend. Recently, one of the authors took part in a group that discussed the best programming for a public television station. He was paid $20. Sometimes the compensation is much more. Sometimes department stores will have a group that receives no more than a free lunch and an opportunity to discuss a favorite topic: shopping. All you can do is to feel your way along, letting experience tell you what payment, if any, is necessary. We did many group sessions with no compensation other than coffee, doughnuts, and cookies. (In one session with men we furnished canned beer. This was a disaster; the noise of the beer cans being placed on the wooden table made the resulting tape sound like a war had broken out.)

Moderator Preparation.   The moderator must have a clear understanding of the question at hand. He or she must anticipate in what directions the discussion may go. And he or she also must know in advance ways of steering the discussion back to the major problems.

The scope of the study must be decided on. Even though the discussion may wander into interesting side roads, the group must be brought back to thinking about the purpose of the group session. The moderator must keep discussion from wandering.

The moderator should have all this well defined ahead of time. He or she should have appropriate questions written on a guide sheet as in Figure 11.1. And the questions may vary a bit depending on where the group discussion goes. It is up to the moderator to allow free discussion—even if it appears to go off the track a bit—just as long as the discussion offers worthwhile ideas to solve the questions on the table.

Moderators do not become completely skilled in the very first sessions they conduct, but this should not frighten them. They will find that moderating skillfully is an art soon learned. And they also will find that moderating a group session can be an interesting and valuable experience.

The moderator must keep the discussion from wandering.

Selection of a Place for the Session

To the extent possible, the group session room should have a "neutral" atmosphere. There should be no pictures to distract attention and no interesting sights outside the windows. A plain table and comfortable chairs are essential.

Available in many places are interviewing rooms fitted out with one-way mirrors so that the client can watch and hear the proceedings without being seen. There are also rooms equipped with videotape recorders so that sound and

SUBJECT: GREETING CARDS

What is funny? What does this age group consider funny?

How much feeling or emotion goes into the purchase of a card?

Find segments. Are there significant differences, characteristics between segments (age groups 18-24, 25-35, male-female, impulse-planned)?

What do people look for in a card? (visuals, message, quality?)

What are purchasing patterns, behaviors, perceptions, characteristics of segment? Where, when, who, why, how?

What really influences the purchase of a card?

Why aren't alternative cards meeting some of the needs of this age group? What are those needs?

How often do you purchase nonoccasion cards?

What kind of message do you look for in nonoccasion cards?

Where do you most frequently buy cards? Specialty, drug, mass merchandisers?

Do you feel there is a difference in quality between the cards in grocer stores, specialty stores, mass merchandisers?

Do you make special trips to purchase cards?

What draws your attention to a particular card?

Do you buy cards while shopping for other items?

How much time do you typically take to select a card?

How much does the card receiver influence card selection?

Do you ever feel inhibited in sending greeting cards?

FIGURE 11.1. *A focus group moderator's guide sheet.*

sight can be retained for future analysis. All these add to the costs and for many group sessions which you might conduct yourself are unnecessary.

If you moderate the group yourself or have one of your people do it, the cost will be considerably less. You can follow up leads much more quickly and thoroughly than a professional, who may not even be aware of the importance of something a participant just said.

Often YMCAs will have a room which they will be happy to rent for a modest sum for your use. The authors have even had sessions in homes of group members. These group members would furnish refreshments and would be paid a modest sum for their efforts.

The very best location, nevertheless, is a quiet room with plain furnishings and no distractions where no interruptions are likely. Almost all businesses have such a location or can find one.

A round table works best, but a rectangular table can be used with the moderator sitting at one end—being "papa" or "mama" as he or she might say out loud to bring a smile and help prevent any stiffness at the beginning.

Chairs should be comfortable, but not too comfortable.

Chairs should be comfortable, not the hard, folding types that become almost unbearable after half an hour. They should not be soporific, however, or you may find one or two of your members "thinking" for a long time with their eyes closed.

If you are using a room not specifically set up for group interviews, rental of adequate electronic equipment (tape recorder or perhaps videotape camera) will be helpful. It is not necessary to hide the mike or the tape recorder. These gadgets help to keep the group on the track; members can see that their every word is being recorded. If you intend to have the tape transcribed, you may wish to caution the group about talking all at the same time. Your poor secretary will have a job keeping the talk straight otherwise.

And if the tape is to be transcribed, when you speak to people either to ask a question or to reply to one, use their names. It would be good to explain to the group why you do this; perhaps they will copy you, and your secretary will be grateful.

How to Find or Develop a Group

Worthwhile groups are generally not difficult to recruit. Here are some of the methods that can be used to get a group together. Local situations, of course, will offer other possibilities.

1. Almost every large city and many smaller ones have marketing research firms that will have interviewers on their staffs. Many of these also can develop groups for you from contacts they have in town. It is possible to get one group of men, for example, who have little interest in sports and another of men who are sports-minded. Or you can have a group of young, married women who are just setting up households. The possibilities are endless. The quality of these local research firms, however, varies. Check them out before using them. See Chapter 16 for guidance. Most of these firms will allow you to do the moderating yourself, limiting themselves to furnishing the groups and the facilities.

2. Often it is easy to use local clubs that are anxious to find some activity that will add to their treasuries. Other possibilities include local women's clubs. Churches offer a tempting way of getting groups together, but a caution must be raised: These groups still have to be well suited to your purposes for the particular problem being studied. Convenience in getting a group cannot excuse getting a poor group for the purpose. In getting a group together you also must clearly recognize the biases that may come with them. Some groups are alike in many ways, but have interpersonal friendships or feuds. Some groups may not actually be in a position to give you the clear thinking you need. We do not say that such groups can never be used, but the chance of bias must be recognized. You want a group that is experienced enough to have ideas on the problem you face, but one that is not so biased that its members cannot make clear judgments.

3. For stores, it is possible to gather a group of charge customers—people whose names are known. The gathering could take the form of a lunch program, possibly even a lunch, a fashion show, and a discussion period. Bias is here because they *are* your customers, but still they will have some good ideas for you. You want to know what they think about *your* store. Few people will worry about hurting your feelings; they will more than likely tell you much that you did not realize about your operation.

The Procedure for the Group Session

The group session is built on a strong foundation of informality. There have been instances in our memories where the moderator was simply unable to bring a group to life. The tape records only the moderator talking—and talking. Fortunately, this is rare. Ordinarily the worst problem is to keep everyone from talking at the same time.

If you find group interviews as valuable as we have, you will probably do a number of them and develop your own style of leadership. However, here is a good sequence to follow:

1. The moderator announces briefly who he or she is, tells something about the company, explains the problem at hand, and tells why it is important to get the participants' help. The group will feel flattered and ready to cooperate.

2. Have each person introduce and tell a little about himself or herself. Even when, in some cases, all members of the group know each other, this forces everyone to open up and talk a little. Some provision for name cards should be made. Blank, folded cardboard cards will do, together with a black crayon for each person. The members should be told to write their names "big and black" and then place them on the table so that the moderator and everyone else can see them. Except in the most unusual circumstances, the more quickly you can get on a first-name basis, the better the session will go.

3. Use an interview guide. This is a list of topics or questions to be covered at the session. It is important that—as far as you can see ahead—these topics

Have each person introduce and tell a little about himself or herself.

be in the best logical sequence. However, you cannot be too definite, since it is the *unexpected* and *new* that is being sought. In a well-moderated session, it is possible that the list of topics may be almost abandoned as the time goes by.

4. Have topics and questions ready so that you can bring a wandering talk fest back to order. Conducting a group takes a little experience. In the beginning you will feel more comfortable with a rather full list of topics or questions.

5. Whether you wander from your list (because something new and important has been introduced) or stay fairly close to it, stay in the area of the main reason for the group session in the first place.

6. Take time to make a summary and ask for confirmation from the group that this is indeed what the members have said and concluded.

How to Handle Problem People at a Group Session

Standard problem types show up at group sessions. Only a little experience is needed to learn how to handle them. If the moderator has explained the reason for the session and the group has accepted this as being sound, the group will discipline itself. However, a few people can be unintentional troublemakers and interfere with the purpose of the group session:

1. One is the person who talks too much and is compulsively dominating. If allowed, this person will fill half your tape with his or her opinions and will intimidate the shy.

2. Another is the person who hesitates too long. While he or she is drawing a breath preparing to speak, someone else has broken in.

3. A third is the accepted "leader" of a session. Groups, like chickens, tend to work out a pecking order. There may be deference shown to the oldest person in the group or to the one who appears most successful, as suggested by dress or mannerisms. There is always a real tendency for certain members to echo the opinions of the talkative person or the accepted leader.

It takes only a few minutes to spot these various types, and it will be up to you to throw questions at the shy ones or to seek persons who do not agree with the "head chicken." The group will be conscious of what you are doing and will aid you as much as possible.

Getting the group members to talk with each other about your problems is not as difficult a task as it sounds. Once interest has been aroused, the group members will disagree with each other and bring out a variety of points.

It will be of great assistance to this free discussion if your opening statement can immediately relate your problem to a problem of interest to the group. The group should have been chosen because of this likelihood. A group of middle-

There is an unfortunate tendency for certain group members to echo the opinions of the talkative person or the accepted leader.

income women who are keeping house for their families can certainly become worked up over the problem of buying draperies and drapery hardware. Soon all their experiences come flooding out: the difficulty in getting advice, the lack of interest on the part of the salespeople, the question of how to measure a window opening for a rod and for the draperies themselves, the changes in style as one fad replaces another, and finally, the difficulty in getting their husbands to install the fixtures and the family fights that sometimes ensue. From all this may come ideas for merchandising or for new products. Once a group has fastened onto a topic such as draperies, you may not have to say very much at all.

How to Analyze the Recorded Tapes

Because every session is different, it is impossible to set up rules for analysis. A few thoughts are in order, however. Analyzing the tapes and preparing the final report are the last steps in the focus group interview process. You may wish to set down on separate sheets of paper the major topics or questions that led you to have the sessions in the first place. How did these people talk about these points? Use actual quotations under each heading. As you slowly work your way through the tapes and the evidence begins to build up on your sheets, important findings and evidence will begin to appear. You may want to use a separate section for brand-new thoughts and ideas that came unexpectedly from the sessions. These new ideas may be the most valuable benefit you will receive.

Since you will likely have more than one group, you can continue to use the same recording sheets, separating each group, but keeping their remarks together in an organized fashion. The odds are that the groups will begin to reinforce each other. There will be some differences, but these will not predominate.

If possible, have a second person do the same analysis. Does he or she perceive something that you missed? Or does he or she read the meanings differently?

A "bull session" will end this part of the research. Can agreement be reached about what has really been learned from these sessions? What have you learned that you did not know before—or half suspected?

Finally, it is necessary for all to reach agreement concerning what actions should be recommended. Have the groups pointed to the need for more thorough and extensive research? Perhaps using other techniques? Or have you received enough from these groups that you can now begin some remedial action?

The final report will be stronger if actual excerpts from the sessions are used. Almost always, a written report should be made, even if you are the boss and have no one else to report to. A written report, if it is done well, requires logical and clear thinking and exposition. If you write the report, you will be the better for it.

Analyzing the tapes and preparing the final report are the last steps in the focus group interview process.

twelve

How to Make Sure You Question the Right People

Sampling is necessary in almost all forms of marketing research. It is rare that you will contact all possible people. You will typically approach only a small number.

This is not surprising or different from most of our living experiences. The physician testing your blood does not drain all the blood from your body! He or she takes a sample, perhaps from a finger or from your forearm. A wine taster cannot finish all the barrels! He or she, too, must sample. We put a toe in the water before swimming to get a "feel."

Sampling in survey research is important. Unless those in a study are representative of the total (the "universe," to use a statistical term), the results mean little. However, the sample drawn by a do-it-yourself marketing researcher will almost surely fall short of a pure sample that would delight the heart of a statistician. Never mind. If our advice in this chapter is followed, the results will be sufficiently accurate for marketing action.

There are four critical aspects of sampling: defining the universe, designing the sampling method, deciding how many to question, and controlling the sampling procedure.

Defining the Universe

The *universe* is the total group you want to study. Let's say you manufacture cake mixes. Your research problem is to determine which of two alternative new mixes you should place on the market, and so you want to do an in-home product test, where people prepare a cake from each of the two mixes and give you reactions.

Michael Yesner, President of G. M. Feldman & Company, advertising agency (Chicago, Ill.), talks about the possible definitions of the universe in terms of your problem. "You don't want all women," he says. "You don't even want all homemakers. Nor do you simply want all women who prepare foods at home. No, you start by wanting women who prepare cakes from mixes."

"Even that's not good enough," he warns. "What you really want is *heavy users*. These are the heart of your market, and the ones whose reactions mean the most."

Whether it is cake mix users or readers of a publication, you need rigorous standards for defining your universe. This is the only way to start planning how to draw your sample.

Designing the Sampling Method

The Basic Sampling Methods. Sampling methods include "pure" sampling (where each element of your universe has a known chance of being part of the sample) and two specific methods which are far less dependable and do not permit any way to estimate so-called sampling error. However, one must be practical in selecting the sampling method. If you have a minor marketing problem, you do not overspend for a highly precise sample.

A wine taster cannot finish all the barrels! He or she, too, must sample.

We shall examine the "purist" methods just a bit later on in this chapter. At the moment, we want only to mention briefly the two less pure methods. One is the quota system, and the other is the haphazard method.

The *quota procedure,* in our opinion, has some definite uses in marketing research. Briefly, you set up what you are looking for in terms of your types of respondents and then find such respondents. The method is especially applicable in mall studies, where you may want only women falling within a stated age group, who are basically homemakers (as opposed to working women), and who have children under 6.

A *haphazard sample* is one in which there is basically no design at all. You take the first 100 people along a street corner or in a shopping mall, for instance. This sort of sampling has no sound basis whatever. Such a sample would be representative only of the street's pedestrians or the mall's shoppers, for whatever either is worth.

Choose the best sampling method for your needs. Be practical. Select the sampling method that will produce a reasonably accurate sample within the practicalities of your situation. Here are some things to consider:

Is a List of the Universe Available? (Statistical Term: "Frame").   There are many possibilities. These include

1. The mailing list

2. The telephone directory

3. The membership roster (a group to which you or others belong)

4. The self-accumulated list of customers or prospects

The mailing list. This has been around for years, primarily for use in direct-mail promotions. There are so many varieties that there may be just the one you are seeking for your particular study. They cover consumers and businesses. Within each broad category there are hundreds of specialized possibilities. If you are looking for consumer owners of air-conditioning, there is such a list. Perhaps you want brides or some other highly specialized consumer group. On the business side, if your universe is funeral directors or independent pharmacies, there's a list. A single example of such a source is Alvin B. Zeller, Inc. (New York City). See your reference librarian to locate the exact kind of list you need and to see what it will cost.

None of these mailing lists is perfect. Most have inaccuracies, and they are rarely up to date. Often there are omissions in the listings. Sometimes the list is too broad to be useful.

The telephone directory. As the telephone became the major way of collecting marketing research information, telephone directories became an increasingly used and reliable list source. In the simplest form, you can use a specific residential directory as a base for drawing a sample in a particular community using a random method of selecting the listings. But not all is well, even here. Directories omit those with unlisted numbers. There will invariably be some

You take the first 100 people along a street corner or in a shopping mall.

businesses in the list. The list is never up to date, even on the first day of publication.

For many communities there is also a reverse (crisscross) directory, listing names, addresses, and telephone numbers by block. This enables you to spot names of residents and businesses in specific areas. This is especially helpful where you must look at results by location or around a particular area (perhaps where you are thinking of locating your business). Your reference librarian is your starting information source.

There are also specialized firms, working from telephone directories, which provide highly specific lists, both for consumers (residences) and for businesses. Since we shall be looking at these in greater detail toward the end of this chapter, we now provide only a brief idea of the kinds of lists such firms can supply. You can get lists, compiled from the alphabetical pages, by geographic area or by income level, age, or type of dwelling. Or by ZIP codes, even ZIP codes with specific characteristics (high condo ownership, for instance). Such lists can be provided with names and addresses (for mail or in-home surveys) or with telephone numbers (for telephone surveys). Compiled from the Yellow Pages, there are lists by SIC categories, by Yellow Page category, and by state, county, ZIP code, and more.

The membership roster. This may be a group to which you belong or some other relevant group. Chapter 4 has already suggested the *Encyclopedia of Associations* as the reference for such group listings, and it is simply a question of whether the particular membership list is useful as your universe and, if so, whether the listing is available.

The self-accumulated list of customers or prospects. This is often one of the most useful lists. The names on such a list are of great importance to you. The list may be comprised of your charge account customers. It may be those who have turned in a coupon for redemption of an offer or a contest designed to get entries from prospects. It may be a list of business firms registered at a trade show or professionals at a convention. There are many more possibilities for a list representing customers or prime prospects. You are the one to decide the nature and origin of such a list.

Other Things to Consider in Choosing Your Sampling Method.

How much will it cost to design and execute the sample? There is no quick way of telling this. You must balance your needs for a tight sample against cost. We merely outline some specifics for you to consider.

How precise must your results be? For a study of major importance to your company, perhaps guiding its new direction or even determining whether it will survive, you cannot take shortcuts on sampling simply to cut costs. This would be like shopping around for the cheapest surgeon when you have a life-threatening problem.

What method of data collection will be used? Methods of data collection have been reviewed in Chapter 10. When your data-collection method is in-home interviewing, personal on-premise interviewing, or telephone, in-mall, or on-the-street interviewing, this limits the sampling methods at your disposal.

If you are doing an in-mall study, you do not have an opportunity to apply probability sampling. Your best choice is quota sampling, where you specify consumer types. If you are doing an in-store study, you can and should control by such factors as day, hour, and point of entrance (or departure).

Selecting the Sampling Method. Fine. You have a basic list from which to sample or you are going the route of a less precise (nonprobability) method. How do you proceed?

Sampling from a list. Select from the list in such a way that you will have a probability sample—so that each item in the list has an equal chance of being selected for the sample. While there are many ways of going about this, two are relatively simple. One is random selection; the other is systematic selection.

With the *random method,* each item in the list is numbered. Then you consult a table of random numbers (or generate these from your microcomputer), and the items are randomly selected for you. In the *systematic method,* you simply divide the total of the items in the list by the number you want to select for the sample and use the resultant figure to tell you that you will need every *n*th item in the list. However, you still need a random starting point. You can ask your computer for this starting point or even take the last of the digits on a dollar bill in your wallet. Your starting point must be within that *n*th range. If you need to select every tenth listing, your starting point must be between 1 and 10.

Deciding How Many to Question

The statistical accuracy of your survey results depends on how many people you have questioned (sample size). As your sample size decreases, the margin of error increases. Set your precision needs early. They should be set in terms of the importance of the study to your company.

The statistical accuracy of your survey results depends on how many people you have questioned.

Setting your statistical needs for accuracy is a lot like betting on the odds. You can state that the odds are that the results of your study will be accurate within stated limits, such as 2 percent, 5 percent, or whatever, but you have to understand the terms.

Accuracy means the consistency of results. If there were 100 studies identical with yours conducted simultaneously, you are talking about the range of results (range of error) that could be expected. The *stated limits* simply specify the range of error you are talking about. The narrower the stated limits, the greater is the sample size.

Let's get down to the nuts and bolts. The statisticians have given us basic tables that show the sample size required for results of a given accuracy (Table 12.1). These tables apply only to probability samples. It is impossible to get down to numbers for the other methods (although practically, most in marketing research use such tables anyway).

Table 12.1 tells you that if 50 percent of your respondents tell you a certain thing, and if you select a sample of 500, your results are accurate within 5 percent.

Table 12.1. Error Range versus Sample Size

Sample size	Range of error	Range of "true" figures*
100	10%	40 to 60%
300	6%	44 to 56%
500	5%	45 to 55%
1000	3%	47 to 53%

*When the figure obtained is 50 percent.

If fewer or more than 50 percent respond in a given way, the error range will be less. Use this table for your error-range prediction; it represents the maximum error.

You will note right off that sampling accuracy is not related proportionately to sample size. It takes four times the sample size to double the accuracy. This is so because probability theory provides a formula about sample size and accuracy that introduces the square root.

If the situation is right, you sometimes can cut back on these number requirements. When your total universe can be stated in terms of numbers possessing a given characteristic, then the *New York Department of Housing* shows statistically that your number requirements are far less. Let's say that there are 500 families living in a particular complex, and that's your universe. Different statistical rules apply. Table 12.2 shows that you can sample only 222 of these families to get results within 5 percent accuracy.

Controlling the Sampling Procedure

It is not enough to define the universe properly, design a good sampling method, obtain or develop a good frame (list), and determine the size of the sample. All is lost if the sampling procedure is not well controlled.

Getting the Right Respondent. Unless you get the right respondent, the sampling procedure is not working. Your sampling procedure must specify exactly who the respondent is to be and must produce that respondent.

Table 12.2 Sample Size Needed to Produce Results within 5 Percent Accuracy When Universe Number Possessing Characteristic Is Known

Universe number with characteristic	Sample size required
500	222
1,000	206
5,000	370
10,000	385
50,000	397

On the consumer side, if you seek the adult male household head and you are doing a telephone survey, your introductory questioning procedures must establish the role of the person answering the call and not allow the interviewer to assume that any male voice responding is the qualified person. If you are seeking that heavy cake mix user, your questionnaire and questioning procedures must be specific to ensure that only a qualified respondent is included. Whatever the consumer qualifications and the data-collection method (in-home interviewing, mall interviewing, mail or telephone interviews), the questioning procedure must filter out only respondents who qualify within the definition of your particular universe.

If you are doing shopper interviewing within a single large retailing establishment, you will need to apply some controls. After making some counts of traffic by day and hour, you could set up quotas for sampling by day and hour that parallel the counts. With careful planning in a mall study—where interviewers intercept mall shoppers to question them—it is possible to instruct interviewers about the proportion of men and women to interview. You can impose age quotas. Or quotas of families versus single shoppers. Or product users, such as cake mixes.

The problem on the business side is no less. If you are doing a telephone survey, the problem is to get past the person—often a secretary—answering the telephone. If you make personal calls to the place of business, the same problem exists. Should you call or write ahead? Calling allows the potential respondent to prepare for the interview. He or she may be able to have materials ready at the time of the call. The prior call makes it possible for the respondent to have someone else there who can provide relevant information in one or more of the areas.

The advance contact also presents problems, however. It is often difficult for the potential respondent to arrange his or her time ahead. It also provides the person with an easy "out" and an excuse for delaying or refusing the interview.

There is no one answer to the problem of making appointments. All we can say is that we made fewer and fewer appointments as we built up our years of experience. Seldom did we strike out completely. More often than not we would complete an unscheduled interview with far more information than we had dared hope for.

There is no sure way of explaining your purpose satisfactorily to someone at an outer desk. The receptionist or secretary will assume that you are a salesperson, no matter what you say. After handing the receptionist your business card, the best approach is to request to see the person you want, since he or she has some information you need, and indicate that you will take only a limited amount of his or her time. This is about all you can do.

When dealing with people at an outer desk, it is often assumed you are a salesperson, no matter what you say.

Getting the Right Proportion of Respondents. If you get fewer than 50 to 60 percent of the sample you are aiming for, you are in trouble. It may not be a good sample. You cannot be sure that those you do not hear from have the same ideas and responses as those who do respond.

How can you be sure that you will get the correct rate? One safeguard is to design your study well. There are two important aspects: sound design of the first contact and a procedure for a follow-up where there has been no response.

In the *design of the first contact,* let's start with mail surveys. An old trick is to use an interesting commemorative stamp on the outgoing mailing envelope—to induce recipients to take an interest, open the envelope, and perhaps save the stamp. The return envelope stamp should be a run-of-the-mill stamp that no one will want to save.

A $1 bill attached to the top of the cover letter is another generally effective device. Use a statement, perhaps in the covering letter, saying something to the effect that "Your time in answering this questionnaire is far more valuable than the dollar bill enclosed. But accept it as a token of our sincere appreciation for your trouble in answering and returning the enclosed form. Give it to the first smiling youngster you see today." Even top executives often respond to such a mail survey appeal. And it often melts some of the most protective secretaries. It is wrong either to appropriate the dollar or to throw it away. Send the whole thing in to the boss and let *him* or *her* decide!

Another device is the promise of a gift to those returning the questionnaire. The nature of the gift should be related to the needs of the sample to be most effective.

It is rare that you can use such appeals in the first-time contact in personal or telephone surveys. The potential respondent wonders whether you aren't really out there with a sales pitch. So your approach has to be a reassuring one: that you are *not* selling and that your interview will be relatively short (or if not the latter, an open admission, with a request for a later appointment time if the present time is not convenient).

Plan the timing of the calls so that you are likely to find the right person at the time you make the contact. In a telephone survey in which your aim is to talk with male household heads, schedule your telephoning times for weekday evenings and weekends. The same goes for working homemakers. Plan differently to reach retired people.

Special Problems of Shopping Mall Interviews.

A moment's thought will tell you that the typical Monday customer is likely to be a different person from the Saturday shopper. The morning customer is different from the evening customer or the afternoon customer. Your schedule of interviewing must be set up to cover all these various types of people.

Consider the reason for these differences. Approximately half of all young married women are working. These women are in the "accumulating" time of life, busy stocking their homes with all the fine things they and their husbands have decided they need. However, they will *not* be buying their wares on any morning except Saturday. On evenings and weekends, young husbands and wives will form a "shopping team," even when buying groceries. The lone woman in a large car who shows up on a weekday morning is important because she will have more money to spend. But for every one of her, there are several working women whose total business is even more important.

A young woman adds her own salary to her husband's, and a family income of,

The morning customer is different from the evening customer or the afternoon customer.

say, close to $50,000 results. An accumulating young couple with $50,000 a year to spend (before taxes) is not a buying unit that can be overlooked.

The *design of follow-up contacts* is just as important. Since even with the best of planning, your first attempt at contact is most unlikely to achieve that 50 or 60 percent of replies, you must make follow-up plans. In all cases you need to keep records and schedule follow-ups.

With mail surveys, follow-ups are fairly cut-and-dried. You keep records of replies and follow a predetermined schedule (how long ago the original mailing was made, and usually you do not wait more than 10 days before the follow-up), and then you send a second mailing or perhaps even make a telephone follow-up to get the information.

With telephone and personal approaches, the procedure is different. First, you want to get an idea as to *why* there is a nonresponse. It may be because no one is at home (or no answer to the telephone) or because the qualified respondent is not available. In the former case, your call-back procedure is a "random" one: you make the follow-up call according to some predetermined plan of your own which you think will help your chances of finding someone there. It may be a different day, a different hour. If the nonresponse is because the qualified person is not available, then the procedure should be to find out when that person will be available and to set up an appointment for the interview.

Should You Build Your Own Sample or Buy One?

By the time you have gotten this far in the chapter, you may have decided that sampling is more than you want to take on by yourself. You do have options in going for outside assistance.

The Sample Designer. This sort of resource works primarily in consumer surveys, where the basic problem is defining the universe and either developing the sampling method or selecting the list (frame). The potential sample designer is often an instructor at a local college or university.

The List Provider. Our earlier discussion in this chapter has already said much about the nature of possible lists for your study. However, the mailing list firm does not provide a sample, it provides a list. The problem of selecting a sample from the list is yours. If you get a complete list, you must still choose the items (people, firms, whatever) from that list to meet the requirements of a good sample.

The List Provider Who Also Offers a Sample. There are at least two firms which not only have lists available, but the capability of drawing a sample from their lists according to your needs. Survey Sampling (Westport, Conn.), working from telephone lists (both alphabetical and Yellow Pages), not only seems to have superbly maintained lists, but offers expertise in providing samples of these lists according to your rigorous specifications. American Business Lists (Omaha, Neb.) offers sampling from telephone business listings.

thirteen

How to Develop a Good Questionnaire

You cannot be too careful in putting together a questionnaire. The way you ask your questions has a major influence on the responses you get. The person may not understand the question in the form in which you put it. The question may be unintentionally biased, leading to an inaccurate response. Constructing the questionnaire is one of the most difficult steps in the research process, yet it is a temptation to think it is so easy that anyone—without a bit of instruction—can handle it. In this chapter we tell you why it is difficult and give you some understanding about how to build a sound questionnaire.

Start by remembering the basics of your study. What is the problem you are trying to solve? Only with this clearly in mind can you begin to think about the nature of the questionnaire. Your first step is to put together a list of the information you need—just the content: do not even think yet about the phrasing or order of the questions. Include only those content items crucial to your problem. Be austere. It is easy to get carried away and to start including "interesting" items that you might as well include simply because you are doing a study. If you go this route, you will end up with a longer questionnaire than necessary and a more costly study. And when other people are looking at your questionnaire, do not let interesting but superfluous suggestions intrude. Make sure that all content ideas are relevant to the problem.

Once your content outline is constructed, you are almost ready to start building your questionnaire. But first you need to understand the three usual parts of the questionnaire: the introduction, the body or content, and the basic data.

1. *The introduction.* In this section you must make sure that the person qualifies for your particular study and persuade that person to answer the questions that follow. How you do this is discussed later in this chapter.

2. *The body or content.* This is the heart of the information you need to help solve your problem. It covers some of the information areas reviewed in Chapters 6 through 8, but only you can say for sure what your particular questionnaire should include.

The content falls into several areas. One is *facts*. A factual question might simply be the make of refrigerator or automobile owned. It might concern buying or other behavior.

As an example of the *knowledge* area, in an advertising study about airlines, a question might ask:

Will you please tell me, if you can, what airline advertises:

- "We love to fly and it shows."
- "We've got your ticket."
- "We give you more."
- "The world's favorite airline."

The *opinion* (*attitude*) area concerns the person's feelings about products, firms, and so on. As we shall show you, you must be especially careful with this

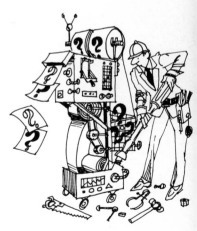

Constructing the questionnaire is one of the most difficult steps in the research process.

type of question. You will not only have to state the concept clearly, but you also must ask the question in an entirely unbiased way that does not "lead" the person to a particular reply.

The *motive* area relates to the reasons underlying behavior or opinion. This difficult area is considered later in the chapter.

Finally, there's the *possible future behavior* area. It is fine to include this sort of content, as long as you realize that results are an expression of attitude, not a prediction of behavior. While people may easily be able to tell you their plans, often those plans are not carried out. "There's many a slip twixt the cup and the lip" is not only classic writing, but sound observation. When you went to work yesterday, you had many definite plans of what you were going to do. Some of them just did not happen. If you are making plans now for a trip to Europe in 2 months, there are many possible events which could change those plans, no matter how definite you think they now are.

3. *Basic data.* This section of the questionnaire covers information you need to know about the person replying. It chiefly includes demographics (age, income, status within the family, and so on). You need it for two reasons: to compare your group of respondents (sample) with known similar data for the particular population (universe) you are studying and to determine whether there are differences in the way that segments of the sample respond. For example, do your younger and older customers react differently to your advertising?

Basic data also typically include identification information such as name, address, and telephone number, where relevant.

General Question Types

We list four question types, according to their structure: *two-choice, list, rating,* and *open-ended questions*. In all except the open-ended type, the question is followed (explicitly or implicitly) by a choice of replies listed on the question-naire form.

Two-Choice Questions. Just so you know the jargon if you talk to a research specialist, he or she may call this the "dichotomous" or "binary question." In this form of question there are only two answer choices provided to the respondent, although in some cases there's a "no choice," "no opinion," or "don't know" possibility. It is easiest to talk about these by providing illustrations:

> Do you *own* or *rent* this home?
> Did you read a newspaper yesterday?
> Of the two local newspapers, *The Times Star* and *The Herald,* which do you prefer?

This sort of question has advantages. It is fast. It is understood easily. It is unbiased. The results can be easily processed by hand or by computer. This is often the way to divide your respondents into subgroups to ask special follow-up questions (such as why those who are no longer customers stopped buying).

Do your younger and older customers react differently to your advertising?

But you have to be careful about using the two-choice question. Avoid asking people to make a choice they are not qualified to make. Do not ask which of two brands a person prefers unless you have already learned that the person uses the product type and that he or she is aware of each of the brands.

Do not misuse this type of question in an overabbreviation of what should be a more detailed question. Suppose you want to divide respondents into light and heavy viewers of television. It would be unfair merely to ask: "Was your television on for more than 1 hour yesterday?" and to place the "yes" respondents into the "heavy" group, with the "no's" going into the "light" group. You have no idea in advance—without special knowledge—of the proper quantitative dividing line. It is risky to set an arbitrary definition in advance. We shall tell you much sounder ways to handle this a bit later on in this chapter.

List Questions.   In the list question, your query is followed by a stated list of categories covering the possible range of replies. Depending on the question, the answer may require selection of a single choice or the person may be asked to choose as many choices as seem relevant. This type of question sounds easy for the respondent and generally is if you have listed the possibilities well.

There are three forms: the name list, the quantitative list, and the qualitative list. The *name list* may contain product categories, brands, companies, or whatever. It may be a list of brands of items owned, for instance, such as automobiles, refrigerators, or televisions. Advantages: It is fast, easy for the respondent, and easy for summarizing (whether by computer or by hand). Just be careful to allow for additional answers that extend beyond your list.

With the *quantitative list,* the person is offered a choice of numerical categories from which to select the reply. The problem is to make the response categories representative so that results will not be distorted. We give you specifics about this later in the chapter.

With the *qualitative list,* you present your respondent—particularly with motive or recall studies—with a list of options for response. If you are doing a motive type of study, you may offer a list of reasons why a particular brand is purchased or preferred. If you are doing a recall sort of study, you may provide the person with a list of aspects to recognize.

Be cautious. Make sure that you include all the right possibilities in the list. Experimental research has shown that if one is omitted, it will be understated in the proportion of responses. Pretesting, discussed later in this chapter, is desirable.

Rating Questions.   These measure a person's degree of feeling about a product category, brand, firm, or issue. There are two types: ranking questions and scaling questions.

In the *ranking question,* the person ranks the items (brand, firm, issue) from top (1) to bottom in terms of some particular attribute. It is easy for the respondent, but average rankings are impossible to interpret, since the differences between 1 and 2 may be very small and those between 2 and 3 could be quite large.

The *scaling question* has the person give an individual rating to each item (product, brand, and so on). The rating may be either on a qualitative or a quantitative basis. The qualitative question— let's assume it is about the price of a given product—might be something like this:

> When you think about the price of this product, how would you describe it as compared to the general market price for the item?
>
> - About as high as it could be
> - Considerably above the market price
> - Slightly above the market price
> - About at the market price
> - Slightly below the market price
> - Considerably below the market price
> - About as low as it could be

Sometimes the question places numbers against each qualitative statement, and in the preceding case, a 7 might be assigned to the first statement, a 1 to the last. This combination of a qualitative scale with quantitative values is known as a "Likert scale," for the psychologist who developed the system.

The straight quantitative approach to the same question would be:

> When you think about the price of this product, how would you describe it as compared to the general market price for the item, based on a scale of 1 to 7, where
>
> - 1 means about as low as it could be
> - 7 means about as high as it could be
> - The other numbers represent degrees of your opinion

Developed as a seven-point scale originally, this method carries the fancy name of "semantic differential," but there is no special magic about having just seven points. You may want fewer or perhaps more (but probably no more than 10, since that's the "ancient" school grading system we all know so well).

We cannot tell you the way to go. The qualitative approach means that you have to be adept at description of degrees. The quantitative approach assumes that all respondents can come up with a neat and accurate numerical self-classification that matches that of other people.

Open-Ended Questions. These are questions for which no answer possibilities are provided for the respondent. The person himself or herself comes up with the reply. The degree of open-endedness can vary. At one extreme there is simply no limit on the possibilities of the range of response; it is all up to the person answering. For example,

> When you bought your car, what were your reasons for selecting that make?

The sky is the limit to the answer possibilities, and that's a weakness. Various people will answer within different boundaries, and when you get a tremendous variety of responses that can be classified under *dealer, advertising, salesperson, financing arrangements,* ad infinitum, this makes it difficult to interpret the results. Furthermore, if you are using interviewers in your study, you need quite skilled workers to be able to ask probing follow-up questions to get an understanding of what the person is talking about.

Generally a wide open-ended question should not be used to try to measure motives. Suppose you ask, after some introductory questions that locate people who have tried Sam's Potato Chips (those who still use, and those who do not):

What do you like about Sam's Potato Chips?
What do you dislike about Sam's Potato Chips?

Some people will simply respond "flavor." Others will mention "saltiness" or "crispness" or whatever. You need more information than this. In short, you should almost always avoid the completely open-ended question. It is vague; it just does not give precise-enough information.

The open-ended question, in our opinion, is useful only when used with boundaries placed on it, without allowing answers to float all over the place. Ask the question about a particular content area. In the case of Sam's Potato Chips, you might want separate open-ended questions such as this:

What do you like (dislike) about

- The flavor?
- The crispness?
- The color?
- The amount of salt?

Principles in Constructing Your Questionnaire

Building a questionnaire is an art, not a science. If 20 research experts were given an outline of questionnaire content and asked to develop a questionnaire, it is almost certain that you would see 20 different questionnaires. All might be equally sound. The principles of questionnaire construction are principles only, not hardbound rules. Your own judgment is important. Despite this observation, we provide a number of principles to follow in questionnaire construction.

Build the right elements into the introduction. There are four ingredients:

1. Introduce yourself and your firm.
2. Qualify the respondent.
3. Give reasons why the person should respond.
4. Start to build rapport.

Introduce yourself and your firm. The starting point is to *introduce yourself*! Whether you are using a mail, telephone, or face-to-face method, this is the first step. Give your name.

The questioner, by name given personally or on the letter, should be ethnically

Building a questionnaire is an art, not a science.

neutral. Like it or not, there is still considerable bias against many ethnic groups, and the introductory part of the questioning cannot afford the luxury of losing some respondents because of this. One simple solution is to use a "neutral" Anglo-Saxon type of name, and at least one research firm handles this by taking common first names and adding "son" to them, so that their interviewers identify themselves by names such as Jackson, Johnson, Peterson, Richardson, Robertson, and Williamson. We really see nothing wrong with this harmless deception. No one is harmed, and it helps make the results of your study more representative. If you are conducting a survey with business respondents, it also might be wise to include the title of the interviewer.

Identify your company. (If giving the name of your firm would provide a bias—a call from IBM might make the person a bit more likely to respond favorably to IBM—that's a special matter, and you might want to have a consultant or a research firm make the study for you.)

Qualify the respondent. The introduction also should check the qualification of the respondent. Is he or she indeed the right person needed for answering your questions?

Give reasons why the person should respond. Tell the potential respondent what's in it for him or her. There has to be at least a *bit* of a reason. With the telephone approach, the reason must be presented quickly or you may lose your respondent. With the mail study, there's a bit more time (with the covering letter) and a chance to offer an incentive as well (see Chapter 12).

Start to build rapport. Finally, the introduction should create a close feeling between you (or the interviewer) and the respondent. The approach should be simple and smooth, relaxed. It should be neutral.

If you are doing a one-on-one interview, the time required for the session should be frankly and honestly stated. In a mail survey, the length (and apparent time required to respond) is at once apparent.

Make sure all questions are clear to the respondent. This is tough. Let's tell you why and what to try to do about it. There are four main points:

1. Use understandable words.

2. Be sure your questions are not ambiguous.

3. Be sure that each question means the same thing to everybody.

4. Gear your questions to the kinds of people in your study.

Use understandable words. Use a vocabulary meaningful to most people. In our younger days, we used to play a family game called "ghosts." In a circle, one person would start with a letter, and the next person would add to it. But each person had to have in mind some real word; otherwise, he or she could be "challenged." If you could not produce a legitimate word when challenged, you lost a point. Well, we had a housekeeper who often played the game with us. When she offered a challenge and got a good answer, her response was "No fair, that's a *college* word!" You have to avoid "college words" in most questionnaires.

Be sure your questions are not ambiguous. Each question should have a specific meaning and one that is the same for every respondent. Consider this question:

> When you last went food shopping, where did you go?

Does this aim at getting store type (supermarket chain, independent supermarket, independent grocery, convenience store, farmer's market, or whatever) or the specific store name?

We have warned you about the potential dangers of open-ended questions. Ambiguity is one of the greatest risks. For example, "Why do you read this particular newspaper?" Some people may answer in terms of an attribute of the product ("It has the best columnists," "I enjoy the comics," "It has the best news coverage"). Others may talk about outside things or people that were an influence ("Almost everyone I asked about it told me this was the only one to get," or "I read about a special subscription price they were offering to new readers"). Still others might mention their own particular attitudes ("I'm basically Republican and was looking for a Republican paper," or "This was the least expensive paper, and I couldn't see spending more than I had to").

If your questioning is to cover such a topic, you might do better to ask at least three questions:

Each question should have a specific meaning and one that is the same for every respondent.

> What, if anything, is there about the newspaper itself that made you decide to get it?
>
> Was there anything you heard or saw about the paper that made you decide to buy it?
>
> What personal feelings or attitudes, if any, influenced you to buy this paper?

Gear your questions to the kinds of people in your study. If you are doing an across-the-board consumer study, questioning people of almost all economic-educational strata, you will have to use simple language geared to the least educated. If you are getting information from a highly trained or experienced group of professional or technical people, use their specialized vocabulary. Such jargon carries specific meaning and shows that your questioning is attuned to the field of expertise.

However, if you are doing a consumer study, avoid the special language of your own field. Consumers will not "get" it. A few examples, just to point out what we mean: "markup," "national brand," "display advertising," "layout," "positioning."

Be sure that questions and their placement in the questionnaire are psychologically sound. The general point: Do not expect your respondent to be able to verbalize all his or her reactions. Often the person is unable or unwilling to give a valid reply. The person may respond to cues you unconsciously provide, rather than to the real intent of the question. Here are the points to keep in mind:

1. Be specific in asking about behavior.

2. Be careful in asking questions where pride is involved.

3. Ask questions in proper psychological sequence.

4. Do not make the questioning too long.

5. Use unbiased questions.

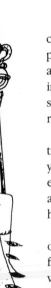

Most people do not intend to lie to you, but pride may make them stretch the truth a bit.

Be specific in asking about behavior. Do not go for generalizations. Most of us cannot generalize our behavior that easily. Do not ask about how often the person visits a supermarket. Too many people cannot make the generalization accurately. Be specific. Ask how many times the person went to the supermarket in the past week. In this way you can project to monthly figures. So long as no seasonal or holiday patterns are involved, your results will average out about right for all families.

Be careful about asking questions where pride is involved. These questions are tricky, yet you often need to include them. Most people do not intend to lie to you, but pride may make them stretch the truth a bit. If you are asking about eating outside the home, do not ask where people generally eat. Not only are you asking for a generalization, but you are almost sure to get an overstatement of higher-priced, "nicer" eating places.

We were conducting a study where it was necessary to determine the amount of beer each respondent consumed so that consumption could be related to such factors as sex, age, income level, and the like and their ideas (images) about various brands. Such information could provide considerable insight into how to build and place effective advertising. We soon found that there were difficulties in what seemed a simple measurement. Not only did people find it difficult to generalize, but more important, there were two elements of pride involved. One was that some people do not like to admit to drinking beer; the other was that heavy drinkers are often unwilling to admit to the real amount consumed.

We came up with a scheme. The first problem was overcome by asking, in rapid-fire style, "What's your favorite brand of soap? Toothpaste? Beer?" The nonuser does not name a brand and reports nonuse, but the beer drinker commits himself or herself without thinking about it.

Then the second rapid-fire query: "Now let's talk about the amount of beer you drink. Into which of these groups do you fall? Just give me the letter of the group." Table 13.1 shows the card each person was handed.

The group descriptions lead the respondents to think that no matter how much beer they drink, there are those who drink more. Even a person drinking up to 36 bottles or cans is labeled a "moderate beer drinker." In addition, the person merely has to use a letter—not a phrase or an amount—in his or her reply. The final question, about consumption in the past 7 days, then presents no response difficulties for the person. The survey produced results paralleling tax figures for the area.

Along similar lines, when you must ask them, *place "pride" and "personal" questions well along in the questioning.* When a question may make your respondent feel "ignorant," "uninformed," or "unintelligent," you face a risk of having the questioning stop then and there. Your first effort is to put those questions in such a way as to minimize the challenge. If you cannot do that, at

Table 13.1. Amount of Beer Consumed Weekly

1. Heavy beer drinker (over 60 bottles or cans a week)
2. Medium-heavy beer drinker (40 to 60 bottles or cans a week)
3. Medium beer drinker (37 to 48 bottles or cans a week)
4. Moderate beer drinker (25 to 36 bottles or cans a week)
5. Fairly light beer drinker (13 to 24 bottles or cans a week)
6. Light beer drinker (7 to 12 bottles or cans a week)
7. Very light beer drinker (6 or fewer bottles or cans a week)

least place them well along in the questioning sequence, after some rapport has been built.

Your study may require a series of questions to measure the brand or company identification of a series of advertising slogans. Some respondents will have to give a string of "I don't know" answers. While you can soften the blow by following such a series of questions with an aided recall (where you use a card showing the names of various airlines), this is still after the fact.

Questions of a personal nature also should be placed well along in the questioning. People hesitate to discuss some topics even with friends, let alone strangers. Yet often your study demands inquiries about the family's annual income or the age of the person. There are *other things you can do in handling pride or personal questions*. One is to state: "We need this information just to help us understand how different kinds of people respond. It will be used only for statistical purposes, and no one will ever be told about this or any other of your replies."

You also can ask what we call "forking" questions. On the age question, for instance, you can start by asking: "Are you, yourself, under 40, or are you 40 or older?" Then, depending on the reply:

If under 40	*If 40 or over*
"Are you under 20?"	"Are you between 40 and 49?"
"Between 20 and 29?"	"Between 50 and 59?"
"30 or older?"	"60 or older?"

Ask questions in proper psychological sequence.   There are several aspects. Use a logical flow of questions. Make each question lead up to the next, setting up a train of thought. It is usually best to start with the general and move to the specific. If you are running an independent shoe store in a downtown area and need to find out what potential customers think of you, you first have to find people who shop in that area. Then you have to find out how often the person visits the area for shopping. Then you must determine whether the person knows your store is there. Only then can you ask about attitudes toward your store.

This use of "filtering" questions is crucial in many studies. Do not assume that everyone in your study is qualified to reply to a question. Do not ask for attitudes about an issue, a store, a brand, or whatever unless you first establish that the person has enough awareness to have a valid opinion.

Avoid a sequence of questioning that may lead to biased replies. Take the case of memory questions. If you are asking questions about the advertising detail that the person has recently been exposed to. you must ask such questions before inquiring about brand awareness or purchase. If you reverse the order, you will stimulate people's memories about the advertising details. You do not want or need this—not if you are truly trying to measure advertising recall.

On the positive side, where you need it, memory can be stimulated by the right sequence of questions. When you ask a question about past behavior, the passage of time can blur memory, particularly if the event was not all that important to the person. If you want to measure the audience of a particular TV show for Wednesday evening and the questioning takes place on Thursday, you might want to use this sort of questioning procedure:

> Did you have your TV on last night?
> [If yes] What time did you turn it on?

Then you can start asking about channels and programs the person had on during each time period until you come to your own. At that point, you want to make sure you are getting real viewers, and it will be a good idea to ask about some of the show elements to establish that the person really has seen the particular show. Only then can you feel safe about starting to ask your advertising recall questions.

Do not make the questioning too long.   You will lose many respondents if it *is* too long. But what is too long? There is no flat answer; it all depends on the topic. If you are talking to a woman about her use of and attitudes about cosmetics and beauty preparations and treatments, you can plan a long series of questions with little risk of early termination. Questioning a man about his new car can also be long. If you want to know how a consumer decided on a tea brand or how an insurance decision was made, the length of questioning will be far more limited.

Do not make the questioning too long. You will lose many respondents if it is too long.

If you *must* have some low-interest questions in the series, place them well along in the questioning. If you are asking a grocery shopper about buying habits and considerations and have to include staples such as baking soda, sugar, and salt, be sure that any such detailed questions are covered late in the procedure. Otherwise you risk losing your respondent.

Use unbiased questions.   The use of certain words or phrasings will—even though you do not intend it—lead some people to respond in a particular direction. These tinged words and phrases could overpower the whole question. Here are just a few examples to alert you (though some of them are unlikely to apply to your particular area of questioning): "big business," "community interest," "socialism," "freedom of the press," "underprivileged," "premium brand."

You must even be careful of your adjectives. Don't ask:

> Do you like the friendly attitude of the employees of Jones Supermarket?

Far more neutral is:

> Do you think the attitude of the employees of Jones Supermarket is very friendly, somewhat friendly, about average, somewhat unfriendly, or very unfriendly?

You also must watch the intensity of your question phrasing. If you ask, "Is the service at Bill's Barber Shop all you could expect?" you will get a high proportion of respondents saying "no," because that's really a strongly phrased question. There are always some service problems beyond the shop's control. A more neutral phrasing would be, "Is the service at Bill's Barber Shop reasonably good?" With this milder statement you will get a more descriptive measure of what Bill's customers really think of his service.

Questionnaire Testing and What It Does for You

Try out your questionnaire before you use it to learn how well it works and to find out how it can be improved. This is like trying out a stain on a piece of wood to make sure it is giving the real color you want. No one, including an expert, can ever be sure that the questionnaire he or she puts together will gather the desired information in a valid, useful way.

Your major aim is to determine if the series of questions is working. Another, possibly important aim—depending on the forms of the questions you are planning to use—may be to help develop answer categories for some of your questions.

We are talking about developing answer categories for list questions (described early in the chapter), particularly for quantitative lists and qualitative lists. With the quantitative list, if your only need is to develop overall consumption, for instance, then all you have to do is to establish groupings where each midpoint (such as 1 to 10) is at some reasonable point and that each grouping is roughly equivalent in range (5 points, 10 points, 50 points, or whatever). You do not need a pretest to do this.

However, quantitative groupings are often used to classify each person by heaviness of use (or exposure to advertising, watching of TV, or whatever), and it is convenient to have a pattern established ahead of time for classifying each person. Thus your pretest can ask an open-ended quantitative question, and the results can be used to give quantitative categories—perhaps two, three, or four, depending on your needs—that will give you the rough proportion of people in each group you need.

When you want to develop qualitative lists, the procedure is similar. Let's say that you want to ask a question—listing alternative responses—about why a particular brand is preferred. By using an open-ended question in your pretest, you can develop a pretty good list of possible replies.

But hold on. Now that we have told you that questionnaire testing can help you set up list categories, we also warn you that for quantitative categorizing you are likely better off waiting until all questioning is complete and then depending on the computer (or hand tabulation), as described in Chapter 14, to put together the groupings.

With qualitative lists, the situation is different. If your pretesting is extensive enough and you categorize the varying responses well (see Chapter 14), it will

How you go about pretesting depends on the nature of your universe.

save you considerable time, trouble, and dollars to list the categories within the question rather than to do it all after completion of the questioning.

Fine. Now that you have some idea of what the pretest can do for you, how do you go about doint it? The answer depends on the nature of your universe (the kind of people you are going to be questioning) and the purpose of your testing.

If you are doing a broad consumer study, a small number of friends and associates may be enough, as long as you can be sure that you are using phrasing that will be understood farther down the educational-income line. If you are doing a study with a highly specialized group (retailers of a given type, medical technicians, or whatever), then your pretest has to be done with those kinds of people.

The questionnaire test should *always* be on a one-on-one basis or a group basis (parallel to a focus group interview, as outlined in Chapter 11). Yes, even if the study is to take the form of a mail survey, only these two testing forms will give the assurance of workability you need.

The purpose of your testing is also an important factor in the form that it takes, particularly in terms of the numbers of people to be included in the test. If your only interest is in workability of the questioning procedure, you can likely limit your test to 10 or fewer respondents. If you need to develop categories for your response questions, you must include more people in your testing, and we can say only that you should continue on—within reason—until you see that patterns of reply are settling down. However, this might take 20 or 30 people or even more.

How do you conduct a test interview? In either the one-on-one method or the group-interview method, follow the procedure most likely to be followed in the later data-collection procedure for the study. If it is to be a mail questionnaire, let each person have a copy and fill it in. If the later procedure will be one-on-one (whether a telephone, mall intercept, or some other procedure that is one on one), then you or an interviewer should ask each question. (When you are using the group-testing procedure, give each participant a blank sheet on which to jot down the question number and his or her response as a basis for later discussion.)

Do not explain in advance (or during the process of participants' replying, if you are asked) the intended meaning of a question or how respondents are expected to decide on a reply. This would destroy what you need from the respondents. Make notes of such comments, but save discussion until they have been through the whole thing.

At the end, ask what gave the respondents trouble. Explain what you were trying to convey with the particular question and seek their advice on how to clarify it. With the questions for which you were trying to develop answer groupings, again seek the respondent's opinions. (You do not have to accept their ideas blindly; use your own good judgment.)

In one particular study, the intent was to determine the extent to which people prepare food at home using a barbecue type of sauce. The first draft of the questionnaire included these two queries:

In just the past 2 months, how many times have you eaten any barbecued food that was prepared at home?

In just the past 2 months, what types of barbecued food have you eaten that were prepared at home?

Testing showed that people were defining barbecued food as anything cooked outside on a barbecue grill. The questions were changed to clarify the meaning:

In just the past 2 months, have you eaten any food that was prepared at home using a barbecue sauce?

In just the past 2 months, what types of food have you eaten which were prepared at home using a barbecue sauce?

We have said that putting together the series of questions is not a simple task. Good pretesting can help develop a good instrument.

An Example of a Poor Questionnaire and How It Might Be Improved

Figure 13.1 shows a hypothetical soup questionnaire constructed merely as an example. It is a poor questionnaire. Look at it carefully and see if you can tell why. Make it a real self-test. Jot down your comments.

First, however, let's explain the hypothetical purpose of the study. It is to determine the role played by soup in lunches eaten at home. It is a telephone survey, made during the day on weekdays, to locate people who are at home for lunch.

Here are our comments on the shortcomings: First, there is no introduction, an unforgivable oversight. Question 1 is poorly placed. If age is to be asked—and the question is presumably included to determine how habits vary by age group—it should likely be asked toward the end of the questionnaire, after rapport has been established. Asking this age question in this form so early in the interview might mean termination of the call.

Question 2 is too difficult for this early spot in the questions. If the person is expected to check the pantry, this should be indicated. But the question should come far later in the questioning, after cooperation has been well established. Further, the question is ambiguous. It could refer to cans (full strength or condensed), powder, cubes, or frozen soup. The question is leading; it assumes that there is soup in the household.

Question 3 is out of sequence. An advertising recall question rarely should be asked this early in a questionnaire. More warming up is required. If the person cannot identify the brand, the question so early in the session might cause enough embarrassment for the person to cut off the questioning.

Question 4 is highly ambiguous. What does the word "kind" mean? Is the meaning flavor or form? The question is also leading, since it assumes that soup was served for lunch.

Question 5 is also ambiguous. What is "how much"? If a reply of "a bowl," "a cup," "a can," or "a package" is given, there is no way to factor it into a standard

```
┌─────────────────────────────────────────────────────────────────────┐
│                      SOUP QUESTIONNAIRE                               │
│                                                                       │
│   1. Into which of these age groups do you fall?                     │
│      18-30 _____  31-40 _____  41-50 _____  51 or over _____          │
│                                                                       │
│   2. How much soup do you have right now on your pantry shelf?       │
│      _____                                    │
│                                                                       │
│   3. What soup advertises, "Mm good!  Mm good!  That's what _____ │
│      _____ soup is, Mm good!"? _____             │
│                                                                       │
│   4. What kind of soup did you have for lunch today?                 │
│      _____                                      │
│                                                                       │
│   5. How much did you have?  _____                 │
│                                                                       │
│   6. Did you have anything else with it? _____        │
│                                                                       │
│   7. How many people in your family had soup more than once last week?│
│      _____                                      │
│                                                                       │
│   8. Do you like soup very much, or do you eat it just because it is  │
│      inexpensive and easy to prepare? _____            │
│                                                                       │
│      Like soup very much ( )   Eat it because it is inexpensive and easy│
│                          to prepare ( )                              │
│                                                                       │
│   9. Who all ate this soup today? _____          │
│                                                                       │
│  10. Where did you get it? _____                │
│                                                                       │
│  11. How often do you have soup for lunch? _____      │
└─────────────────────────────────────────────────────────────────────┘
```

FIGURE 13.1. *Example of a poorly constructed questionnaire.*

quantitative pattern, such as ounces. Unless you are doing a face-to-face interview (where a measuring cup can be used to help the reply), the question might better be omitted.

Question 6 is another ambiguous one. Does it mean a snack (crackers or potato chips) to be eaten along with the soup, or does it mean something much more substantial, almost a separate course, such as a sandwich?

Question 7 puts a strain on the memory and does not mean much unless total family size is known.

Question 8 is leading. The two options are presented as opposites, which they

REVISED SOUP QUESTIONNAIRE

INTRODUCTION. Good afternoon. This is _____ , of the Standard Research Company, calling from _____ . We are making a survey on prepared soups, and I would like to ask you a few questions.

or dinner at home today

1. Did you, personally, eat lunch at home today?

   Yes ☐   No ☐
   (GO TO Q. 2)   (GO TO Q. 8)

prepacked frozen microwave meal

2. Did you, personally, happen to have prepared soup -- not home-made -- for lunch today?

   or dinner today

   Yes ☐   No ☐
   (ASK Q. 3)   (GO TO Q. 8)

3. What flavor of soup was it? (CHECK WHICH)

   Bean _____   Onion _____
   Bouillon _____   Oxtail _____
   Chicken broth _____   Pepper pot _____
   Chicken gumbo _____   Scotch broth _____
   Chicken noodle _____ Split pea _____
   Chicken rice _____   Tomato _____
   Clam chowder _____   Vegetable _____
   Consomme _____   Other (specify) _____
   Mushroom _____

4. Was this prepared from a can, a powder or a cube, or a dry mix?

   Can (Condensed ☐   or Regular ☐)
   Powder or Cube ☐
   Dry mix ☐

5. In terms of measuring cups, about how much soup did you, personally, eat at lunch today?

   1/4 cup ☐   3/4 cup ☐   over 1 cup ☐
   1/2 cup ☐   1   cup ☐

FIGURE 13.2. *The soup questionnaire revised.*

6. Did you have any snack to go with the soup at the very same time you were eating it, such as saltines, other crackers, potato chips, or the like?

Yes ☐   No ☐
(ASK Q. 7)   (GO TO Q. 8)

7. (IF YES) What was it?

Saltines ☐   Potato chips ☐
Other crackers ☐   Other (specify) ☐

8. Will you please tell me all the members of your household living at home, by sex. Please tell me the age of each, starting with oldest.

(RECORD BELOW)   (CIRCLE AGE OF RESPONDENT)

9. (ASK FOR EACH FAMILY MEMBER) Did _____ eat lunch at home today? (RECORD BELOW)

10. (ASK FOR EACH FAMILY MEMBER WHO HAD LUNCH AT HOME) Did _____ have soup for lunch?

	Q. 8	Q. 9	
	Age	Yes	No
Males	____	☐	☐
	____	☐	☐
	____	☐	☐
	____	☐	☐
Females	____	☐	☐
	____	☐	☐
	____	☐	☐
	____	☐	☐

11. During the past 7 days, including today, how many times have you, personally, had soup for lunch?

    7 ☐   6 ☐   5 ☐   4 ☐   3 ☐   2 ☐   1 ☐   0 ☐

12. When you last bought soup, at what kind of store did you purchase it?

    Chain supermarket ☐   Independent supermarket ☐
    Independent grocery ☐   Other (please specify)_____

13. Please tell me how much you like soup generally. A rating of 7 means that you *like it about as much as you possibly could*; a rating of 1 means that you *dislike it about as much as you possibly could*. The numbers in between stand for feelings in between. Now, where would you rank your liking for soup, between 7 and 1?

    7 ☐   6 ☐   5 ☐   4 ☐   3 ☐   2 ☐   1 ☐

14. Compared with most other foods you prepare at home, would you say that preparation of soup is:

    one of the easiest foods to prepare ☐
    easier than most foods to prepare ☐
    about the same as other foods to prepare ☐
    less easy to prepare than other foods ☐
    least easy of any food to prepare ☐

15. Compared with most foods, would you say that soup per serving is:

    one of the most expensive ☐
    more expensive than most ☐
    about the same price as most ☐
    less expensive than most ☐
    one of the least expensive ☐

Name of respondent: _____ Date: _____

St. and number: _____ Inter's init.: _____

State and zip code: _____

Telephone number (include area code): _____

Your questions should not strain the memory.

are not. The words "inexpensive" and "easy to prepare" are two quite separate entities. The person could respond favorably to each alternative.

Question 9 is too colloquial. No questionnaire should be so localized that it seems to be a discussion with a neighbor over the back fence. Further, the form of measurement is not precise. All family members should be included, listed by sex and age. Those who had lunch at home that day should be listed, and those having soup with the meal should be specified.

Question 10 is ambiguous. The person could properly reply "off the pantry shelf," but that would not be very helpful. What is really wanted is a store name or a store type. There is still another problem. If the soup has been on the pantry shelf for very long, chances are the person cannot be sure where it was bought.

Question 11 is also ambiguous. It asks for a generalized reply, not about specific behavior. You—and your respondent—simply do not know the meanings of "often," "frequently," "seldom," and "occasionally." So there is no solid way of interpreting numbers of answers in each category. And what is "home-made" soup? Does adding noodles to a canned or other product qualify?

Finally, the questionnaire is poorly arranged psychologically. All questions about today's lunch should be placed together.

Common sense shows you how poor the questionnaire is. When one of the authors gave this questionnaire to his secretary without saying anything about it, she made no comment. When he gave her a revised version later, along with an explanation, she did comment. "My," she said, "I *thought* that was a bad questionnaire. I'm glad it was supposed to be bad!" Take a look at the revised questionnaire shown in Figure 13.2. It is not perfect (as we have said, no questionnaire is), but you will see that it is a big improvement.

fourteen

How to Summarize the Results of Your Study

Because of the computer, the most common term for summarizing results is *data processing*. If you do not understand the computer, do not be dismayed. We shall use the term *data processing* simply as a shortcut, but do not be intimidated. What you need to know about the computer—at your choice—is limited, and we shall provide that background. Besides, we include one method of summarizing which (while not used often) has nothing to do with computers. However, our basic approach is a discussion of data processing through use of the computer. Toward the end of this chapter we shall describe hand tabulation (no computer) and fill you in on the basic differences from what we have said about computer processing of results.

Data processing, broadly defined, is counting the number of people who respond to a question in each particular way. Let's take a hypothetical question, as shown in Table 14.1. In this question you will definitely want a numerical count of those reporting that they belong to a specific type of group. You will want a count of those who belong to no social group at all. And, to make sense of the whole array of data, you will want percentages of the total group of respondents who fall into each category.

That's the minimum. Other calculations may be made. (You may want to calculate the average number of social groups to which a person belongs, for instance.) Additional analyses may be needed. You may want to look at the differences in frequency and nature of social club membership by factors such as age and sex. It is also possible to do a lot of fancy statistical analyses, but not unless you are an expert in survey statistics. We shall spare you that. If you opt to use a specialist survey data-processing firm, ask it for any recommendations about such analyses.

The broad purpose of data processing is to put meaning into the data. It provides summary figures so that the results are easily grasped and understood. If you had to examine each one of 1,200 questionnaires for these results on social groups to which the person belonged, you would come out with your head spinning and no clear idea of the major results. Even if you made a mental generalization, you could easily be wrong.

The immediate product of data processing is a table. Figure 14.1 is a dummy computer printout reproduced as a table. While this is fairly typical of computer printouts in the form of tables, you may not need anything so elaborate in your study. This particular printout shows the total results for an answer (where age is shown as the answer), but also provides an analysis for each answer by ownership (undefined), income, sex, and city community. The table shows the number of replies in each category and, more important, the percentage. These percentages, as we have said, make it easy for you. You would have a rough time if you tried to make mental comparisons of the numbers of respondents. If you want an array similar to this from your study, show your data-processing source this sample table. Of course, you will have to make your own listings both for the question answers down the side of the table and the "breakouts" (factors of analysis and the groupings within each) across the top of the table.

If you do not understand the computer, do not be dismayed.

Table 14.1

To which of these types of groups, if any, do you belong? As I mention each one, please tell me whether you are currently a member.

Church group	Yes ( )	No ( )
PTA	Yes ( )	No ( )
Fraternal group	Yes ( )	No ( )
Civic club	Yes ( )	No ( )
Charitable or fund-raising group	Yes ( )	No ( )
Musical group other than church	Yes ( )	No ( )
Sports club	Yes ( )	No ( )
Political club	Yes ( )	No ( )
Card club	Yes ( )	No ( )
Volunteer group (where you provide time and service without pay)	Yes ( )	No ( )
Other social group	Yes ( )	No ( )
Belong to no such group		( )

Data processing should be planned at the time of building the questionnaire. There are three reasons.

1. *To make sure that data needs will be thought of in terms of the purposes of the study.* Giving careful thought to the kinds of data specifically needed may suggest addition or deletion of questionnaire content and help ensure that all data processing needed to do the job has been considered.

2. *To make sure that time and costs of data processing are held to a minimum.* You will save time and money if the data-processing plan has been well thought through in advance, so that you do not have to go back to the questionnaires or computer to locate the source of errors and then correct them. With the computer, it's not the running time that's expensive. It's the setup cost. You want to avoid setup costs past the first.

3. *To precode the questionnaires.* This means providing "coding" indications directly on the questionnaire. (*Coding,* as we explain later in this chapter, is the assignment of a number for each reply. It has nothing to do with quantity, but is merely an identifying symbol to provide a system of classifying the particular response.)

Wherever possible, as suggested in Chapter 13, possible replies to the question are listed on the questionnaire. Each answer should then be preassigned a code, printed on the questionnaire. Let's use that earlier example of membership in social groups. Table 14.2 shows how the questionnaire might preassign codes for each response.

We shall tell you more about the setting up of these codes later in the chapter. Right now all we want to do is to give a brief idea of what coding is all about. There are three steps in data processing: coding, editing, and tabulation (where you have the choice of doing it on the computer or by hand—although the choice in almost all cases today is the computer).

If you had to examine each of 1,200 questionnaires, you would come out with your head spinning and no clear idea of the major results.

Sample computer printout with the following cross-tabulation. Column groups: OWNERS (NOW, NON, FORMER), INCOME (UNDER 25000, 25000 &OVER), SEX (MALE, FEMALE), CITY COMMUNITY (KETTERING, CENTERVILE, MIAMI TWP., WEST CARROLLTON, MIAMISBURG, MORAINE, OAKWOOD, WASHINGTON TWP., BEAVER CREEK).

	NOW	NON	FOR-MER	UNDER 25000	25000 &OVER	MALE	FE-MALE	KETT-ERING	CEN-TER VILE	MIAMI TWP.	WEST CAR-ROL-LTON	MIA-MIS-BURG	MOR-AINE	OAK-WOOD	WASH-ING-TON TWP.	BEA-VER CREEK
SAMPLE SIZE NO ANSWER	300	300	75	236	233	195	397	109	109	109	58	58	58	58	58	58
PERCENT BASE	300 100%	300 100%	75 100%	236 100%	233 100%	195 100%	397 100%	109 100%	109 100%	109 100%	58 100%	58 100%	58 100%	58 100%	58 100%	58 100%
DEMOGRAPHICS--AGE																
24 YEARS & UNDER	32 10.7	10 3.3	9 12.0	20 8.5	13 5.6	17 8.7	28 7.1	12 11.0	7 6.4	11 10.1	4 6.9	4 6.9	6 10.3	4 6.9	2 3.4	1 1.7
25 TO 34 YEARS	73 24.3	48 16.0	24 32.0	61 25.9	58 24.9	38 19.5	85 21.4	12 11.0	23 21.1	27 24.8	15 25.8	18 31.1	15 25.9	12 20.7	9 15.5	14 24.1
35 TO 44 YEARS	91 30.3	42 14.0	19 25.3	38 16.1	80 34.3	48 24.7	93 23.4	18 16.5	31 28.4	31 28.4	9 15.5	11 19.0	9 15.5	8 13.8	18 31.1	17 29.3
45 TO 54 YEARS	65 21.7	54 18.0	11 14.7	29 12.3	48 20.6	40 20.5	75 18.9	15 13.8	26 23.9	14 12.8	11 19.0	14 24.1	9 15.5	19 32.7	10 17.2	12 20.7
55 TO 64 YEARS	28* 9.3	80 26.7	7 9.3	48 20.3	25 10.7	34 17.4	66 16.6	32 29.4	16 14.7	17 15.6	8 13.8	6 10.3	12 20.7	4 6.9	13 22.5	7 12.1
65 YEARS & OLDER	11 3.7	66 22.0	5 6.7	40 16.9	9 3.9	18 9.2	50 12.6	20 18.3	6 5.5	9 8.3	11 19.0	5 8.6	7 12.1	11 19.0	6 10.3	7 12.1
MEDIAN	40	54	37	45	41	44	44	53	43	40	46	41	44	48	45	43

FIGURE 14.1. Sample computer printout.

Table 14.2.

To which of these types of groups, if any, do you belong? As I mention each one, please tell me whether you are currently a member.

Church group	Yes ( ) 7-1	No ( ) 7-2
PTA	Yes ( ) 7-3	No ( ) 7-4
Fraternal group	Yes ( ) 7-5	No ( ) 7-6
Civic club	Yes ( ) 7-7	No ( ) 7-8
Charitable or fund-raising group	Yes ( ) 7-9	No ( ) 7-0
Musical group other than church	Yes ( ) 8-1	No ( ) 8-2
Sports club	Yes ( ) 8-3	No ( ) 8-4
Political club	Yes ( ) 8-5	No ( ) 8-6
Card club	Yes ( ) 8-7	No ( ) 8-8
Volunteer group (where you provide time and service without pay)	Yes ( ) 8-9	No ( ) 8-0
Other social group	Yes ( ) 9-1	No ( ) 9-2
Belong to no such group		( ) 9-3

Coding

Coding, as we have said, is the assignment of a number (occasionally some other symbol, such as a letter) to represent each reply to a question on a questionnaire. Coding is a necessary step for two reasons. First, it gets the raw materials—the replies—into shape to be counted and otherwise processed. Second, it makes processing of results of the study reasonably simple. Therefore, you have to know what coding is all about.

Since the computer is so widely used in data processing of results, our discussion centers on that kind of coding. The code is used to get totals for each set of replies to a question (and for other kinds of analyses as well).

Let's first give you an idea of how this numerical coding system works. Visualize, if you will, a coding scheme that offers you 80 or more basic locations (columns), and think of these as 1 through 80. Within each of these columns there are 10 specific positions. Think of these as running from 1 to 10 (10 in this case becomes a 0, since we want only a single-digit code). Now you have a coding framework within which you can assign specific replies to each question in your study. If you will look at the codes assigned in Table 14.2, you will see exactly how this works. The 7-1 means column 7, position 1; the 8-3 means column 8, position 3.

Precoding. We have to start by telling you about precoding and precoding for identification of a particular questionnaire. *Precoding* consists of printing codes on the questionnaire in advance of their use in collecting information. It shows the column and the specific number within the column opposite a prelisted reply. In Table 14.2, each indicated number—for both the column and the position within the column—appears opposite the response category, just as shown.

A special case is the identification of the particular questionnaire. Each questionnaire should be consecutively numbered at the time of duplication, in advance of questioning. Often the first three or four columns are reserved for this. Therefore, an 0001 would mean that the first questionnaire received a position of 0 in each of the first three columns and a 1 in the fourth column. If the last questionnaire were 1000, there would be a 1 in the first column and a 0 in columns 2, 3, and 4. You need such identification should summary errors be detected, for the only way of resolving these is to go back to the original questionnaire for reference.

Determining List Codes. Here we are talking, as explained in Chapter 13, about having a list of answers on the questionnaire (which may be provided to the respondent or, sometimes, in the case of a personal interview, only for the interviewer to check off the category into which the answer falls). You have to be pretty sure of yourself to provide such a list, which can then be precoded on the questionnaire for easy data-processing entry and handling.

As we said in Chapter 13, such lists take three forms: there's the name list, the quantitative list, and the qualitative list. The name list is one where you know in advance exactly the names you need in the list. If you are doing a product study, it is simple enough, for each category, to prelist the names that will account for the great majority of replies; it is quite safe to list and precode them on the questionnaire. If you are doing a study in which you are getting responses naming particular firms (manufacturer, media, retailer, or whatever), you can quite safely provide the listing in advance on the questionnaire.

With quantitative and qualitative lists, the problem is not quite so simple. An earlier study may show what categories you need for comparison. You may decide to set up categories paralleling government or other reports, so that you can make direct comparisons. In the absence of either of these situations, we recommend that you follow the procedures outlined in the following several pages.

Determining Codes for Open-Ended Quantitative Questions. Here we refer to a question that asks for replies in terms of numbers (not the numerical scaling type of question outlined in Chapter 13, which provides a stated list of predetermined numbers, where coding is automatic and needs no adjustment). We are talking about questions such as the following:

> How many times have you eaten dinner at home in the past 7 days, not including today?

> What size and width of shoe do you yourself wear?

> Do you own a car? If so, what model year is it?

The model-year response can be converted to the car age. Let's suppose that the car ages calculated on this basis showed, for 10 owners, the following sequential replies: 4, 1, 7, 3, 8, 2, 1, 6, 5, and 1. Such an array provides no meaning. The way to handle it is to arrange the display by size:

Age	Number
1	3
2	1
3	1
4	1
5	1
6	1
7	1
8	1

Now the array makes more sense. If you wanted to, you might even make the age classes read "1 or 2," "3 or 4," "5 or 6," and so on and thus end up with fewer categories, depending on your needs in the specific survey. In this example there is no possible reply of 0, but many numerical questions contain a legitimate possibility of a 0 category. In these cases, you should assign 0 a specific numerical category of its own, for it indicates lack of possession, ownership, or whatever and has a totally distinct meaning from any other numerical response. Zero is qualitatively distinct from all other numbers.

Setting up quantitative class intervals is not always the easy task it may appear. While it is not as difficult as setting up categories for qualitative questions, there are still rules to keep in mind. The categories must *be representative of the particular series*. Unless you take care, the data may be distorted through use of nonrepresentative class intervals (numerical groups). Assume that the raw answers range from 1 to 10 and that two replies fall into each of the 10 possibilities. Now assume that the class intervals selected are as follows:

The common retailing practice of "psychological" pricing can affect the representativeness of your responses.

Value	Number of cases
1–2	4
3–5	6
6–10	10

These intervals distort the data. The classification makes it superficially appear that there are many more cases in the heavy end of the values; only a really careful observer will notice that there are 10 cases in the lower end of the list and 10 in the higher end.

The appropriate categories are not always obvious in marketing surveys. Sometimes people's responses tend to cluster around particular numbers. Consider the question, "At what time did you first turn on your television yesterday?" The class intervals you set up must consider that most viewers tune to a program at the hour or half-hour, when the program begins. You would have to set the intervals to show each hour and half-hour during the day.

You would have a different (though similar) problem if you were asking about the price paid to buy a particular item, because of the common retailing practice of "psychological" pricing. For example, many retailers feel that a price of 99 cents is far more appealing than $1, that $1.39 is better than $1.40, and so on—that the customer thinks that such prices are significantly lower than the next figure. While this assumption has never really been proven, it does mean that use of a category such as 90 to 99 cents would not likely be representative of the responses. Thus many replies would be at the upper end of the grouping.

With the computer, the way to put together numerical categories is to enter each specific reply into the program, tell the computer to give you such runs for the entire survey, and then, after reviewing the detailed results, make up your mind on the categories, instructing the computer how to put the groupings together. A less precise way was suggested in Chapter 12. That is to have a sufficient sample of people in your pretesting of the questionnaire to permit precoding of the numerical groupings right on the form itself.

The numerical categories must be *logical*. Let's say that you asked a question about how long ago a consumer last bought fresh beef. Let's also say that there is a clustering of answers around 4 days. This is not an indication that the class interval should run from 1 to 7 days. This would be so broad a range that you would have little sensitivity of reply in your results. Meeting the technical requirements of a range around the cluster is not enough; common sense is required as well. In the case of fresh beef, perhaps there should not even be class intervals.

The categories must *tie in with the purposes of the study*. There are many ways in which the purposes of the study affect the selection of quantitative class intervals. Let's look at just one. A study of beer drinkers asked about beer-drinking preferences and situations. The brewer wanted to analyze results by heaviness of beer drinking, using equal numbers of heavy, medium, and light drinkers. The brewer needed to know the amounts of beer consumed by individuals so that these three groups could be defined in advance of the production of "final" tables from the study. The computer handled it in the manner already outlined.

The categories must be *mutually exclusive*. This seems so obvious that it is scarcely worth mentioning. Yet even trained marketing researchers sometimes violate this principle, so do not fall into the trap. Let's make sure you understand the trap we are warning about. Suppose two income categories are shown as

$30,000 to $35,000

$35,000 to $40,000

Where does an income of $35,000 fall under this arrangement?

When appropriate, class intervals should be of *equal size*. If all previous requirements have been met, and this one can reasonably be followed, it should be. Equally sized intervals make the whole package neater, easier to understand, and easier to treat statistically (calculation of an arithmetic mean or average, for instance). However, this is more an ideal than a requirement. There are many situations in which there are good reasons why the numerical class intervals cannot be of the same size.

Suppose that on a study about beef a woman gives an answer of 0 when asked about how many pounds of ground beef she has bought within the past 7 days. This puts her into an entirely different category of reply from all those giving a reply in pounds. It would be distortion to show this reply anywhere but by itself, in its own class interval. Also, the top-level answer category may have to be virtually open-ended. If you ask a question about the number of hours of weekly television viewing, the top category you show in tables for the sake of simplicity and stringing out of small groups of replies might be "20 hours or more." It might be desirable to handle the total annual mileage put on a car in a similar manner. (The problem of calculating an arithmetic mean can be solved by following the earlier described procedure of letting the computer take all the raw, ungrouped answers first and then setting up the groups. In cases such as these, however, a median—the value of the middle item in the whole array—might be better anyway, and in such a case, the detailed distribution of answers in the top category does not matter.)

Determining Qualitative Codes.   Here we are talking about classifying a tremendous variety of qualitative, explanatory replies. A typical question might be, "Why do you shop there?" The replies can simply bounce all over the place, and it is often difficult to make sense of them. You have to categorize, compress, and summarize to get an overall understanding of the result. Setting up such codes is one of the most difficult parts of your survey effort. If the question is truly open-ended, your classifications must meet at least three requirements.

First, the classification must *put interpretive sense into the array of responses*. The categories selected should represent the best possible scheme for comparisons of the responses. People drink beer. They comment on their reasons for doing so. If these comments are simply listed in the order in which they come in, they will seem to vary all over the lot and make little sense. People drink beer to feel good, yet if they drink too much, it is going to make them feel rather bad and may even harm their health. People drink beer because it is sociable, yet some are solitary drinkers (while watching TV, for instance, or while working on a project in the garage or as a break in mowing the lawn—almost as a reward). People drink beer because it is refreshing or has a good flavor. A few drink it because they cannot afford the "hard" stuff. Yes, all this seems confusing, but if you classify the reasons under only a few headings, the pattern of replies will start to make sense. Headings such as "social reasons," "rewarding," "physical effects," "flavor," "refreshing," and "economy" might just do it. You simply have to give a bit of thought to your classifications. We cannot tell you exactly how to go about it, since the nature of the classifications will depend on the question and your purpose in asking the question (how you intend to use the results).

Second, the classification must *consider the respondent*. Your categories should represent the respondent's point of view; otherwise, your groupings will be misleading. If you are running a study on why people eat at your restaurant, answers might range over a wide area, such as "to save money," "you have plenty of parking space," "the food is good," "I like the service," "it's near to where I work," "it's the best place in town for steaks," or "you're close to where I live." With the answers strung out like this, it is difficult to see a pattern. But start thinking of these replies from the customer's viewpoint. Now you can begin to visualize categories such as "good food," "good service," "reasonable prices," and "convenience." Things begin to fall into place both from the customer's point of view and from yours (for interpetation and possible action).

Finally, there are some almost *mechanical requirements* to be met. One is the number of categories. You do not want too few, for that will prevent you from

People drink beer for a variety of reasons.

seeing all you should in the findings. You do not want too many, for that will make it difficult to understand the findings. Unfortunately, we have no magic way of telling you the right number of categories. You will have to solve it for yourself, as you go, in terms of the purposes of your study. But as Peggy Kelcher, of McKerracher Data Processing Services of Toronto, Ontario, says, "It is always easy to group categories on the final print-out of the report, but if the categories are grouped at the coding stage, it is impossible to expand the category after data entry without going back to the original questionnaires and recoding and reentering the data."

Each category should be mutually exclusive. If there is some question about where a particular response fits, there is something wrong with your groupings.

We have talked about the standards for setting up these qualitative codes. But what is the actual process of doing it? How do you examine the range of responses you get and proceed to set up these codes? Unlike the quantitative categories, you cannot leave it to the computer. This takes considerable personal effort.

The only really sound way is to do a test tabulation. This is a visual task. By hand, a proportion of total questionnaires is examined and replies are listed, in detail, to the question. From this a coding structure meeting the preceding requirements can be set up.

You have to do this well. Not only must you—or whoever does it—understand all the preceding standards, but the person also will have to have a sound understanding of the purposes of the study. Perhaps the best way to handle this physically is to use a small (3- by 5-inch) library card for each response. As additional responses like it are obtained, tick marks can be made on the card. This is far better than trying to make a list—on one or more sheets of paper—of each response as it is recorded. This gives you flexibility in shuffling the answers to come up with reasonable categories.

Be sure to get a good cross section of respondents in this sample tabulation. If you take the first day's results, these may represent—depending on the data-collection method—a highly unrepresentative subsample (those most easy to reach, those most interested, a particular geographic group, or whatever). Ideally, you should wait until all results are in and then make a "random" or "near-random" choice of questionnaires.

How many? Our suggestion: Start perhaps with 50 or 100. Take another 50 or 100 and see how stable the variety of response is. The coding of these qualitative questions should be entered in red on the questionnaire opposite the precoding of the particular column or columns left for that purpose.

Editing

Editing is the inspection and modification or correction of the recorded replies on the questionnaire. Its general purpose is to make the material more meaningful and to make clear to all involved in subsequent stages of data processing the exact meaning of each reply. The problem: Survey data, as obtained and recorded, are rarely perfect, no matter how skilled the interviewers, how perfect the questionnaire. Editing serves four specific purposes as well:

Editing increases consistency and accuracy. The specific purpose of editing is to eliminate replies which are inconsistent or downright incorrect. To be conservative, follow the policy of eliminating a reply when you are not sure how to correct it. Make corrections only when there is convincing evidence that the modification is really warranted. Otherwise there is too fine a line between true survey results and those which are a figment of someone's imagination.

Let's see how this works. A liquor study asked what *brand* of whiskey was last purchased. One respondent named "Old Overholt." Since this brand has not been marketed for some years and there was no way of figuring what the correct reply should have been, the response was edited to "Don't know."

In that same liquor study, once the brand name was obtained, the *type* of whiskey was asked: blend, bourbon, Canadian, Scotch, Irish, or other. One Dewar's user responded that the type was bourbon. Since Dewar's is a Scotch and one could assume that the user knew the brand, then either the respondent or the interviewer had made an error and the type could safely be edited as "Scotch."

This type of editing also makes it possible to eliminate the incorrect asking of (and therefore inappropriate answers to) filtering questions. In one study, five questions about attitude toward smoking risks on various aspects of health were to be asked only of smokers. If any person recorded as a nonsmoker gave answers to the subsequent questions, the answers to those five questions should be edited out. Better to discard them than to make the dubious assumption that the person was a smoker. Be conservative in editing; play it safe. "Creative" editing should be avoided.

Editing increases the rate of usable responses. Even the best interviewer sometimes fails to ask a particular question or to record a reply. The editing process sometimes provides a chance to complete replies where omissions occur by referring to another part of the questionnaire (although sometimes there is no corresponding part of the questionnaire that permits this).

For example, in a study of women's use of flatware, an early question concerned brand and pattern. This was followed by a question about type: sterling, plate, stainless steel, or other. Since brand and pattern are important to most women only in the case of sterling or plate, it was possible to set up an editing pattern (with advance knowledge of the makes and their various patterns). It was simple to set up an editing pattern that would correct for specific makes and patterns by whether they were sterling or plate. The other types do not really matter by make and pattern.

Another study asked about the brands of television sets known to participants. A later query inquired about makes of set ever owned. A few people named previously owned makes they did not mention in the knowledge question. How to edit? Should you edit to include makes previously owned, or should you edit to show separately those makes previously owned but not spontaneously mentioned in the brand-recall question? The way you go depends on the purpose of your study.

Editing increases clarity.   Editing may help to remove ambiguities of response (or recording). If editing cannot eliminate ambiguities about the responses to a question, it is better to forget the results of the question rather than to make unwarranted assumptions about how to clean things up.

In the same liquor study mentioned earlier, Scotch drinkers were asked their opinions on the largest-selling brand of Scotch in the United States. Some mentioned more than a single brand, and the interviewer duly recorded these multiple answers. What editing choices are there?

One is elimination of the person's answers, on the logic that the question had not been answered. A second is to accept all the person's answers. Third, the first-named brand could be taken as the reply, with the logic that the first name that comes to mind carries the most weight. In this particular study, the first-named brand was taken as the reply. The editing decision depends on the purpose of the study.

Editing provides uniformity.   In designing your questionnaire, you naturally do your best to see that the questionnaire will provide comparable replies from each person questioned. But even the expert sometimes fails. You may ask how many miles an automobile owner gets to a gallon. You expect the interviewer to record the whole number, whatever it is.

The respondent who is a meticulous record keeper may refuse to respond within any such bracket. He or she may insist that it is 23.5 miles, and that's that. The good interviewer will record it that way, and it is up to you to have an editing system to handle it. Our suggestion on handling replies ending with .5: raise the first case, lower the second, and so on.

Preparing for the Editing Process.   There are two steps. One is to try to figure out, in advance of the start of your study, the procedural problems and solutions. Do this at the time of questionnaire development.

Your best-laid plans cannot foresee all these problems. So you—or your survey contractor should you go that route—also should review a number of the questionnaires as they come in on your survey. Despite all your best efforts, you cannot foresee all the editing problems that may arise.

The interrelationships of questions and responses should be considered. It is the only way to get a real handle on all your editing needs.

In these days of computer processing of survey data—by all odds the common method—we have some special comments. Editing today is essentially a computer process. You or your data-processing firm tell the computer how to edit, and except for questions that you have not resolved in advance—and where the computer may have to throw back the question to you—it is virtually an electronic process, as long as all the instructions are written in. In the case of telephone surveys, many telephone data-collection firms also have programs with a videoscreen and a terminal unit (keyboard), both connected with a computer,

The computer may have to throw back the question to you.

to be used by the interviewer as the calls are made. The videoscreen shows the interviewer, question-by-question, exactly how each is to be phrased. The display also shows the possible response categories. The interviewer punches in the reply. The next question—whether the follow-up to a filter question or simply the next general question—appears on the screen. At any point where the interviewer punches a reply inconsistent with the editing program, the screen flashes that, and the interviewer—through questioning or rerecording of a wrong response—makes the correction. Thus the editing process is simultaneous with the questioning.

If the telephone research firm does not offer this process, or if another form of questioning is used (such as in-mall questioning), the data-processing system or firm can provide similar, though after-the-fact, program editing. Of course, such a process lacks the self-editing procedure during the questioning procedure.

Some Final Comments on Data Processing by Computer

We have intentionally kept this computer discussion of processing pretty simple. But there are two additional areas we want to tell you about.

1. *There are advanced statistical computer analyses available.* We make no effort to describe these, but merely alert you that there are highly specialized computer analytical methods. Talk to an expert about these and how they may be of assistance to you in getting a better understanding of what the data mean in terms of your particular problem.

2. *You have a choice of going to an outside computer firm or doing it yourself.* Only if you have your own computer and you—or someone else—have the time and enthusiasm to undertake it should you think about computer processing of your own survey. If this situation applies to you, however, there are computer programs you can buy—at relatively modest prices. While Chapter 16 tells you specifically how to locate such programs and what they can produce for you, we mention here just four of the basic survey programs which will serve as examples: P-STAT (Princeton, N.J.), SPSS (Chicago, Ill.), Microtab (Newton, N.J.), and UNCLE (World Research Systems Limited, Marina Del Ray, Calif.).

If you decide not to do it yourself, there are many computer firms specializing in analysis of surveys. Most are quite competent in recommending procedures and tables to meet your needs. We suggest that you start by referring to Chapter 16 to learn the listed firms and what they offer.

We do have a suggestion when you talk to such a firm. Do not take for granted that they have a complete quality operation. Most do, but check it out. For one thing, find out if their keypunching operation (a typewriter-like keyboard is used to input the code material) provides quality control. The method is verification of some stated proportion of questionnaire input—perhaps 10 percent, selected on a random basis. In this case, a second keypuncher, using a sample of the original questionnaires, independently makes entries into the system. These are then compared with the original punching and the discrepancies are noted and checked out, making it possible to calculate the percentage of correct punches.

Hand Tabulation

Rarely will you tabulate your survey by hand in this computer age. It is not often worth it if you have over 100 questionnaires; the advantages, including cost, simply are too great in favor of the computer.

There are two additional considerations beyond number of questionnaires. One is the *cross-tabulations* (*cross-tabs*). A cross-tab breaks out the replies to a question by demographics or by results to another question. In a newspaper readership study you may want to analyze why readers buy the paper, for instance, by how long they have been reading it or by sex of the reader. In either case, you are into cross-tabs. If you have more than one or two factors by which to cross-tab, then you are simply getting into too many hours of work and checking of accuracy to make hand tabulation worthwhile.

Then there's the number of questions and the variety of answers to each. While we cannot give you hard answers on these, generally hand tabulation just is not worth the time if there are very many questions or very many varieties of responses within questions. As we explain the hand tabulation process, you will understand why.

What Hand Tabulation Is and How to Do It. Hand tabulation is just what the name implies. It is doing the whole counting process by hand. You might think that the simple way to do this is to set up a tally sheet showing the possible answers to a particular question and then just enter a stroke for each reply as you run through the questionnaires, adding a cross-bar for the fifth entry. Then all you need do is to multiply the number of cross-bars by five and add the extra single strokes.

You would be using poor judgment if you did this. Suppose that at the end of a 200-questionnaire survey you found your total answers to a question were 199 instead of the 200. The only way to clear this up is to start from scratch, and with poor luck it might come out to 201 this time! Interruptions in the middle of the process can be devastating.

It is much better to use what the writers term the "sort-and-count method." Let's say you are dealing with a question about how many radios a family has in the home. The answers range from 1 to 7, and you have decided that you do not want to set up group categories here, but that you will just report totals for each number of sets, from 1 through 7.

Sort the questionnaires by answer. You will end up with seven piles. (If you also happen to have a zero and a no-answer group, there will be two more piles.) Then pick up and count the number in each stack.

You are right that this is going to take more time than the tick method. In the long run, it may take less. Under the sort-and-count method, if your figures do not add up to the total questionnaires, it is relatively simple to recount each stack and find out where you made your error. There is the added advantage that as you

Interruptions in the middle of the hand-tabulation process can be devastating.

count each pile that first time it takes only seconds to eye the code (or answer) and make sure it is in the right pile, so you have a built-in check on classification.

The method gets a lot more complicated when a person may properly have given more than a single reply to a question, as might be the case with the membership in social groups discussed earlier. In this case, your first sort is by the lowest code number (the first group named). After getting the total count for the first group, all the questionnaires in that pile must be resorted for the next lowest code (adding them to the pile already accumulated for that category), with those not naming a second group put into a discard pile. The process is then repeated until all the categories have been duly sorted and counted.

Precoding.   The precoding process is no different from that for computer processing.

Coding.   Here there is often a difference. With hand tabulation, there is no chance to have the computer run totals for you from raw data, so that you can then tell the machine what categories to set up and to repunch the information. With hand tabulation, it is by hand all the way, and you have to go through the detailed process—described under qualitative coding within the computer discussion. This is necessary even for more quantitative questions. Once the categories have been set to your satisfaction, then the codes must be hand-entered on each questionnaire.

Editing.   Editing is also far more time-consuming than when you use the computer. The same standards must be applied and stated. But now the editing all must be done by "hand"—examination of the cross-relations, errors and omissions, and all the rest—for each separate questionnaire. Once again, entries (this time they are response changes) must be made in red, to distinguish them from the replies originally entered on the form.

Final Comment

All in all, doesn't it seem a lot simpler to go the computer route rather than hand tabulation?

Section Four

Additional Considerations

fifteen

How to Write or Present a Report That Will Get Action

Several weeks ago one of the authors went to a lecture by an eminent Washington-based news reporter. Everyone looked forward to the talk, believing, of course, that we would hear "juicy" inside news about the Capitol.

Apparently everything was prepared. Signs directed visitors to the right auditorium. The hall was filled. *But,* someone forgot to check the microphones. The poor speaker spent the first 10 minutes asking the audience if they could hear. "How about this mike on the right?" "How about this one?" Shouts came from the audience to speak louder—or that the back rows could not hear at all. A dreadful experience for the reporter and the audience. The talk was much less interesting, and people leaving at the end were heard to say how disappointed they were.

Furthermore, the speaker, a substitute for the one who had been first asked, apparently wrote his talk on the back of a piece of scrap paper on the flight from Washington. After a very short talk, the speaker asked for questions from the audience; after an embarrassing silence, a few questions were offered by women with tags on their dresses, indicating that they were officials of the group that had organized the program. Obviously, these were planted questions of no particular interest to the rest of the audience. The speaker then called one question the last, hurried out to his car, and left for the more comfortable atmosphere of the beltway.

We only mention this unhappy instance because it illustrates so clearly how a presentation can go wrong because someone forgot to check details. Even though the speaker was a quickly chosen substitute, someone should have made sure that he knew what the audience wanted to hear. The microphones should have been working properly, and the lighting should have been properly set. In fact, almost everything that could go wrong did go wrong. And it was not the fault of the moon and stars or wrath of gods; it was the fault of *people.*

How many times have the readers of this book sat in meetings where slides were to be shown on a screen. Almost inevitably, the printing is too small for people in back rows to see clearly. Then the usual happens: the apology by the speaker for not making the slides better. The restlessness in the back because half the program is being lost to them. Speakers at meetings often wonder why some of the audience begins to walk out during the presentation (perhaps down to a bar). It is not always indifference by the hearer—it is the fault of the speaker himself or herself in many cases.

We have come a long way together in this book. We hope that you have gained new insight into what you can do for yourself. Whether by mail questionnaire, telephone study, focus group interviews, in-office interviews, or point-of-sale interviews, you know now that there is a large amount of solid fact finding that does not necessarily require the help of a professional researcher. The principal aim of these chapters was to convince you that you can do the job and to give you some practical advice on how to go about it.

If this book has succeeded in this aim, then you have decided to make an attempt at research into one or more of your problems. If you are new at

If a presentation is to go right, someone must check all the details.

research, you will take special pride in your first job. This is especially so when your findings and recommendations are put into a report that is convincing enough to get the whole "team" behind you. It is a rare company in which the person who does the research is also the sole writer and reader of the report and the sole person to act on it. In most cases, others have to be convinced. Even if these others are your subordinates, you know in your heart that they must believe in the correctness of the research methods, the facts that have been found, and the actions that are urged as a result of these facts.

A good report, a good presentation, is almost always necessary. In some cases it will be presented to someone higher in the organization than you. In others, the selling job must be done with subordinates. Many a top-management person, even a sole owner of an establishment, has found to his or her surprise that subordinates need more than an order to render effective cooperation.

Thus the report and the oral presentation must be as well done as possible. The microphones must work. The slides must be visible. Of course, good grammar, spelling, and good English always must come without question.

How to Analyze and Evaluate Your Data

It is necessary, before beginning to write at all, to take a clear look at what you have found.

Another Look at the Problem.   Now is the time to go back to the beginning of your planning and take a fresh, new look at the problem and how it was stated. What were the major questions and the minor ones? Does it appear that the gathered facts will satisfy the problems and answer the questions? Patently, there is no point in writing a report about a study that has not done the job. However, if you have carefully supervised or carried out the study while it was in progress, the chances are that you have indeed satisfied all the possible doubts. Before putting a word on paper, it is good to do a little meditating about the meaning of what you have found (in this case, the word "meditating" does not mean a blank mind).

One caution: It is extremely doubtful in any study that you will get everything you wished for. There will be some lingering doubts about some matters. The *big* question is answered, but you wish that you had done a little more work on some other phase. This lack of completeness must be pointed out in your written report or oral presentation. It is always good to declaw, early on, those who will be quick to point out flaws in your research. You should be able to point out reasons for any omissions. Perhaps they were not important enough for your purposes to spend extra money and time filling them. To try hiding a small omission by not mentioning it is to invite uncertainty about the validity of the whole report. It is perfectly satisfactory to describe things left out, give the reasons why, and suggest further research at some future time.

One thing to realize about groups of people who hear your report or read it is that many feel a subconscious need to feel and act important. They will seek

You know in your heart that your subordinates must believe in the correctness of the research methods, the facts that have been found, and the actions that are urged as a result of these facts.

opportunities to appear thoughtful and analytical in front of their peers. Allow them this satisfaction; agree with whatever you can without destroying the important conclusions of the report, and you will gain friends and backers. However, do not compromise on the matters that really count.

What alternative actions can be recommended? Now that all the scores are in, what do they mean? What alternative actions can be recommended? Is there a clear yes or no? Or go or no-go?

Many studies end in some lack of clarity. They may show that sales of a product increased nicely when displayed at the end of an aisle in a supermarket, but it also could be true that sales of a more profitable item were cannibalized. It becomes a question of cost- and profit-effectiveness—but even that may not be wholly clear. Customers may want the display of certain items which are related to others, such as gourmet foods, with other such delicacies. Sales may increase at the end of an aisle, but to the confusion of customers who buy such high-markup merchandise. Since it is not always clear what the right course is, the study may do no more than point out the factual problems that must be solved by management.

How clear are the results? In a sense, this topic is a bit repetitious, having been partly covered in the last section. However, it is important for you to realize how strongly the results of your study lean one way or another. If you get an overwhelmingly positive reaction to the idea of producing a new form of widgets, a clear road for action has been unfolded. If the response is 60 to 40, say, or split about even, further thought will have to be given to the true meaning of the results. Remember, too, that you almost certainly do not have what is called a "probability sample." But your "nonprobability sample" was well conceived and you have faith that the results are good. If about half the respondents said, "Yes, go ahead," the recommendation might still be positive, depending on other factors such as anticipated volume and profit or on actions being taken by competitors. Even a lower positive reaction might still result in a recommendation to proceed.

It is always good to declaw, early on, those who will be quick to point out flaws in your research.

Of course, for other kinds of research, such as focus group interviewing, there is no real question of going or not going. How people *think* or their emotional attitudes are what we are after there—not a signal to do something or not to do it. A focus group may tell a manufacturer of a new toothpaste that prospective customers really do not like the new pumps being introduced by competitors. This is not projectable to all people who scrub their teeth, but it may lead to new thinking about how the new toothpaste will be packaged.

If the research needs a clear negative or positive attitude before you or your management can make a decision and this clear reaction did not come about, further research may have to be recommended—perhaps even another small-scale study much like the one you just completed. Does this new research produce the same split in opinions? If so, then that is the way life is, and you and your management will have to make a decision on the best evidence possible from all sides. If further research produces different results, then perhaps the whole project was done carelessly and inadequately, and you may have to start all over again. Or perhaps the successor in your job.

If further research produces different results, then perhaps the whole project was done carelessly and inadequately, and you may have to start all over again.

What alternative actions can be recommended?   Again, some repetition. But now that all the scores are in, what do they mean? What alternative actions can be recommended?

We cannot enter into all the variations that may occur in study results. However, let us say that a shopping center study has shown that almost all the center's customers come from a small area. A more affluent (according to census figures) group from another area is not patronizing the center. Since you talked to people who *did* come there for shopping, you have no evidence about all those who did *not* come.

Several recommendations are immediately apparent. First, you are now in a position to consider a study of the nonshoppers. This involves further research, more time, and more money. Second, the findings may show a satisfactory condition. There is enough potential business from the area now being served. Third, the differences between the people of the area being served and the people in an adjacent area may seem minimal. A little more advertising effort (perhaps in a local "give-away" suburban newspaper) can win new business. What we are saying is that very few studies produce clear recommendations for only one course of action. There are alternative or supplementary actions that can be taken, and all these have to be thought out before the report is written and presented. The final report will have to be quite direct, but you will have to spend some prewriting time going through an "on the one hand, on the other hand" stage of thinking.

If other people in your company feel there are some holes in your work, they will be only half-hearted in fulfilling your recommendations.

Can you benefit from again consulting other people in the company?   Most of the time, yes! Go to the people who will have to put your recommendations into action. Show them what you have, what you think the returns mean, and what actions you believe should be recommended. If you have solid rapport with these people, you will benefit from their advice. Executives have different mind sets. You may be warned that such and such a vice president tends to dislike a certain way of doing business. You can be set to disarm him or her a little if he or she raises an objection at a meeting—or after reading your report.

You also may feel aggrieved and hurt, since almost certainly some fault will be found in your work. But two points are important. First, if these people feel that there are some holes in your work, they will be only half-hearted in fulfilling your recommendations. Second, if they point to missing material, you have a chance to repair your study a little. Then you will have all the people on your side. This may seem a small point, but it has saved many studies from oblivion. A small argument now is better than an unpleasant scene later.

One more point: God did not make any human who did not like to have his or her advice sought. Having given advice, the advisor will much more likely be "on the side" of the advisee. Never miss this opportunity.

How should the report be written?

1. From the first sentence, the report should be addressed strongly to the needs and desires of the listener or reader. A business problem needs solving.

The report addresses itself to this problem—some guidance for action is given. And this should be the whole concept and organization of the report. Listeners and readers are likely to have a very short attention span if their interests and needs are not addressed clearly and at a very early point in the report. And from the very beginning of the report, the emphasis should be on actions that should be taken. A research report is whistling in the wind if it does not lead to something being done with the findings.

2. A report can be too long. No one in business likes a report that is long and wordy. There are no exceptions. Avoid wordiness completely. One fault that is prevalent in young report writers is a tendency toward "fine writing." Probably a result of college training, it must be weeded out and destroyed. Reports can become the kind of efforts that once pleased college professors. We have been on both sides of this fence. A professor, facing a pile of term papers, may subconsciously equate length with quality. Skipping through the massive sentences, somehow he or she sees completeness and thoroughness staring him or her in the face. Not all professors by any means have this weakness, but students have told us about getting good grades by writing reams about "what the professor wanted."

No one in business likes a report that is long and wordy.

3. Good, clear English is required. There is great merit in short sentences. And there is as much merit in the use of simple, familiar words.

4. A report can have too many details. The people who read and act on your report will assume that you knew what you were doing. The research methods used can be described at the end of the report. Some will glance at these, but simply to assure themselves that you had built a strong foundation for your recommendations. Tables and charts must accompany some research reports. But again, *keep them simple*. The point of a figure should be immediately grasped by the audience or reader.

5. A report can fail to come to the point. These suggestions are all related. It is difficult sometimes, especially for an inexperienced report writer, to come to the point in any paragraph. After the first draft of a report, it is vital to edit severely, weed out unneeded words, eliminate "on the one hand, but on the other" types of waffling. The last thing you want is for your readers to wonder, with considerable exasperation, what on earth you are trying to say. You are not a politician trying to be on everyone's side until after the election.

6. A report can give conclusions and recommendations at the wrong point. Where to put the conclusions and recommendations has been an area of disagreement.

- Some say that the report should lead toward the conclusions and recommendations. Logically, recommendations should be at the end of the report—a result of the facts that have been presented. Clearly this is a reasonable way of doing things. The trouble is that many readers of your report will be interested solely in the conclusions and will not want to take the time to get to them.
- Another possibility is to start with the major conclusions followed by the

A report can have too many details.

recommendations, all on one or two pages. After that will come the report itself.

Still another way is to write a separate and highly condensed report, merely covering the most important questions at issue. A larger report could then go to people who are more concerned with details. Those getting the condensed version can be told that the larger version is available to them upon request. An "executive summary," either at the beginning of the report or as a separate version, as mentioned earlier, is probably now used more frequently than formerly. The only real trouble with this method is that many people will read nothing else. The main report is left for those lower-echelon folks who have to do something about the lesser matters. The major point of this discussion is that those people who are most important to the reader or the listener are likely to be persons with a great deal to do and a great impatience with less important details.

7. A report can fail to communicate with the people who must accept and act on it. Even if you are the boss—you own the business—your report should take into account the human foibles, weaknesses, and prejudices of the people who must act on it. Knowing these people as you do, does it not make good sense to write directly to them? Persuading them, selling them?

We are not recommending pandering to your readers or departing in any way from the truth, but there are ways of making truth more palatable. For example, say a department manager in your small manufacturing company believed that one of her new products was being awaited breathlessly by the world. No research was done while the product was being developed. The manager was supremely confident in the product's appeal. Now it is not selling well and your research shows why this is so: it does not do a very good job, and almost no one wants it. Your report will show that the favorite new product is a puppy rapidly growing into a dog.

You may have a wild temptation to say it just like that in your report. But don't. Be very gentle to the department head—and lead her carefully to the point where she must conclude that the product never *will* sell. After seeing the facts, she can make her own conclusions and her face will be saved. Maybe you have also "saved" an employee who is otherwise good, loyal, and productive and who makes a mistake only occasionally.

Think then of all the people who will be reading the report. You have an organization which you need to keep productive and happy. What is the best way of breaking the news to Mr. A? How best to bring help to Mr. B? How best to pacify the highly emotional Mr. C? Truth tempered with wisdom and discretion is the best medicine.

8. A report can fail to consider legal problems in certain terminology. These days, with Uncle Sam watching every business move, it is quite possible that a completely innocent statement may wind up in a low court years later. An almost idle question about whether a component part ought to be strengthened might lead to a perfectly honest conclusion that the part is O.K. Then someone gets hurt and brings suit. The report is seized and used against the company. It is wise to

It is quite possible that a completely innocent statement may wind up in a law court years later.

think of such possibilities in advance and avoid possible future trouble. Perhaps a report should be examined, in some cases at least, by someone in a legal capacity before it is committed to final form and final filing.

Steps in Writing a Strong Report

Early in the study you should have written a tentative outline of what the final report would be like. If you did do this, you will be thankful. The next step will be to add to this first outline. Certainly the intervening days of work have added much to your knowledge; the outline can now be expanded and made complete.

The best help, for some at least, is what is called a "sentence outline." Major headings and subheadings are placed in their usual positions, but the supporting topics are written as phrases or sentences. In a sense, such an outline is a half-report; it could almost be used as it is. Forcing yourself to write a sentence outline helps to clear your mind regarding just exactly what you have and what you do not have.

A preliminary outline would never win you a good mark in college, but it will prove most useful when actual writing of the final report gets underway. The thing that must be remembered in writing a report for businesspeople is their possible difficulty in reading. At a time when the results of college entrance examinations show less and less verbal ability, you really cannot assume that every important reader can, with ease, follow through all the clauses, phrases, and five-syllable words that you might like to use.

Business ability is not necessarily coordinated with high reading ability. People who read easily and quickly will not be offended by a simple report. People who read with difficulty will be happy not to be required to work so hard. After the report is written, it is wise to go through it, breaking up long sentences where possible, substituting short words for long ones, and simplifying the mathematical presentations. What we have been saying again and again in different ways is: Do not make your readers work hard. Make your report a joy to read.

One hundred percent accuracy is just a dream. You simply cannot be completely sure that you are right. One thought that has sustained many researchers in moments of doubt is, "At this moment, in this company, I know more than anyone else about this particular problem." For one, bright, shining moment, you are the hero, the expert. This attitude of authority will help you later as the study is put to use. You never need apologize to anyone if your research was well and thoroughly done. The research needs to be pure, unbiased, thorough, and complete. Then, and only then, can you hold your head up and be impressive—even in your own organization with your own employees.

Especially when you reach the point of describing the most important findings and recommendations, it is extremely necessary to speak and write with authority. Do not ever forget that people tend to accept you at your own evaluation. If you believe in what you have done, others also will believe. Say what you have to say with firmness, with authority, and with no self-doubts in your voice or between the lines of your report.

Strength can come from anticipating objections and answering them before

For one bright, shining moment, you are the hero, the expert.

they arise. It does not take much sagacity to forecast what Nancy, Bob, or Jim will probably say. If you reflect for a moment, you can almost hear them voicing some prejudice, some habitual mode of thought. It is wise to have answers for such attitudes before they are brought out publicly. Thinking in advance about such objections also will force you to make your research that much better and more complete. If a sales manager believes that most new trends in consumer goods start on the West Coast, and you are investigating a "trendy" sort of item, you had better have an answer ready in case he or she asks you why you did not investigate the west—if you did not.

A strong report will bring up alternative actions that might result from the findings. It will also show which is the best alternative and why.

A strong report will openly discuss its shortcomings. It will say that this or that topic was not covered and here is the reason. Perhaps it was a question of money or time. Perhaps a little beginning research showed that certain topics, geographic areas, or other matters simply were not important for the purposes of this research. A great element of weakness is introduced when a cover-up is attempted to hide insufficient or poorly done research.

Once in a while the nature of the study demands thought about the effect of your recommendations on the competition. If your company does this or that, what counteractions are competitors likely to take? This is another example of the need for forethought and meditation. If we do this and competition does that, how can we counter the counteraction? If we bring out our product XX, how soon are we likely to face competition? And so on.

If a shopping center takes certain steps to attract more trade from a wider area, what will the shopping area a mile away do about it? Will our actions simply mean that everyone spends more money with no resulting benefits? Can we get the jump on our competition—a jump with which they can only catch up with difficulty? This kind of thinking sometimes distinguishes a good report from a weak one. At least the recognition of these problems, even if no answer is presently possible, will show that you have done your homework.

How to Make a Good Oral Presentation of Your Report

Ordinarily, a report that has taken a significant bit of time and money deserves more than just being put into the company mail or left on someone's desk in the morning. With such handling, it would probably take its place in the usual pile of advertising, minor matters of all kinds, and some crucial matters that demand instant action. Where will your report stand in this hierarchy?

At the very least, a finished report deserves personal delivery. The first receiver will be your supervisor, if you have one. If you are the boss, the owner, then you can determine who should get copies and in what order.

Much better, if at all possible, is an oral presentation of the study. Even a report that is small and relatively unimportant to the company as a whole can still be presented to a few members of middle management.

An oral presentation can emphasize the importance of the findings and

A finished report deserves personal delivery.

recommendations. It gives people their opportunity to voice objections and questions and gives you the chance to answer them before they spread like a cancer. Only in the give and take of a meeting can you be reasonably sure that everyone understands what has been said. Insist on an oral presentation if you can, although a delay of a week or so may be necessary to get everyone in the same room at the same time.

An oral presentation will benefit from imaginative visual material. It should never consist of having the report just read out loud. In fact, it is a very good idea not to distribute the written report until the oral presentation has ended. With a report in front of them, many listeners will be leafing through the pages rather than paying attention wholly to you. Distributing the report in advance also causes some disruption from rattling of paper and turning of pages. Members of the audience may whisper to each other about some points you have made on paper.

Here are some suggestions for helpful activities in connection with an oral presentation:

1. Make an outline of the points to be covered, but if at all possible, refrain from preparing anything that has to be read aloud. Notes can be used, perhaps on 3- by 5-inch cards to be held in your hand. A lectern is always good. It hides notes. It also may hide shaky knees and sweaty palms. However, a lectern is not always possible. Your presentation may be made in someone else's office. But you should still use notes, not prepared material to be read aloud.

2. Avoid details as far as possible. The listening group knows that it will get a written report. For the most part, your report should cover only findings and recommendations—and these should be boiled down to the most important and interesting.

3. It is always better to have two people present a study, or even three. Any audience will get tired of just one person unless that person is an unusually professional speaker. A change in voices or a change in manner of speaking will hold interest longer.

4. Hold any presentation to a maximum of an hour, except under the most unusual circumstances. The span of human attention is short. The report itself can be read later. Your oral job is to interest and convince the listeners. Questions may run the meeting beyond an hour, but this is the option of the group, not you. If you receive many questions, you know your report has aroused interest and may even have achieved success.

5. Without making an obvious thing of it, a good speaker (especially, of course, in a small group) can refer to some members of the audience by name. The more the speaker can involve particular people, the more likely he or she is to be convincing: "As Marcia said 3 months ago, we really do not know enough about the XX market. Now, Marcia, I think we can say we really know a little more." Marcia is pleased at having her thinking publicly mentioned. "I'm glad that Joe steered us to that man in Milwaukee. We really got a lot from him—and he sends

A lectern is always good for hiding notes, shaky knees, and sweaty palms.

his best regards, Joe." This can be carried too far, but a little may help ease tension in the room, both for the listeners and for yourself.

6. There are so many visual aids that it is impossible to mention them all. If time allows, slides can be prepared of some of the charts and tables in the report. Slides showing store displays, parking difficulties, or other scenes related to the report can make a meeting much more interesting. If slides are to be used, *please* practice ahead of time for the sake of everyone. All our working lives we have had to watch upside-down slides, projectors that were too far away, print that could not be read on the screen, and bulbs that burned out when no replacement was available. There is absolutely no excuse whatsoever for such happenings.

Now that we are talking about practice, let us continue. Any oral presentation should be practiced. It is absolutely stupid to get a group of people together and then muff your presentation.

Even what some of your listeners may call a "dog and pony show" can have its advantages. Putting on a good show, corny as it may be, can be amusing. The audience may be grateful for a change in their day's routine, and you will win respect for your presentation, partly because you are so plainly right and partly because you amused your people.

Various devices are readily available in most cities, if your company does not already have them on hand. You can use a projector that shows printed pages from the report transferred to film. A good slide projector is always useful.

You can use a felt board to grasp signs or other paper objects. Using a felt board, it is possible to build your presentation toward a climax, adding one object after another.

It is not good to remain in one spot during the entire presentation. After a few moments behind the lectern to hide the shaky knees, move about a little. Not too much, or your audience will begin wondering where you are going next. Go to a blackboard to write something. Hold up a sign. Do not operate your own projection equipment if you can possibly get out of it. Interest should center on you and not on your struggles with mechanical equipment.

Almost any presentation deserves a full-scale dress rehearsal. This includes going over everything you plan to say and making sure that the machine operator knows what he or she is to do and when.

Probably the major fault of most business presentations is their tendency to drag. Keeping the pace up is vital if you are to grasp and hold the attention of your group. How to keep the pace up deserves some thinking ahead of the actual presentation. Have you ever noticed that people whom you know very well will change their voices and mannerisms in front of a group? A much better relationship between speaker and audience will come about if the speaker is perfectly natural. Speakers' voices at a meeting tend to take on a monotone which rapidly becomes monotonous. For most of us, the best thing we can do is to speak in a perfectly normal way, as though we were talking about last Sunday's golf game.

All these things help to establish rapport with the audience. Without rapport, much of the meaning and importance of what is being said is lost. Following

Keeping the pace up is vital if you are to grasp and hold the attention of your group.

these suggestions is not at all difficult. Anyone can become an interesting speaker. First, of course, the person must have something to say—and you do! Second, some deliberate effort must be made to form a good relationship with the group—and you can do it!

Summary

This chapter has not talked about the "meat" of your study. It has only discussed how to "cook" and present that meat. Some of the hints and suggestions are so plainly true that we wonder why we have had to sit through dull, boring, and everlasting meetings for so many years—and have had to read equally dull and boring reports. To make a dull presentation of an important study is inexcusable when you can so easily turn it into an interesting, spritely, amusing, and thoroughly convincing performance. There is nothing wrong with a little laughter. Not jokes filched out of an old joke book, but laughter that comes from hearing serious things told with just a little unexpected twist. If this chapter can keep anyone in any company from yawning and squirming while you make a bad presentation, then it has done its job. What we would like from you, the reader, is a promise that never, never, never will you be guilty of conducting a bad meeting. At least promise that you will try your very hardest to be interesting.

sixteen

How to Find and Use Outside Help in Your Study

Do you need or want outside help in your study? Since you are reading this book, you had hopes that you could do it yourself. If you had wanted to build your own house and bought a do-it-yourself book, you may have decided by this point in your reading that your proposed project was too much for you. This can occur with a survey, too. You may come to the conclusion that your particular study is simply too complex or too time-consuming.

You may decide that your other company duties are far more crucial. If so, it would be financially unwise to spend your days and hours on a marketing research study, just as you would not take time off from your job to build your own house. Ordinarily it would cost you less to do the work on the house—or the survey—yourself, but you will in the long run save money for your firm by putting your efforts where they provide the greatest financial return. If you have better things to do for your company, using outside research help means dollar savings. Just do not rationalize. If you can do the job more economically yourself, you should. Maybe you can find the time if you try.

Sometimes a neutral outside research source may be needed. If your study is intended to settle a major policy or operating dispute, it is possible that your associates who dislike the survey results might well dispute those results, arguing bias or poor research quality. Your time and the firm's money would have been wasted. A neutral source is far less likely to be disputed.

Similarly, if you intend to use results of the study outside the company (such as with advertisers or potential advertisers or perhaps with one or more potential investors in your firm), there's a believability advantage in having an outside firm do the research.

Some Basic Considerations

Types of Outside Resources. These include the research contractor (often called the "research firm") and the consultant. A *research firm* is a company—generally incorporated—that takes on part or all of a marketing survey. It is a business firm—just as is your own company. It is in business to make a profit through doing part or all of marketing survey studies.

There is an amazing variety of research firms. We will not even try to tell you all the types. But to give you a brief idea, there are small local firms, regional firms, national ones, and even international. Some are extremely specialized, tackling only specific types of work. Others are generalists. Some have national reputations and charge accordingly. But there are others who do quality work but charge only moderate prices.

The kind of firm you go to depends on your own particular needs. We shall try to show you how to make some preliminary decisions as to type of firm you might want to consider.

We shall classify these firms as simply as we can. The *generalist* (general contractor) takes on the entire study from study design through the report, with all other steps in between (as discussed in Section Three). The *subcontractor*

You may have decided by this point that your proposed project is too much for you.

takes on one specific segment of the total survey process: it may be design of the sample, the field work, the data processing, and so on. The *specialist* firm offers expertise in a narrow range, such as focus group interviewing or collecting data through a particular technique (telephone interviewing, mall questioning, or mail surveys). There will be more about these three basic types later in this chapter. There are still other types, but the do-it-yourselfer can find out about those for himself or herself. We'll be telling you how.

The *consultant* (an individual or firm) does *not* undertake studies (or any part of them), but does provide—for a fee—guidance for the entire project or a part of it (such as sampling). Depending on your needs, the consultant may design the study and act as your agent in handling any or all of the relationships with research firms. There are several types of consultants. The individual consultant is often a marketing professor. At least two types of business firms offer research consulting: the advertising agency and the management consultant firm. More about these later in this chapter.

Your Basic Choice: Consultant or Not?   If you choose to use outside help, then you must decide before doing anything else just how much help you need. If you opt for help the whole way through the study and want to leave almost all of it to an "architect," you still face a basic choice.

Should you go to an overall consultant who has no research facilities or to a generalist research firm that has the apparent facilities to do everything you need, from designing the study right on down the line to the report?

The authors' recommendation: Go for the consultant. The generalist research firm makes money from using its special know-how and special facilities. As honest and ethical as it may be, these considerations—conscious or not—are built into its recommendations. The consultant, on the other hand, earns income only through time spent on advising and working with you on your study. Another point: The consultant, by definition, is happy to allow you to put in whatever amount of interest, time, and effort you consider relevant. He or she adapts to your needs.

This chapter discusses, in sequence, how to locate and decide on a consultant, how to locate and evaluate contractors, how to obtain and evaluate submissions from contractors, and how to work with contractors.

How to Locate and Decide on a Consultant

The Possible Types of Consultants.   If your company is large enough to have its own advertising agency, the agency may have a research specialist, perhaps even a research department. If so, this may be the best possible source of a consultant. The firm knows your company. It wants to be sure to do all it can to help you, in whatever area. It is surely not going to overcharge for its services.

We have some reservations about the management consulting firm as a source, mainly because unless you are a pretty big firm, it is unlikely to be interested in your one-shot marketing survey. Despite our reservations, specialists in these firms can offer considerable help in a marketing survey.

If yours is a small firm, the marketing professor may be the way to go. He or she will be available and generally not too expensive. But there is a real risk. He or she may not be knowledgeable. Unless the professor is actively involved in marketing research—not merely teaching it—he or she will not be current on research contractors who can fill your needs and may not even be current on techniques. A strong word of warning: Unless the school has some sort of well-run research bureau, do not let the professor sell you on the idea that students can do the interviewing. Both authors have been professors of marketing. Both have seen student interviewers do sloppy, undependable, even dishonest work. It is a lot of fun to fill in the forms in a pub and be paid for it. You will get the field work done less expensively, but you may not be able to count on the results. There is a major exception, however, which we talk about now.

It is the *Small Business Institute*. This is a program under sponsorship of the *Small Business Administration* (SBA) of the federal government. If your local or nearby college or university offers this service (telephone the 800 number for SBA to find out the nearest source), you may be able to arrange a well-planned, well-monitored survey at extremely low cost. The student team, after consultation with you, will deliver a report to you. All this is within 6 months.

Management consulting firms are unlikely to be interested in your one-shot marketing survey.

Locating and Deciding on a Particular Consultant. The *college professor* who may be a consultant is easy to locate. There may well be a college in your community or nearby. If not, a telephone call to the college you attended will tell you whether the school has a marketing department and someone in it who teaches or claims knowledge of marketing research.

If you have an *advertising agency,* it is even simpler. Your agency will advise you whether or not this is within their field of expertise. As to the *management consultant firm,* we still reluctantly say that unless you are already dealing with one, for purposes of a single survey, forget it. Let's say you *do* have several possible consultants lined up to consider. How do you decide on which one meets your needs? This is not that difficult.

How well does each one seem to understand your problem and needs? How does each show survey expertise against what you have already learned from this book? How much knowledge does each show about the kinds of contractors that might be needed for your study?

Ask for the names of clients. While the individual or firm will provide names only of satisfied clients, this is still a necessary check you should follow through.

How to Locate Contractors

Locating the names of pertinent research contractors is a different story. There are several steps.

Define your needs. You wouldn't think of asking for an appointment at a medical clinic before you knew what sort of physician you needed, and you shouldn't look for a survey research firm (contractor) that way either. Just what *are* your needs?

How wide is the market area to be studied? Do you need all stages of the study to be done by the contractor or only such specific steps as building the sample of respondents, developing of the questionnaire, data processing, or analysis and reporting of results?

Get names and performance of possible contractors. There are "informal" sources for such names. These are personal contacts. The major resource, we think, is a peer in another firm. There are other possibilities, however: your advertising agency, the local newspaper (particularly the advertising department), or your trade association.

If you approach your contact in the right way, you will get immeasurable help. You can describe what your general research needs are—without revealing your specific problem—and get suggestions on research firms that might meet your needs. Has your contact used outside research firms? Which one or ones?

There are also "formal" sources for names of contractors. These are published lists of firms with some description of their background and capabilities (generally based on information provided by the contractors). A listing from any published source is no assurance of quality.

There are published lists of firms with descriptions of their background and capabilities.

The most readily available published list is in the Yellow Pages. Look under "Market Research and Analysis." In a smaller community you may not find any listings, so go to your next largest community nearby. But note that except for the possibility of a display ad for the firm, you are unlikely to be able to determine whether the contractor offers the specific kind of help you are seeking. A telephone call may set you straight on that.

There are three published lists (each published annually)—often available in larger libraries—which tell you more about the firm. One is the *International Membership Directory & Marketing Services Guide* of the American Marketing Association (Chicago, Ill.). The marketing services portion covers 142 pages, of which 86 are devoted to marketing research contractors. The pages are divided into topical headings, making it reasonably simple to use. If you need a telephone survey, a focus group, or whatever, you will find firms listed for that sort of activity.

The *MRA Research Services Directory* is published by the Market Research Association (Chicago, Ill.). It provides specific listings for firms that handle one or more aspects of focus groups (recruiting of groups, conference rooms for groups, audiotaping, videotaping, projector, and one-way mirror with observation room, with even the room capacity reported). If it is a telephone survey you think you need, the number of lines is reported, along with the days open weekly. If you are thinking of a mall study, you can tell for each firm offering these whether it has its own installation in the mall or is there only by specific study arrangement and, if it has its own facilities, their nature (such as a test kitchen and booths). The directory also lists firms that do in-store interviewing and observation. Also covered are firms with other specialized interviewing capabilities, such as executive, professional, black, Hispanic, and door-to-door. All these are cross-indexed geographically, making the list easy to use to answer your specific needs.

This particular list provides chiefly the names of firms willing to take on one or more specific segments of the study. Excluded are nationally known firms interested only in a total study from start to finish. However, many of the firms in the MRA list definitely will and can handle your complete study, if that's what you want.

Perhaps most valuable of these list sources is the *GreenBook: International Directory of Marketing Research Companies and Services,* a publication of the New York (City) Chapter of the American Marketing Association. The listing includes some 1,300 firms from 53 countries. The basic information about each company is provided alphabetically by company name. Each listing provides the firm name, address, telephone number, and key executive contacts within the group. A short paragraph describes its services. In addition, there is helpful cross-indexing by more than 100 "company services" (the "kind" of marketing research), such as advertising research, audience research, and concept testing. To help you locate nearby firms, there's an alphabetical listing within each state.

How to Make a Preliminary Evaluation of Contractors

Now you have a list of possible contractors who can likely fill your needs. But you are not quite ready to ask them for plans or prices. You need some more information about them first. You have three basic information sources: networking, the firm's clients, and the prospective firms themselves.

Networking. Here we are talking about those people and organizations which we discussed as personal sources of names of research contractors that might meet your needs: peers in other firms, your ad agency, your trade association.

Ask whether any of the firm's past or present clients are known. You will want to check some of these. If you make contacts like these, be sure to ask with which research firms the person had bad experiences. If these requests are made by telephone, with no written record, your source will usually tell you what you need to know. After only a few telephone calls you can ask about both good and bad aspects of the firm names coming up most often. A key question to ask: "Would you have this firm do another study for you if you had a need for their kind of service?" Hemming and hawing is an obviously negative response. On the positive side, too, you will know when you are getting an enthusiastic "yes."

The Firm's Clients. Once you have a short list of some of the firm's clients, be sure to check them out. As we have said, make the contact by telephone, so that there is no written record required of the person replying. Talk to the person—so far as you can determine—most closely associated with the project. Then ask the kinds of questions suggested in the preceding paragraph. Some of this checking will have to follow your first session with the prospective research contractor.

Check with the research firm itself. While distance and cost may offer problems in following what we suggest, there are definite things you should check out about a potential research contractor before seriously considering the firm as a possibility to help you.

One is its *policies*. If you are a first-time buyer of marketing research, it is unlikely that the research firm is going to change or modify any of its policies for you. Determine the ground rules before you get them into your game. We do not have all the questions, but we can suggest a few.

Basic, we think, is their attitude toward your role. You must have the right to make the final research decisions, not the other way around, just as you have the right with your physician to reject his or her recommendations. Of course, the professional researchers are the experts, and you are generally likely to accept what they recommend. While this will not be a factor in your dealing with most contractors, the prestigious national firm may not accept this idea.

A few research firms also may want to reserve the right to permit you to cite results and interpretations to those outside your staff only with their approval. You may want to think this over.

You will also want to check the *pricing* policies of the potential contractor. There are three basic ways in which a research firm may quote a price. One is a *cost-plus method*. The firm tells you that it will do as you say and bill you after it gets its costs. Forget it; this is writing a blank check. But there are exceptions.

The major one is where you do not know what proportion of the general population falls into your needs. For example, your firm offers computer supplies, catering to the home market, and you want to do a telephone interview study. The problem is that you have no good figures for your market area about the proportion of homes with computers. So the only way your research contractor can preprice your study is to show price if there are 50 percent of computer homes, 40 percent, and so on. This parallels the well driller who charges on the basis of number of feet required to get to water. You have no choice but to accept this particular kind of "blank check."

There's another form of blank check you should be more wary of. You may be buying only interviewing from a so-called local supervisor (a person typically working out of his or her home with names of local interviewers available) who has few assets. Here you will be billed an hourly rate for interviewing (make sure you know in advance what the rate is). You will typically be billed for the time the worker takes to get to the place of work or travel on a door-to-door basis. The supervisor will add a percentage for supervision. You will also have to pay for automobile mileage, tolls, and the like, even meals if the interviewer has to pay for them because of the nature of the assignment. The supervisor may give you an estimate in advance, but it is only a rough approximation. You will have to pay cost-plus.

This is risky. While it is unfair to ask the local supervisor to take all the risk, it is fair to put some limits on the possible cost.

You must determine the ground rules before you get any research firm into your game.

A second method of pricing is the *flat rate,* where you are given a flat contract price for your survey. This is rare. There are too many unknowns in the survey business. If you find a contractor who will offer you a flat rate and you think the price is reasonable, you should probably take it.

The third and most common form of pricing is a *dollar figure with a range of plus or minus 10 percent*. If the quotation is $4,000, the actual billing might run between $3,600 and $4,400. You can be almost certain that your bill will be on the high side of the $4,000, so you should budget the top figure of $4,400 and hope for the best.

You are typically asked to pay the research firm a third on authorization, a second third on the start of data gathering, and the final third on report delivery. There are many variations of this arrangement. In group interviewing, where the going-in expense of the research firm is such a great proportion of the total cost, your first bill may be a much higher proportion of the contract price because of the heavy going-in costs of the research firm. But like most buyer-seller service relations, it also depends on your power position vis-à-vis your contemplated research source.

A second major area of the policies of the research firm is its *procedures*. These tell you a great deal about the quality of the work they turn out. Ask the firm about the specific sampling method proposed for your study. How will the firm go about developing the questionnaire? Will they test it, and if so, how? What is the nature of the interviewing staff? Have they been trained? If so, how? What kind of training is proposed for your particular study?

Ask about the proposed completion rate for your particular study. The completion rate is the proportion of the listings (the "frame") with which questioning has been completed. It should be at least 60 percent, as discussed in Chapter 12. What editing and coding procedures are followed? (See Chapter 14 for what they *ought* to be doing.)

There is the crucial area of *personnel*. People are the heart of a research firm. It is they who make the policies and procedures of the firm work. They determine how good (or poor) the end product will be.

You need knowledge about the account executive and processing department heads. The account executive—regardless of title—is the person who handles relationships with you and typically acts as project director of your particular study within the research firm. He or she sees that the study is properly designed (if that is a part of the assignment) and goes through on schedule and that each department head understands and executes his or her portion of the work and the report (if that is a part of the contract).

Make sure that the person you first deal with is the one you will be dealing with throughout the study. Some research contractors put in a second-team person as your contact once the project has been authorized.

You will also want to talk with the heads of departments within the firm. These may include the sampling department, the interviewing or data-collection department, and the data-processing department. While you are likely not an expert in survey research (otherwise you wouldn't be reading this book), you can still make some reasonably fair assumptions about these people (and the firm's

Talking with heads of departments will quickly give you an impression as to whether they are glib and how thorough their operation is.

procedures) just by talking with them. Ask them, for instance, to tell you about the operation of their departments and the steps they take to ensure quality. You will quickly get an impression as to whether they are glib, how thorough the operation is, and whether they give much thought other than to the day-to-day operation.

There are *other considerations*. One is the geographic distance between you and the research contractor. It should not be great, since you are likely inexperienced in dealing with a research firm. There simply are too many possible problems. Continuing communication between you and the research firm is essential. You have to know what is going on. Even an experienced research buyer may go wrong if there is not a constant flow of communication. In one case—yes, one of the authors—an experienced research buyer dealt with a research source some 750 miles away. The study went sour—not because of competence of the research firm, but because of lack of communication. Do not risk it unless you are willing—rather than the research contractor—to take on the prime responsibility for continuing communication.

You *should* assume such responsibility. But you also should let the firm know that you definitely want to be kept informed. Even if you deal with a local firm, make sure that you are kept well informed about your study. Let them know in advance that you want to hear about anything that goes wrong with your study, even minor things. As we have been saying, marketing surveys are far from truly scientific studies, and there are many, many possible problems involved. You need to know of these, and your supplier needs to realize that you want to know about them. It may involve problems due to a questionnaire containing errors, poor interviewing, poor completion rates, or many of the other things outlined previously in this book. The point is that you and your research contractor should be partners and share problems. You have to make sure in advance that this type of communication will happen.

How to Obtain and Evaluate
Submissions from Contractors

There is a basic difference between a proposal and an estimate. A *proposal* is a project plan developed by the contractor once it understands your problem and how the proposal submitted can help answer your problem. It is a plan for your entire study, and it tells the dollars involved to do that. The proposer, with your acceptance, runs with the ball. The study is all his or hers.

The *estimate,* on the other hand, is a quotation based on job specs. You describe specifically what your requirements are: the universe, the sample and the sampling method, the questionnaire, the precise data processing required, and so on. Your estimate request might be for the entire study or for one or more portions of it. The request might go to several groups of subcontractors, depending on how you have decided to handle things.

Do you want a proposal or just an estimate? The answer depends basically on how much effort and money your firm is willing to allocate to the study. If you and the firm have plenty of time to put in, you will save money by developing a stated list of specs. But if you and the firm decide the better route to go is to leave it all to the research contractor—of course, with your own important input—then you should go the route of the proposal.

Asking for and Evaluating a Proposal. In fairness to the research firm, do not ask for a proposal unless you are serious about doing the study. Making a proposal costs money—there is considerable (and expensive) creative time required. And typically, the research firm does not charge for the proposal.

You need to do a lot of homework before asking for a proposal. You have to be ready to state your problem, to provide considerable background about your company, and to provide what you know about the competition. Do not worry about revealing confidential information. If you have chosen your proposers well, you have no fears that any of your information will be leaked to others.

You should know what to expect in the proposal. It typically includes a statement about the background of the problem. It describes the marketing environment of the study and the research firm's understanding of the specific problem for which an answer is sought. While it is typically a playback of what you have told the potential supplier, it reflects the research firm's understanding of your problem.

The longest and most detailed section of the proposal deals with the research methods. It describes how the firm plans to handle the aspects described in Chapters 10 through 13: how the data will be collected, the size and nature of the sample, the questionnaire, and the summary of the data. Of course, the proposal also specifies the price and the terms of payment.

If this is the first time you are getting a proposal from a particular research firm, expect some promotional material as well. Any bonuses the firm offers—special competencies in sampling, data-collection methods, data processing, and the like—will be included. The firm may indicate major clients for whom it has worked. It may tell you about its size, history, and current major personnel.

How do you judge a proposal? We think there are three bases. One is the *soundness of the plan*. How can you, probably a novice in research, make such a judgment? It may not be all that difficult. Most of us know glib writing when we see it—and glib writing might just be a caution sign. Common sense is another good guide.

The *content and organization* are certainly a guide, too. The plan should provide a concise statement about how the study will be conducted, as well as providing an indication of the researcher's planning ability and practical experience. The proposal should include all study aspects relevant to the problem and its solution. If there are major oversights in the first proposal, you would probably be right to forget the research firm as a possibility.

There are three bases for judging a proposal.

If you are expecting a written report, the *writing style* in the proposal should be a major consideration, particularly if there are other executives in the company who will be reading the report. Chapter 15 has already outlined some of the important considerations in a report presentation. If the proposal communicates poorly, it is unlikely that the findings will be any more clearly presented. There should be little research jargon. Occasional technical terms may be acceptable,

Beware of the researcher who throws around big words or overimpressive, hard-to-decipher sentences and paragraphs.

but only because of their precise meanings and word economy. Beware of the researcher who throws around big words or overimpressive, hard-to-decipher sentences and paragraphs. If you have trouble understanding the proposal, you will have even more trouble understanding the report. So will your associates.

From a proposal submitted by an unnamed research firm (to protect the guilty), here is an example of how not to express an idea:

> What is needed is a structural program to encompass all measures of the gestalt of the market's assessment of the contestants in the particular product field.

In simpler terms, what might have been said:

> We plan to have consumers rate all major brands in this product category.

Sorting out the poor proposals from the good one sometimes is not that difficult. One of the authors, as a consultant to an association, solicited proposals from three research firms. Copies were sent both to the consultant and to the association officer designated to make the recommendation to the association. When the consultant was met at the airport, the association officer said, somewhat timidly, that he thought one of the proposals was not very good. He was absolutely right; that proposal was discarded at once. You need not be a research expert to spot a poor proposal.

Asking for and Evaluating an Estimate. If you go the route of an estimate, the major burden is on you rather than on the contractor. You have to be really specific in your specs. Otherwise the low estimate, technically correct, will not be likely to produce just what you expect. Admittedly, it is tough if you are not an expert—or working with an expert consultant—to foresee all the possibilities. If your specs call for a telephone survey, you not only have to specify the universe (including qualified respondents and how to determine them), but you also must specify the follow-up procedure and the rate of completion required. Even then you have no idea of the interviewing quality. Just what training and supervision are applied? How much of this should be a part of your specs?

Providing specs is not easy. If you go the route of asking for estimates from specs, keep an open mind. Also ask for ideas. It is quite possible that one of the research contractors you approach will have just a great idea about how the study might be improved. Thus, when you ask for estimates, be sure, too, to describe the problem. The supplier may come up with a really creative idea for improving the study. Be sure that the cost estimate plays back your specs. Otherwise it may not be a binding contract, if accepted.

How to Work with the Research Contractor

Once you have selected your research contractor, your problems are just beginning. Now you have to make sure that what you contracted for and expect are what you get. To manage this, there are two major steps.

Work properly with the research firm. Your problems with the research firm are not necessarily over once you have selected your contractor. You have to make sure that you and they work well together to produce the study you want. You must not lose sight of the fact that these people are strangers to you and your company. You may have had lunch with one or more of them a number of times, had some drinks, made small talk, even done some kidding. Still, you lack intimate knowledge of how they work, even how good they are. Projects that start in the most friendly atmosphere may end in distrust and hostility. If this happens, it may be as much your fault as that of your research contractor. It is up to you to see that this does not happen.

One of the worst things you can do is to give an assignment to a research firm then leave it all entirely alone until close to its completion. By that time it may have gone down the wrong road so far that there is no hope for it. From the very start of a research study assigned to a contractor, you need frequent and continuing contacts to check on its progress and problems. If your contractor is within reasonable distance, it might even be a good idea to schedule meetings at stated intervals and to get written progress reports.

Projects that start in the most friendly atmosphere may end in distrust and hostility.

You will have one major contact person in your research firm, but do not let it go at that. If you have followed our earlier suggestion in this chapter, you will know the name of every executive working on your project. Keep in touch; otherwise you may find out—much too late—that things are going wrong.

You will want to know not only how the study is going technically, but also in terms of timing. If there are delays, you need to know about them early, and what the research contractor is doing to rectify or minimize them.

There is also the issue of cost. If you have followed our suggestions, you are protected on costs. But if you are dealing with a very small research contractor and he or she runs into cost problems on your study, the study could be in trouble. Sometimes neither you nor your research firm can foresee the cost problems. Your focus group firm may have been wildly optimistic on the number of hours required to recruit 15 people meeting your requirements. You could insist that they stick to their estimate. But that would not likely be wise. They are in business, just as you are.

In your dealings with your research contractor—assuming that you have made a good choice—remember that they are professional researchers. You would not visit a physician and tell him or her what medications and treatment you wanted. You would not tell the physician during the treatment what changes in medication and procedures you thought were necessary. He or she wouldn't take it.

Do not expect a truly professional research firm to take it either. They are the experts, not you. Of course, they will take suggestions, but only up to a point. Naturally, this does not mean that the good research firm will not even listen—of course it will, and it should. But generally be ready to accept their expert opinions and use your power as the client only when you are completely convinced they are wrong. This should be rare.

You would not visit a physician and tell him or her what medications and treatment you wanted.

How to Recognize Good or Poor Work. If you have done all we have recommended, it is unlikely you will get a poor study. You will have planned and supervised so thoroughly that the results of your study will be dependable.

Be sure to look at completed data-collection forms. How thoroughly they are filled in will tell you a great deal. Be prepared for some opposition from the research firm. According to industry ethics, it is improper for the research firm to reveal respondent identity, particularly when associated with specific replies. You should be able to meet this challenge by looking at the forms in the office of the research firm or having all forms submitted to you after deletion of specific identification material.

What you will need to check: (1) question skipping (the rate of omission to answers to questions), (2) the probing of open-ended questions (see Chapter 13), and (3) the internal consistency of replies. None of these quality checks on interviewing will be clear from the data tables.

Where possible, you will also want to compare your company, industry, or government figures with any that come out of your particular study. For example, one research study showed a gross understatement of the dollar sales of a particular manufacturer. This made all other results of the study suspect, and the company rejected the study completely. If your study shows telephone ownership in your consumer study is 80 percent and government data show it well over 90 percent, your study lacks credibility.

But be careful in judging results that do not come out according to your expectations. They are not necessarily wrong. If the results seem outrageous, do a bit of work on your own. Make your own check. We have suggested other methods.

Index

About the Authors

GEORGE EDWARD BREEN, former Director of Marketing Research at The Stanley Works (one of *Fortune*'s 500), holds a B.A. degree from Yale University, an M.B.A. from the Harvard Graduate School of Business Administration, and a Ph.D. from New York University.

Mr. Breen has at various times served on programs for the Conference Board, the American Management Association, and other organizations. He is the coauthor of two previous books on marketing and has written a number of magazine articles. He founded the Connecticut Chapter of the American Marketing Association and served as its first president.

Mr. Breen is now Professor of Marketing at Miami University School of Business Administration.

AL BLANKENSHIP is Professor Emeritus of Marketing, Bowling Green State University. His Ph.D. is from Columbia University.

Previously, Mr. Blankenship has been a vice president, a director, and an owner of Canadian Facts Company, Limited (Canada's largest survey research firm). He also has been secretary-treasurer of the American Marketing Association and is a fellow of the Professional Marketing Research Society (Canada).

His interest in small business is reflected by former membership on the Board of Directors of SCORE (Service Corps of Retired Executives), a national volunteer group dedicated to assisting small business.

Mr. Blankenship has published seven other books. His works have been published in several foreign countries, including Canada, Mexico, England, Sweden, Germany, Spain, Italy, the Philippines, and India.